In accordance with the latest syllabus prescribed by the
Council for the Indian Certificate of Secondary Education Examination, New Delhi.

ICSE CERTIFICATE GEOGRAPHY

CLASS IX

Edition-Cordinator

ManuscriptEdit
by Reseapro

Rakesh Rai
Department of Geography
St. Paul's School
Darjeeling (W.B.)

Keshab Sharma
Department of Geography
St. Joseph's School
North Point, Darjeeling (W.B.)

Edited By

Sharmila Ghosh
Saifee Hall
Kolkata (W.B.)

OSWAL PUBLISHERS
1/12, Sahitya Kunj, M. G. Road, Agra-282 002

No part of this book can be reproduced in any form or by any means without the prior written permission the publisher.

Edition: 2021

ISBN: 978-81-95133-31-4

Printed at: Upkar Printing Unit, Agra

OSWAL PUBLISHERS

Head office : 1/12, Sahitya Kunj, M.G. Road, Agra-282 002
Phone : (0562) 2527771- 4, +91 75340 77222
E-mail : contact@oswalpublishers.com
Website : www.oswalpublishers.com

PREFACE

Geography is the study of physical and human aspects of our environment and their linkages. All human actions have an impact on the realm of the earth and are, equally, influenced to a great extent by the Earth's physical domain. Geography is therefore an exciting exploration into how our planet Earth was formed, the natural forces that shape the land, the effects of weather and climate and how we are damaging our precious environment.

This edition is customized to meet the academic needs of the Indian Certificate of Secondary Education (ICSE), as prescribed by the Council for the Indian School Certificate Examination (CISCE).

All efforts have been made to envelop the syllabus comprehensively, in a lucid, simple and straight forward language. The text has been supplemented with features such as illustrations, maps, diagrams, tables and photographs to simulate interest, enhance understanding, enable review of concepts and promote self-evaluation of progress.

Learning Objectives at the beginning of each chapter outlines the scope of each chapter as specified by the CISCE.

Key Terms list the most important terms which are shown in bold letters, in each of the chapters

Points to Remember provides interesting pieces of information relevant to a particular topic within the chapter

Review Exercise at the end of each chapter contains various questions carefully framed to meet the requirement of board examination.

Map Work and Practical Work section prepare the students for examinations by providing suitable examples and practical applications.

The book has been innovatively designed to make the study interesting. It aims to connect students and teachers with the real world by providing them a sound knowledge of geographical concepts and ideas.

Progress will come to a grinding halt if we cease efforts to improve. All constructive suggestions for the further improvement of the book are welcome and we shall try to incorporate as many of such suggestions as possible in the future editions.

–Publisher

SYLLABUS CLASS IX

Aims :

- To develop and understanding of terms, concepts and principles related to Geography.
- To explain the cause-effect relationships of natural phenomena.
- To understand the use of natural resources and development of regions.
- To acquire knowledge of and appreciate the interdependence of nations and different regions of the world.
- To know the availability of resources, understand, explain their uses and appreciate the problems of development in India.
- To understand and encourage human efforts made to conserve and protect the natural environment.
- To acquire practical skills related to the meaning and use of maps and their importance in the study of Geography.

- There will be **one** paper of **two hours** duration carrying 80 marks and an Internal Assessment of 20 marks.
- The question paper will consist of Part I and Part II.
- **Part I (compulsory)** will consist of **two** questions. Question 1 will consist of short answer questions from the entire syllabus and Question 2 will consist of a question based on **World Map**.
- **Part II :** Candidates will be required to choose **any five** questions.
- Candidates will be expected to make the fullest use of sketches, diagrams, graphs and chart in their answers.
- Questions may require answers involving the interpretation of photographs of geographical interest.

PRINCIPLES OF GEOGRAPHY

1. **Our World**

    (i) Earth as a planet

    Shape of the earth. Earth as the home of humankind and the conditions that exist.

    (ii) Geographic grid : Latitudes & Longitudes

    (a) Concept of latitudes : main latitudes, their location with degrees, parallels of latitude and their uses. (b) Concept of longitudes : Prime Meridian, time (local, standard and time zones, Greenwich Mean Time (GMT) and International Date Line (IDL). Eastern and Western hemisphere, (c) Using latitudes and longitudes to find location. Calculation of time. (d) Great Circles and their use.

    (iii) Rotation and Revolution

    Rotation : direction, speed and its effects (occurrence of day and night, the sun rising in the east and setting in the west, Coriolis effect)

    Revolution of the earth and its inclined axis–effects : the variation in the length of the day and night and seasonal changes with Equinoxes and Solstices.

2. **Structure of the Earth**

    (i) Earth's Structure

    Core, mantle, crust : meaning, extent and their composition.

    (ii) Landforms of the Earth

    Mountains, plateaus, plains (definition, types and their formation):
    Mountains : fold, residual and block.
    Plateaus : intermont and volcanic.
    Plains : structural and depositional.
    Examples from the world and India.

    (iii) Rocks : difference between minerals and rocks, types of rocks : igneous, sedimentary, metamorphic, their characteristics and formation; rock cycle.

- (vi) Volcanoes

    Meaning, Types : active, dormant and extinct.
    Effects : constructive and destructive.
    Important volcanic zones of the world.

- (v) Earthquakes

    Meaning, causes and measurement.
    Effects : destructive and constructive.
    Earthquake zones of the World.

- (vi) Weathering and Denudation

    Meaning, types and effects of weathering.
    Types : Physical Weathering : block and granular disintegration, exfoliation;
    Chemical Weathering : oxidation, carbonation, hydration and solution;
    Biological Weathering : caused by humans, plants and animals.
    Meaning and agents of denudation; work of river and wind.
    Stages of a river course and associated land forms : V-shaped valley, waterfall, meander and delta.
    Wind : deflation hollows and Sand dunes.

3. **Hydrosphere**

    Meaning of hydrosphere.
    Tides : formation and pattern.
    Ocean Currents : their circulation pattern and effects. (Specifically of Gulf Stream, North Atlantic Drift, Labrador Current, Kuro Shio and Oya Shio.)

4. **Atmosphere**

    - (i) Composition and structure of the atmosphere.

        Troposphere, Stratosphere, Ionosphere and Exosphere; Ozone in the Stratosphere, its depletion, Global warming and its impact.

    - (ii) Insolation

        Meaning of insolation and terrestrial radiation.
        Factors affecting temperature : latitude, altitude, distance from the sea, slope of land, winds and ocean currents.

    - (iii) Atmospheric Pressure and Winds.

        Meaning and factors that affect atmospheric pressure.
        Major pressure belts of the world.
        Factors affecting direction and velocity of wind : pressure gradient, Coriolis Effect.
        Permanent winds : Trades, Westerlies and Polar Easterlies.
        Periodic winds : Land and Sea breezes, Monsoons,
        Local winds : Loo, Chinook, Foehn and Mistral.
        Variable winds : Cyclones and Anticyclones
        Jet Streams : Meaning and importance.

    - (iv) Humidity

        Humidity : meaning and difference between relative and absolute humidity.
        Condensation : forms (clouds, dew, frost, fog and mist).
        Precipitation : forms (rain, snow, and hail).
        Types of rainfall : relief/orographic, convectional, cyclonic/frontal with examples from the different parts of the world.

5. **Pollution**
    - (a) Types : air, water (fresh and marine), soil, radiation and noise.
    - (b) Sources

        Noise : Traffic, factories, construction sites, loudspeakers, airports.
        Air : vehicular, industrial, burning of garbage.
        Water : domestic and industrial waste.
        Soil : chemical fertilizers, bio medical waste and pesticides.
        Radiation : X-rays; radioactive fallout from nuclear plants.

(c) Effects : on the environment and human health.
(d) Preventive Measures
Carpools, promotion of public transport, no smoking zone, restricted use of fossil fuels, saving energy and encouragement of organic farming.

6. **Natural Regions of the World**

   Location, area, climate, natural vegetation and human adaptation.

   Equatorial region, Tropical grasslands, Tropical Deserts, Tropical Monsoon, Mediterranean, Temperate grasslands, Taiga and Tundra.

7. **Map Work**

   On an outline map of the World, candidates will be required to locate, mark and name the following :

   1. *The major **Natural Regions** of the world : Equatorial, Tropical Monsoon, Tropical Deserts, Mediterranean type, Tropical grasslands, Temperate grasslands, Taiga and Tundra.*
   2. *The Oceans, Seas, Gulfs and Straits : all Major Oceans, Caribbean Sea, North Sea, Black Sea, Caspian Sea, South China Sea, Mediterranean Sea Gulf of Carpentaria, Hudson Bay, Persian Gulf, Gulf of Mexico, Gulf of Guinea, Bering Strait, Strait of Gibraltar, Strait of Malacca.*
   3. *River : Mississippi, Colorado, Amazon, Paraguay, Nile, Zaire, Niger, Zambezi, Orange, Rhine, Volga, Danube, Murray, Darling, Hwang Ho, Yangtse Kiang, Ob, Indus, Ganga, Mekong, Irrawaddy, Tigris, Euphrates.*
   4. *Mountains : Rockies, Andes, Appalachian, Alps, Himalayas, Pyrenees, Scandinavian Highlands, Caucasus, Atlas, Drakensburg, Khinghan, Zagros, Urals, Great Dividing Range.*
   5. *Plateaus : Canadian Shield, Tibetan Plateau, Brazilian, Highlands, Patagonion Plateau, Iranian Plateau, Mongolian Plateau.*

INTERNAL ASSESSMENT
PRACTICAL WORK/PROJECT WORK

1. A record file having any **three** of the following exercises will be maintained. (This file will be evaluated out of 10 marks).

    (a) Uses of important types of maps.

    (b) Direction and how to identify them : an illustrative diagram.

    (c) Reading and using statement of scale, graphic scale and scale shown by representative fraction method (No drawing work, only explaining their meanings).

    (d) Reading of one town guide map or an atlas map. (Recognising the symbols and colours used, identifying directions and distances).

    (e) Drawing and recognising forms of important contours viz. valleys, ridges, types of slopes, conical hill, plateau, escarpment and sea cliff.

    (f) Drawing at least one sketch map to organize information about visiting an important place, a zoo or a monument.

2. Candidates will be required to prepare a project report on any **one** topic, The topics for assignments may be selected from the list of suggested assignments given below. Candidates can also take up an assignment of their choice under any of the four broad areas give below. (The project will be evaluated out of 10 makrs).

Suggested list of Assignments :

(a) **Weather records :** Maintaining and interpreting weather records as found in the newspaper for at least one season.

(b) **Collection of data form secondary sources :** {Using Modern techniques i.e. Global Positioning System (GPS), Remote Sensing, Aerial Photography and Satellite imageries} : Preparing a Power Point presentation on current issues like : use of earth resources/development activities/dangers of development and ecological disasters like droughts, earthquakes, volcanoes, floods, landslides cyclones and tornadoes in the world.

(c) **Physical Features :** Collection of data from primary and secondary sources of taking photographs and preparing notional sketches of features found in the vicinity or areas visited during the year as a part of school activity.

(d) Find out the sources of pollution of water bodies in the locality and determine the quality of water.

(e) Collect information on global environmental issues and problems and communicate your findings through appropriate modes (posters, charts, collages, cartoons, handouts, essays, street plays and PowerPoint presentation).

(f) **Area Studies :** Choosing any aspect from World Studies and preparing a PowerPoint presentaion or a write up on it.

(g) **Meteorological Instruments and their uses :** Six's maximum and minimum thermometer, mercury barometer, aneroid barometer, wind vane, anemometer, rain gauge and hygrometer.

CONTENTS

1. Earth As a Planet — 11–17
2. Latitudes and Longitudes — 18–27
3. Rotation and Revolution — 28–34
4. Structure of the Earth and Internal Processes — 35–39
5. Landforms of the Earth — 40–46
6. Rocks — 47–55
7. Volcanoes — 56–63
8. Earthquakes — 64–70
9. Weathering and Denudation — 71–79
10. Hydrosphere — 80–90
11. Atmosphere — 91–98
12. Insolation — 99–104
13. Atmospheric Pressure and Winds — 105–115
14. Humidity Precipitation — 116–123
15. Pollution and Environment — 124–139
16. Natural Regions of the World — 140–164

CHAPTER 1
EARTH AS A PLANET

Shape of the Earth : Earth as the home of Humankind and the conditions that Exist.

ORIGIN AND EVOLUTION OF EARTH AS A PLANET

Our solar system (including the Earth) is formed from the collapse of a large, rotating giant cloud of dust and gas called, 'Solar Nebula'. It started its collapse and core formation, some 5–5.6 billion years ago. As the nebula shrank in size, it spun faster. This rapid rotation consequently prevented its collapse and a large number of smaller units were formed from it. The center of the nebula that moved slowly formed the Sun and the smaller units formed the planets about 4.6 billion years ago.

The planet Earth was initially a barren, rocky, and hot object with a thin atmosphere of hydrogen and helium. Due to a gradual increase in density, the temperature inside increased. As a result, the heavier materials sank towards the centre of the Earth, and the lighter ones moved towards the surface. With the passage of time, it cooled further and solidified, and led to the development of the outer surface in the form of a crust. During the cooling of the Earth, gases and water vapour in the atmosphere started to condense and caused precipitation. Thus, Oceans were formed. Then life began to evolve in the ocean. It can be assumed that life began to evolve sometime 3,800 million years ago.

EARTH : AN OVERVIEW

Earth is the densest and fifth largest planet in the solar system and the third planet with respect to distance from the Sun. *(Fig.1.1)* Being at an advantageous distance from the Sun, neither too close like Mercury and Venus nor too far like Uranus and Neptune. Earth is the only planet that supports life with its moderate climatic conditions. Earth's biosphere and other biotic conditions enable the formation of the ozone layer, which blocks harmful solar radiation, thereby permitting life. Earth was formed 4.54 billion years ago, and life appeared on its surface within one billion years. It is otherwise referred to as the blue planet. Earth orbits the Sun at an average distance of 150 million kilometers.

Fig. 1.1 : Planets in the Solar System.

Earlier Notions about the shape of the Earth

Fig. 1.2 : Ferdinand Magellan

Fig. 1.3 : Christopher Columbus

The shape of the Earth has intrigued people since the early days. The Babylonians thought the Earth was hollow to provide space for their underworld. The Egyptians believed that the Earth is a square (with four corners) with mountains at the edge supporting the vault of the sky. Most ancient cultures during the Middle Ages have had the view that the Earth is flat. Some mathematicians and explorers of ancient and medieval times viewed that the Earth was round. Pythagoras, a Greek philosopher and mathematician stated that sphere was the perfect figure, fit for a man's habitat. Aristotle supported the view of Pythagoras and put forth several arguments in its favour. However, Ferdinand Magellan's *(Fig. 1.2)* round-the world expedition and Christopher Columbus *(Fig. 1.3)* exploration proved the earlier notions wrong.

In 1519, with the help of King of Spain, Magellan set out on his expedition with five ships. Although he was killed by the natives, his crew completed the voyage. They broughts his ships back home after going across the Indian Ocean, South Africa, from Atlantic to Spain, thus proving that the Earth was not flat, but spherical in shape.

Earth's outer surface is divided into several rigid segments, or tectonic plates. The surface of the Earth consists of three layers: (i) Lithosphere, (ii) Hydrosphere, and (iii) Atmosphere. The lithosphere is the Earth's surrounding layer that includes the land surface and ocean floor. Vast oceans, inland seas, lakes, rivers and underground waters that contribute to the hydrosphere cover about 71% of the surface. The atmosphere is a layer of gases surrounding the Earth.

SHAPE OF THE EARTH

In the present space age, the Earth's spherical shape is an established fact. A new term 'Geoid' is used to describe shape of the Earth, which means earth-shaped.

Proofs of the Earth's Spherical Shape

A number of factors that prove the spherical shape of the Earth are :

- **All Celestial Bodies are Spherical :** In the solar system, Sun, Moon and all other celestial bodies appear to have a circular outline. Since Earth too belongs to the same system, it should not be an exception.

- **Circumnavigation of the Earth :** People travelled round the world in different directions, but again came back to the starting point. Ferdinand Magellan and his crew were the first to go around the Earth in a ship and complete the voyage without encountering a sharp edge. Now, aircrafts make trips round the world on scheduled flights.

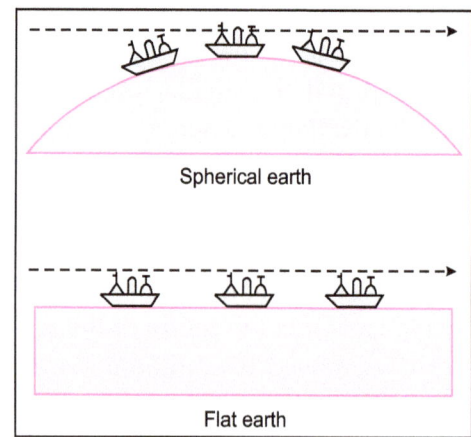

Fig. 1.4 : Ship viewed from Horizon

- **Line of Visibility Increases with Height :** When an observer observes an approaching ship from a higher place, he first sees the mast of the ship, then its funnel and finally the hull *(Fig. 1.4)*. If the Earth was flat, then he would have seen the whole ship at once.

- **Sunrise and Sunset :** The time of Sunrise and Sunset varies all over the world. If the Earth would have been flat, then the Sun would have risen and set at the same time for all the people of the world *(Fig. 1.5)*.

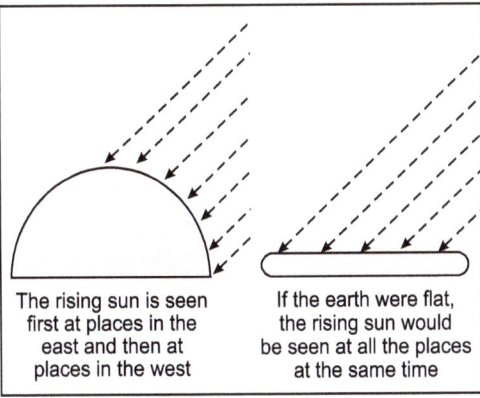

Fig. 1.5 : Rising Sun on spherical and flat Earth

- **The Variation of the Sun's Elevation with latitude :** By noting the angles of shadows in two cities on summer solstice, and by performing the right calculations using his knowledge of geometry and the distance between the cities, Eratosthenes was able to make a remarkably accurate calculation of the circumference of Earth. If the Earth were flat, then there would have been no variation in the Sun's elevation *(Fig. 1.6)*.

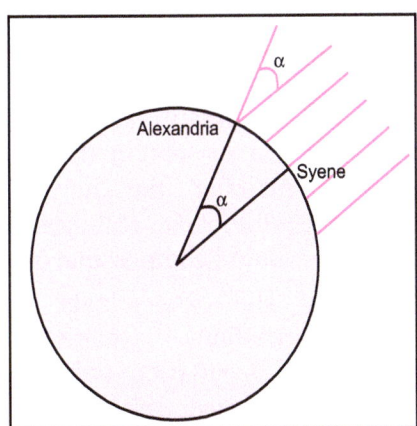

Fig. 1.6 : Eratosthenes' Calculation.

- **Shadow of Earth during Lunar Eclipse :** The shape of the curved shadow of the Earth on the moon during lunar eclipse proves that the shape of the Earth is spherical *(Fig. 1.7)*.

Fig. 1.7 : Lunar Eclipse

- **Aerial Photographs :** The aerial photographs of the Earth sent by artificial satellites and various spacecrafts prove that the Earth is round *(Fig. 1.8)*.

Fig. 1.8 : Photo of Earth taken from Apollo 17

- **Force of Gravity :** Newton discovered and measured the force of gravity. Since the force of gravity is roughly the same everywhere on the globe, it could be surmised that the Earth must be spherical.

Earth as a Spheroid

Actually, Earth is not a perfect sphere. Its shape is described as an 'oblate spheroid'. The measurement at poles and equator shows that it is shaped like an orange, slightly flattened at the poles and with a bulge at the equator. Hence, based on the measurements and established facts, it is accepted that Earth's shape is an 'oblate spheroid' *(Fig. 1.9)*.

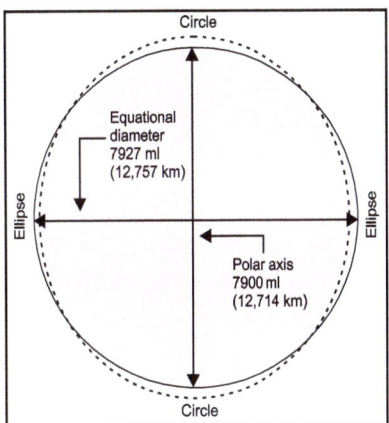

Fig. 1.9 : Earth as a Spheroid.

Size and Measurement of the Earth

In the third century B.C., the Greek mathematician Eratosthenes measured the circumference of the Earth. He measured it with the help of the shadows casted by the Sun during the summer solstice at different locations, and performed a bit of clever geometry. Thus the circumference of the Earth, could be measured in kilometers, which is approximately equal to 39,600 km. The actual circumference as per latest measurement is 40,077 km. Therefore, it is astonishing that Eratosthenes' measurement is so close to the actual one considering the time (200 B.C.) and the methodology available at that time.

EARTH : ITS UNIQUENESS IN THE SOLAR SYSTEM

- **Abundance of Land and Water :** The Earth is often referred to as the 'blue planet' because it is the only planet where water covers (71%) area almost twice that of land (29%). Thus, the distribution of land and water is uneven. There is an antipodal balance between the land and water on the directly opposite sides of the Earth. The areas of land and water are equally distributed in the Northern Hemisphere, whereas Southern Hemisphere is mostly dominated by water, nearly fifteen times more than land. The present distribution of land (continents) and water (oceans) on the surface of the Earth shows that if there is land in one part of the globe, then there is water on the opposite side of the Earth. Even the Northern polar ocean is opposite to the Antarctic landmass.

- **Earth as a home to Mankind/Habitability :** The most remarkable feature of Earth is that it is the only planet where life exists. The biosphere is the space near the Earth's surface that contains and supports living organisms and ecosystems which spreads over the Lithosphere, Atmosphere, and Hydrosphere. Biosphere supplies the essential requisites of life, viz. light, heat, water, food and living space or habitat.

Air, water, human beings, animals, plants, plantations, soil and bacteria – all are interlinked in a life-sustaining system called environment, and all these have survived by adapting themselves to the environment. Therefore, a balance among the different cycles like energy cycle, oxygen cycle and water cycle is necessary on which our environment depends.

- **The Largest of the Terrestrial Planets in the Solar System :** Earth is the largest of the four terrestrial planets (Mercury, Venus, Earth and Mars) in size and mass. It also has the highest density, surface gravity, the strongest magnetic field, and the fastest rotation and active tectonic plates. The Earth is unique among other planets because of its biosphere, with rich amount of oxygen and liquid hydrosphere. It has one natural satellite, the Moon, which is the only large satellite of a terrestrial planet in the solar system.

To sum up, Earth's location in the solar system, the appreciable amount of oxygen, the moderate temperature, and the water cycle on Earth are favourable for the existence of life. Tectonic plate activity and volcanism, Biosphere and relatively strong magnetic field are some unique features that differentiate the Earth from other Planets.

Conditions Favouring Life on Earth

- **Right Position in the Solar System:** It is the third planet with respect to its distance from the Sun. It is neither too near to the Sun like Mercury and Venus nor too far like Uranus and Neptune. Hence, it receives just the right amount of heat conducive for life.

- **Earth's Atmosphere:** Extending up to 1600 km around, its atmosphere contains adequate amount of Oxygen (21%), and Nitrogen (78%), along with a trace amount of other gases like Hydrogen, Helium and Ozone. The tiny amount of Carbon dioxide present in the atmosphere helps in maintaining the Earth's surface temperatures. Without it, the oceans would freeze and life would be impossible on Earth.

- **Ozone Layer:** The ozone layer in Earth's atmosphere contains relatively high concentrations of ozone (O_3). It absorbs 97–99% of the Sun's high frequency ultraviolet radiations which is damaging for the life on Earth. It also retains the heat radiated from the surface of the Earth.

- **Biosphere :** The biosphere is the biological component of Earth, which includes parts of Lithosphere, Hydrosphere, Atmosphere and other 'spheres' (e.g., Cryosphere, Anthrosphere, etc.). It is the space that contains and supports living organisms and ecosystems. It includes living organisms along with the dead organic matter produced by them.

- **Chemical Composition:** Iron-nickel core and silica rich mantle surrounded by a thin crust are just the right combination to have an active, but not overactive volcanic system which are required for the seafloor spreading to occur.

- **Molten Core of Iron:** The core of the Earth generates a magnetic field that keeps cosmic rays away from entering our atmosphere.

- **Water :** The abundance of water on Earth's surface is a unique feature that distinguishes the 'blue planet' from other planets. It is the only planet where water covers (71%) area of the Earth, almost twice that of land (29%).
- **Water Cycle :** Water cycle is another unique feature of the Earth. It is a vital mechanism to support life on land. But, it is also a primary factor of erosion and weathering of the Earth's surface *(Fig.1.10)*.

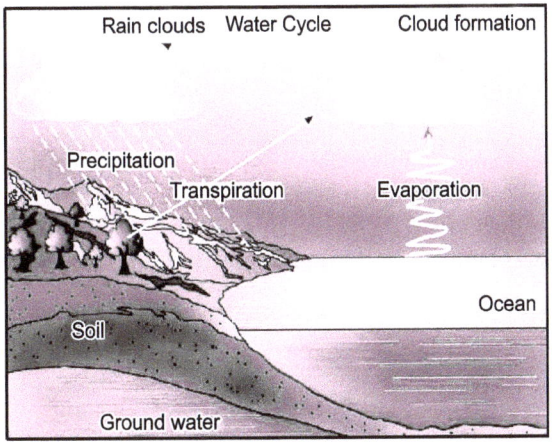

Fig. 1.10 : Water Cycle

MOON – EARTH'S SATELLITE

The Moon *(Fig.1.11)* is the Earth's only natural satellite and the largest natural satellite in the solar system relative to the size of its planet. Most of the planets have satellites, but they are very small in relation to their own size, whereas the Moon has a diameter of approximately one quarter that of the Earth. In fact, Earth and Moon are often referred to as 'double planets'.

Fig.1.11 : The Moon.

The Moon revolves around the Earth in $27\frac{1}{3}$ days (27 days, 7 hr, 43 min and 11.47 sec) and rotates on its own axis in exactly the same time. That is why only one side of the Moon is visible from the Earth. The Moon does not have light of its own. It looks bright to us because the Sun's rays get reflected off its surface. During the day, we cannot usually see the Moon because the Sun is brighter. The Moon's gravitational influence produces ocean tides and causes lengthening of Earth's day by about 23 µs a year.

Moon At a Glance	
Diameter	3,474.8 km
Mean distance	Apogee (maximum distance) from the Earth 406,499 km Perigee (minimum distance) 356,399 km.
Atmosphere	It has no atmosphere, as its gravitational pull is too weak to hold down gases.
Temperature	100°C (Day time); –180°C (At night)
Orbital period	27 days 7 hr 43.7 min
Average orbital speed	1.022 km/s speed
Circumference	10,921 km (equatorial)

Earth At a Glance	
Axial tilt	23.44°
Rotation	23 hr, 56 min and 4 sec
Revolution	365.2425 days
Average orbital speed	29.78 km/s–1,200 km/h
Circumference	40,077 km (equatorial)/ 40,009 km (polar)
Diameter	12,756 km (equatorial) / 12,714 km (polar)
Surface area	510,072,000 Km² (In Total) 148,940,000 Km² land (29.2 %) 361,132,000 Km² water (70.8 %)
Surface temperature	Min : 89.2°C, Max: 57.8°C Mean : 14°C
Composition of atmosphere	78.08% Nitrogen (N_2), 20.95% Oxygen (O_2), 0.93% Argon (Ar), 0.038% Carbon dioxide (CO_2), About 1% water vapour (varies with climate)
Volume	1,084,000 million cubic km
Mass	5.98 x 10^{21} metric tonnes
Density	5.52g/cm³
Satellite	1 (Moon)

 **SUMMARY**

- **Axis :** It is an imaginary line, extending from the geographic North Pole to the geographic South Pole, around which the Earth is imagined to be rotating.
- **Atmosphere :** It is a layer of gases surrounding the planet Earth.
- **Biosphere :** It is the space on and near the Earth's surface that contains and supports all kinds of living organisms and ecosystems.
- **Ecosystem :** Ecosystem is a group of organisms and the environment with which the organisms interact.
- **Equator :** An imaginary line around the Earth forming the great circle that is equidistant from the North and South Poles.
- **Geoid :** The Geoid is an equipotential surface that serves as a reference surface from which topographic heights and ocean depths are measured.
- **Hydrosphere :** The combined mass of water found on, under, and over the surface of a planet is called Hydrosphere.
- **Lithosphere :** The outer solid layer of the Earth is called Lithosphere.
- **Northern Hemisphere :** The hemisphere that is to the north of the equator is called the Northern Hemisphere.
- **North Pole :** The point at which the northern end of the Earth's axis of rotation intersects the Earth's surface is called the North Pole.
- **South Pole :** The southernmost point of the Earth's axis is called South Pole.
- **Southern Hemisphere :** The hemisphere to the south of the equator is called Southern Hemisphere.
- **Solar System:** The Sun along with its planets, and their satellites, comets, meteors etc. form the Solar System.
- **Solar Nebula :** The rotating flattened cloud of gas and dust from which the Sun and the rest of the bodies in the Solar System are formed is called Solar Nebula.
- **Water Cycle :** The natural cycle of evaporation of water, and subsequent condensation and precipitation as rain and snow is called water cycle.

 **EXERCISES**

A. Answer the following questions

1. What is the position of Earth with respect to Sun?
2. Name the three layers of the surface of the Earth.
3. Name the early mathematician who held the view that Earth was spherical in shape.
4. Why is the Earth called as an oblate spheroid?
5. State two evidences that prove the spherical shape of the Earth.
6. What is the importance of Earth's magnetic field?
7. What is the surface distribution ratio of land and water on Earth?
8. What is the significance of the atmosphere of the Earth as compared to other planets?
9. How many satellites does Earth have, and what are they?
10. How long does the Moon take to revolve around the Earth?

B. Explain the following terms

1. Solar Nebula
2. Ozone Layer
3. Water Cycle
4. Biosphere

C. Give reasons for the following

1. The Earth is a habitable planet.
2. Earth is a unique planet.
3. The shape of the Earth is not exactly a sphere.

D. Diagrams

1. Draw a sketch showing lunar eclipse.
2. Draw a diagram to show water cycle.

E. Board Questions

1. What conditions favour life on the Earth ?
2. What is Geoid ?

CHAPTER 2
LATITUDES AND LONGITUDES

> **Concept of Latitudes :** Main Latitudes, their location with Degrees, Parallels of Latitude and their uses.
> **Concept of Longitudes–**Prime Meridian, Time (Local, Standard and time zones, Greenwich Mean Time (GMT) and International Date Line (IDL). Eastern and Western Hemisphere. Using Latitudes and Longitudes to find location. Calculation of Time, Great Circle and their use.

Planet Earth's spherical shape can be represented by means of a globe. Globes are maps represented on the surface of a sphere. Earth is having a vast equatorial circumference of approximately 40,077 km. This vast expanse of land consists of a number of villages, towns, cities, countries within the great continents. In this case, how does one find out a specific location on the globe? This is where maps are considered extremely useful. A map is a graphic representation of a portion of the Earth's surface (area of land, or sea showing physical features, cities, roads, etc.) drawn to scale. It provides information on the existence, the location and the distance between the ground features such as populated places, and routes of travel and communication. Major types of maps include topographic maps, showing features of Earth's land surface, nautical charts, representing coastal and marine areas, hydrographic charts, which represents ocean depths and currents, and aeronautical charts, which detail surface features and air routes. During the Earth's annual orbit around the Sun, four cardinal points – North, South, East, and West – are reached. These four cardinal directions are the guidelines for locating places on the globe and are indicated on every map.

EARTH'S GRID

A grid system allows the location of a point on a map (or on the surface of the Earth) to be represented in a way that is easily and universally understood. It is a pattern of horizontal and vertical lines drawn on a map, which intersect at coordinates. Geographers use these coordinates to locate places on Earth, on maps, and on globes. The vertical lines are called lines of longitude or meridians, and the horizontal lines are called lines of latitude or parallels.

LATITUDE

Latitude is the angular distance (in degrees, minutes, and seconds) of a point, north, or south of the Equator. Lines of latitude are often referred to as parallels. The Equator is an imaginary line that runs around the surface of the Earth, perpendicular to its axis of rotation. It is located equidistant from the poles. The northernmost point is known as the North Pole, and the southernmost point as the South Pole.

Equator is the 0° latitude, while the North Pole and South Pole are 90°N and 90°S latitude, respectively. The lines of latitude are circles of different sizes. The longest circle is the Equator, while at the Poles, the circles shrink to a point. As latitudes run parallel to the Equator, they are also known as parallels of Latitude. *(Fig. 2.1)*

The total circumference of the Earth is 360° and the distance from the Equator to the poles (North and South) is one-fourth of this. If the parallels of latitudes are drawn at an interval of 1°, there will be 90 parallels in the northern and southern hemispheres respectively. Thus, there would be 181 latitudes including the Equator. The distance between two adjacent latitudes is equal throughout except near the poles, where it is slightly longer than near the Equator due to the Earth's polar flattening. Each degree of latitude is approximately 69 miles (111 km) apart (the Earth represents 360° and the circumference of the Earth is 40,000 km approximately: so, 40,000/360° = 111 km). For precision purposes, the degree is further subdivided into minutes (') (1 min = 1.85 km) and seconds (") (1 sec = 30 m), there are 60 minutes in each degree, and each minute has 60 seconds.

Eg.: Mumbai lies on 18°55′ N latitude. So, its distance from the Equator = [18 × 111 km (55 × 1850 m)] = 2100 km.

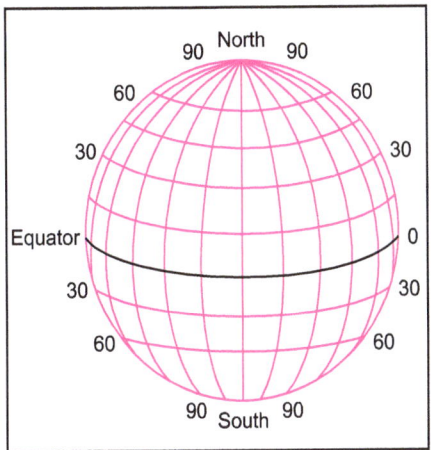

Fig. 2.1 : Parallels of Latitude.

The Five Parallels of Latitudes

- **Equator (0°)** : It is the 0° latitude, which divides the Earth into two halves: Northern Hemisphere and Southern Hemisphere. It is also the only line of latitude, which is also a great circle. *(Fig. 2.2)*

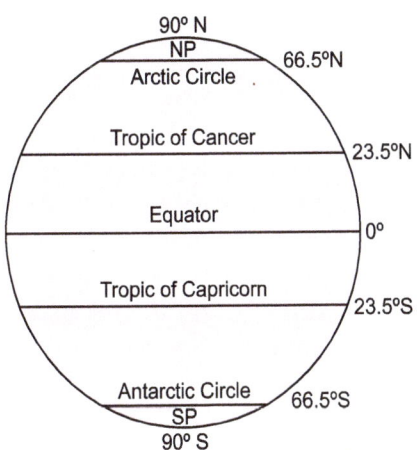

Fig. 2.2 : Some important lines of Latitudes.

- **Tropic of Cancer (23½°N)** : It is located 23½° North of the Equator. It is the farthest northern latitude at which the Sun can appear directly overhead. It runs through Mexico, Egypt, Saudi Arabia, India, and southern China. The Sun is directly over the Tropic of Cancer at noon on summer or northern solstice.

- **Tropic of Capricorn (23½°S)** : It is located 23½° South of the Equator. It is the farthest southern latitude at which the Sun can appear directly overhead. It runs through Chile, southern Brazil, South Africa, and Australia. The Sun is directly over the Tropic of Capricorn at noon on the winter or southern solstice.

- **Arctic Circle (66½°N)** : It is located 66½° North of the Equator. The Arctic Circle marks the southern extremity of the polar day (24-hour sunlit day, often referred to as the 'midnight Sun') and polar night (24-hour Sunless night).

- **Antarctic Circle (66½°S)** : It is located 66½° South of the Equator. Antarctic Circle experiences at least one whole day during which the Sun does not set, and at least one complete day during which the Sun does not rise (during the solstices). The area south of the Antarctic Circle is known as the Antarctic.

The latitude of a place can be determined by :

❑ **Observing the Pole Star :** The Pole Star is the only star in the northern hemisphere, that does not change its position, and this has been recognized by sailors for hundreds of years. *(Fig. 2.3)* If you are at the Equator, the star will be just above the horizon, if you are at the North Pole, it will be directly above your head. The angle between the star and the horizon indicates the latitude. This angle can be accurately measured with a device called *Sextant*.

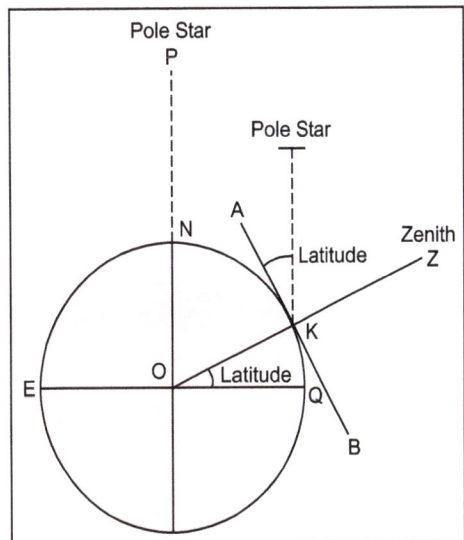

Fig. 2.3 : Finding Latitude by observing Pole Star.

- **Observing the Sun :** When the Sun is overhead, one should note :

- **Zenith Distance :** It is the angle that the Sun makes at noon with the zenith (the point in the sky, which is vertically above the observer). This can be obtained with the help of instruments.
- **Declination of the Sun :** It is the angle that the Sun makes North or South of the Equator on a particular day. This information can be obtained from the Almanac (book of astronomical data).

Northern Hemisphere

Latitude of a place = zenith distance + declination of the Sun

Southern Hemisphere

Latitude of a place = zenith distance − declination of the Sun

Example : See Fig. 2.4 :

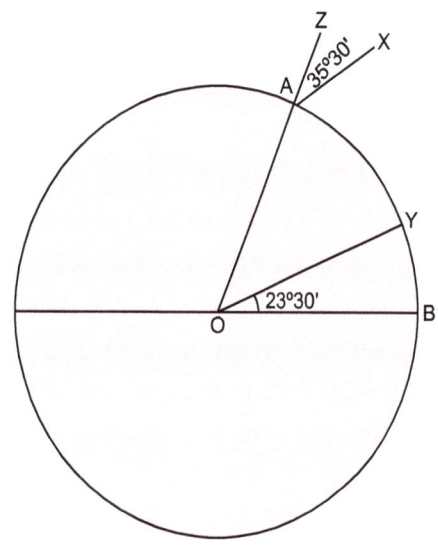

Fig. 2.4 : Finding Latitude by observing the Sun.

Latitude of place A = zenith distance (35°30′) +
          declination of the Sun (23°30′ N)
        = 59°N

Importance of Latitudes

- Latitudes help to locate places on the Earth's surface very easily. Economic and industrial developments of various countries depend upon their interaction and communication across the world. This is possible only because we know the exact locations of these places.
- It helps us to locate the position of a place away from the Equator, which is the only Great Circle. Sailors and aircrafts all over the world use the Great Circle route to save time and fuel. This route is mapped with the help of latitudes.
- Latitudes also result in extreme seasonal differences because the angle of the Sun vary at different times of the year which causes change in weather, depending on the latitude. This affects the temperature and the types of flora and fauna of that area. For example, tropical rainforests are the most biodiverse places in the world; while harsh conditions in the Arctic and Antarctic make it difficult for many species to survive.
- Latitude is of significance also because it helps navigators and researchers to understand the various patterns found on Earth. E.g., High latitudes have very different climates than low latitudes. In the Arctic, the climate is much colder and drier than in the Tropics.

Climatic Zones of the Earth

Latitudes help us to divide the Earth into different climatic zones *(Fig. 2.5)*.

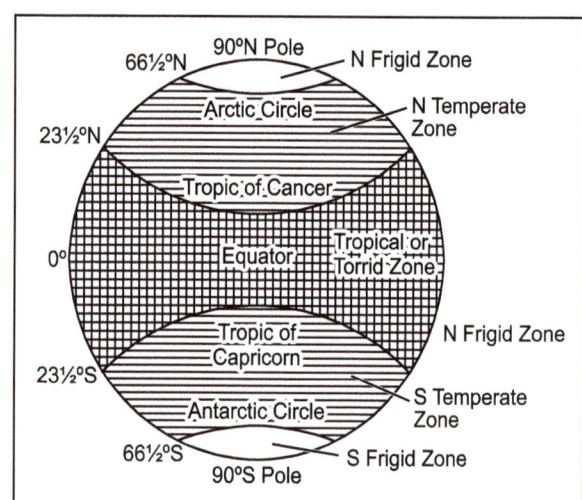

Fig. 2.5 : Climatic Zones of the Earth.

The climate is determined based on these Temperature Zones, as the amount of heat received from the Sun varies due to the inclination of the Earth. The three main climatic zones can be classified as under :

- **Torrid/Tropical Zones:** The geographic region lying in between the Tropic of Cancer (23½°N) and the Tropic of Capricorn (23½°S) is called as the Torrid Zone. The Sun's rays fall vertically over this surface almost throughout the year. Therefore, very high temperature prevails during the summer and mild temperature during winter. The areas 5°N and 5°S of the Equator are called the Doldrums or Equatorial Zones. The Torrid Zone includes most of Africa, southern India, southern Asia, Indonesia, New Guinea, northern Australia, southern Mexico, central America, and northern South America.
- **Temperate Zones :** The North Temperate Zone extends from the Tropic of Cancer (23½°N) to the Arctic Circle (66½°N). The South Temperate

Zone extends from the Tropic of Capricorn (23½°S) to the Antarctic Circle (66½°S). The Sun's rays fall at an inclined angle over this surface throughout the year. Therefore, mild temperature (neither too hot nor too cold) prevails in this zone round the year. However, at times, erratic weather patterns can be seen in this zone. The North Temperate Zone includes Great Britain, Europe, northern Asia, North America, and northern Mexico. The South Temperate Zone includes southern Australia, New Zealand, southern South America, and South Africa.

- **Frigid Zones :** The region between the Arctic Circle (66½°N) and North Pole (90°N) in the northern hemisphere, and the Antarctic Circle (66½°S) and the South Pole (90°S) in the southern hemisphere, is called the 'Frigid Zone'. This zone receives the Sun's oblique rays throughout the year, as a result of which the temperature remains very low. The Frigid Zones are the coldest parts of the Earth, and are covered with ice and snow. The North Frigid Zone (the Arctic) includes northern Canada and Alaska, Greenland, northern Scandinavia, northern Russia, and the Arctic ice. The South Frigid Zone (The Antarctic) is filled by the continent of Antarctica.

LONGITUDE

Longitude is an angular distance between the Prime Meridian at Greenwich and a point on any meridian on the surface of Earth *(Fig. 2.6)*. It is an angular measurement, ranging from 0° at the Prime Meridian to +180° eastward and –180° westward and usually expressed in degrees, minutes, and seconds.

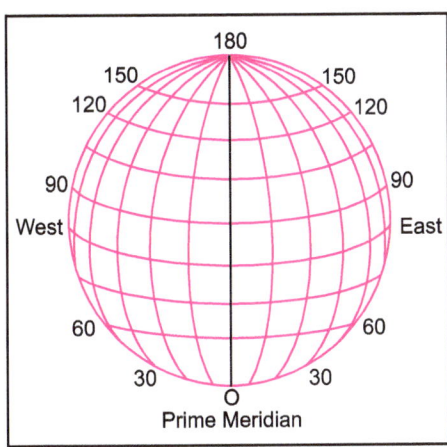

Fig. 2.6 : Meridians of Longitude.

Longitudes are a series of imaginary vertical lines connecting North Pole to South Pole, passing through the Equator. Since Earth is taken as a circle, the longitudes are drawn 1° apart on the Equator, with 1 to 179° towards East of Prime Meridian and 179° towards the West. These lines are called Meridians, which literally means as 'mid-day'.

Prime Meridian

The longitude that passes through the Royal Astronomical Observatory, Greenwich (near London, UK) is called the Prime Meridian (Greenwich Meridian). There are 360 meridians of longitude. All meridians, unlike latitudes, are complete circles dividing the Earth into Eastern and Western Hemispheres.

Unlike latitudes, with the Equator as a natural starting position, there is no natural starting position for longitudes. Therefore, a reference meridian had to be chosen. An international meridian conference in 1884 adopted the prime meridian as the universal Prime Meridian or zero point of longitude. The distance between adjacent meridian is uneven. At the Equator, it is 1° apart, (equivalent to 111 km) but this distance gradually decreases towards the poles and becomes zero at the poles as they converge into a point.

Importance of Longitude

- **To Locate the Position of Certain Place and Time Zones on the Earth's surface :** The measurement of longitude along with latitude is important to fix the location of a certain place or time zones on the surface of Earth. For example, Delhi can be anywhere on 28° 38' N latitude. But, the exact position of Delhi can be fixed where the 77° 12' E longitude intersects this position on 28° 38' N latitude. For example, 77°E longitude intersects Delhi's position on 28°N, therefore, we can say that the exact location of Delhi on the globe is 28° 38' N 77° 12' E. Therefore, only with the help of both latitude and longitude, the position of all the places on the Earth can be detected.

- **To Define the Great Circle Routes :** The measurement of longitude is important to define the Great Circle routes. Ships and aircrafts use Great Circle routes for safe navigation. Flight lengths can often be approximated to the Great Circle distance between two airports.

- **To Determine the Local Time of a Place :** Longitude is used to determine the local time of the place.

The Great Circle Routes

If the plane contains the center of the sphere, then the circle is called a Great Circle; otherwise, it is a Small Circle. The 0° latitude is the only Great Circle as its plane passes through the center of the Earth. On the contrary, all the meridians (two opposite meridians forming semi-circles together form one circle, example 0° and 180°) are Great Circles as they divide Earth into Eastern and Western Hemisphere. There can be infinite longitudes, but for our convenience, only 360 meridians are drawn, 1° apart, on the Equator.

Importance of Great Circle Routes

- The most famous use of Great Circle routes *(Fig. 2.7)* in geography is for navigation because they represent the shortest distance between two places on the Earth.

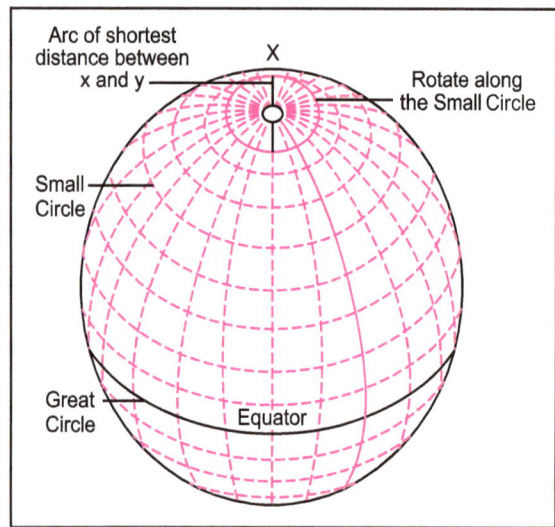

Fig. 2.7 : Great Circle.

- Due to the Earth's rotation, sailors and pilots not using Great Circle routes must constantly adjust their route, as the heading changes over long distances. The only places on Earth where the heading does not change are on the Equator or when traveling due north or south.

- Since Great Circle routes lie on the arc of a Great Circle, they are mainly used to save fuel and time, as it is very economical to travel through these routes since they are the shortest routes or distances between places.

- It is most advantageous for aircrafts. For example, over the northern hemisphere, planes travelling West normally follow a Great Circle route that moves into the Arctic to avoid travelling in the jet stream.

Longitude and Time

The Earth takes 24 hours to complete one rotation (i.e., 360° of its rotation). Therefore, to turn through 1° of longitude, the time taken is $\frac{24 \times 60}{360}$ minutes, or 4 minutes, or 240 seconds. Earth rotates from West to East. So, places in the East see the Sun first, white the places in the West see it later. Thus, for each degree of longitude towards East, a time of 4 minutes is added; and for each degree of longitude towards West, 4 minutes is subtracted.

Example 1 : Calculation of time on 30°E when it is noon at GMT *(Fig. 2.8)*.

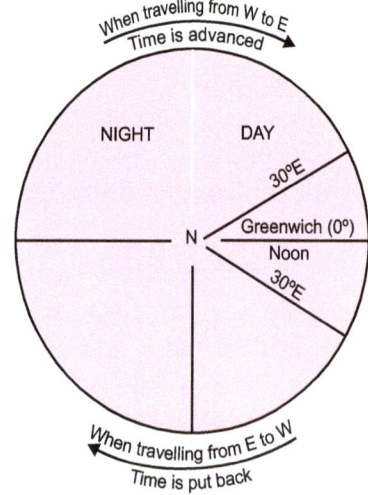

Fig. 2.8 : Longitude and Time.

$$1° = 4 \text{ min}$$

∴ $15° = 15 \times 4 = 60 \text{ min (1 hr)}$

∴ $30° = 2 \text{ hrs.}$

The place is east of GMT, so 2 hrs are added.

∴ The time on 30°E is 2:00 PM

Similarly, for 30°W, 2 hrs. is subtracted.

∴ The time on 30°W is 10:00 AM

Example 2 : Calculate the time of a place when the longitude is given :

(i) When the local time is 6 AM on Monday at Alexandria 30° E in Egypt, What will be the local time at New Orleans 90° W in USA? Refer *Fig 2.8.1*.

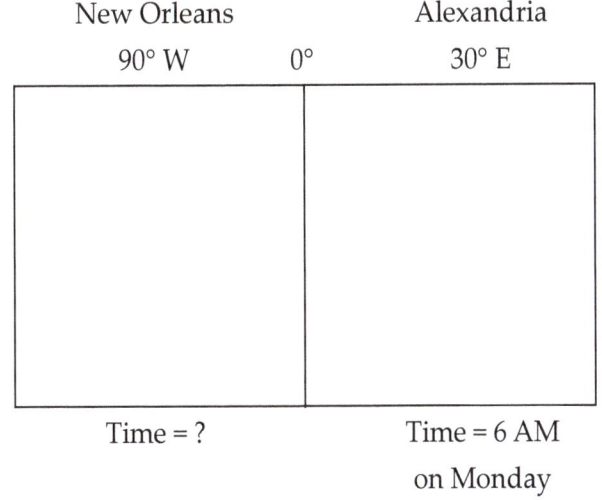

Fig. 2.8.1

Time at Alexandria 30° E = 6 A.M or 0600 hrs on Monday

Difference in Longitude between two locations
= 30 + 90 = 120°
= 120 x 4 = 480 min = 8 hrs
(For every 1°, time difference = 4 min.)

Difference in time has to be subtracted as New Orleans is to the West of Alexandria (locations to the west log behind in time from locations in the east)

Time in New Orleans
= 0600 hrs – 0800 hrs
= (2400 hrs + 0600 hrs = 3000 hrs)
= 3000 hrs – 0800 hrs
= 2200 hrs or 10 PM on Sunday
(the previous day)

(ii) A cricket match commences at Delhi 77° E at 10 AM on Sunday and the radio commentary is received at Sydney at 2.52 PM. Calculate the Longitude of Sydney. *(Fig 2.8.2.)*

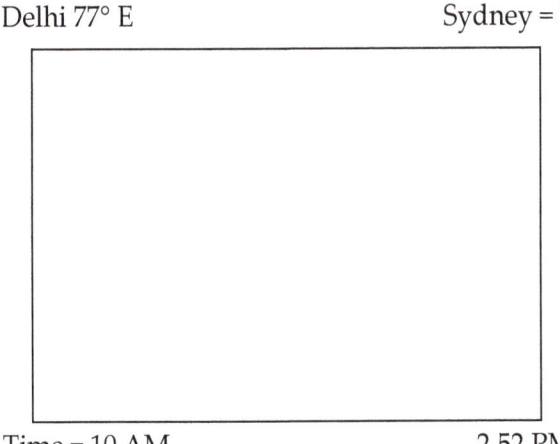

Fig. 2.8.2

Difference of time
= 1452 hrs (Sydney) – 1000 hrs (Delhi)
= 0452 hrs
= 0452 hrs = 292 min

Time difference of 4 min = 1° of Longitude

Therefore, time difference of 292 min = 292 /4 = 73° difference of longitude.

Sydney being to the East of Delhi, time at Sydney is leading, so also the longitude.

Hence, the longitude of Sydney
= 77 ° E (Delhi) + 73 ° E
= 150 ° E

Local and Standard Time

Local Time (Noon time) : Local time of a place is that time when Sun is overhead in its Meridian. For example, if Sun is overhead 60°E longitude, all the places on that longitude will have noon at that time. As the Earth rotates, Sun is overhead successive degrees of longitude every four minutes until it completes 360° in 24 hours. Thus, local time varies for each successive longitude by 4 minutes. The places located east of Greenwich see the Sun earlier and are ahead in time., whereas in the West people see the Sun later and lag behind. For example, when it is noon in London longitude 0°,the local time of Chennai (80°E) will be 5 hours 20 min ahead of London. Thus, due to the rotation of the Earth, different places on the Earth's surface experience a different time of day. Since it is not possible to have our own local time, a system of standard time is observed by all the countries.

Standard Time : Since it is not possible for all places to follow their own local time, while travelling East to West or West to East, we have adopted a standard time for each country, meaning fixed time as per schedule. The local time of the Standard Meridian of a country is called Standard Time. It remains same for that particular country–usually, it either was offset from Greenwich Mean Time, or was the local mean time of the capital of the region. The difference between local mean time and local apparent time is the equation of time. The place on the same longitude has a different standard time. Most countries adopt their Standard Time from their

Central Meridian. Indian Government has accepted the meridian of 82½° E for the Standard Time, which is 5 hours 30 minutes ahead of GMT. Nepal and Sri Lanka also follow the same Standard Time.

Greenwich Mean Time (GMT)

Greenwich Mean Time (GMT) is a term originally referring to mean solar time at the Royal Observatory in Greenwich, London (0° longitude). Noon Greenwich Mean Time is not necessarily the moment when the noon Sun crosses the Greenwich Meridian and reaches its highest point in the sky at Greenwich because of Earth's uneven speed in its elliptic orbit and its axial tilt. Its time is taken as the Standard Time of England. International time follows GMT worldwide, and is adopted uniformly by all the countries and International Airlines.

Coordinated Universal Time (UTC)

Coordinated Universal Time (UTC) can be considered equivalent to Greenwich Mean Time (GMT) (when fractions of a second are not important). UTC is the system used to indicate time in meteorology, and is recommended for all general time keeping applications. Time on most weather maps is given in UTC. It uses 24-hour (military) time notation and is based on the local standard time on the 0° longitude. Due to the irregularity of the Earth and the Sun's movements, the exact time need to be modified occasionally through the use of leap seconds. UTC takes into account the leap seconds as they are added to our clock every so often. Midnight in Greenwich corresponds to 00:00 UTC, noon corresponds to 12:00 UTC, and so on.

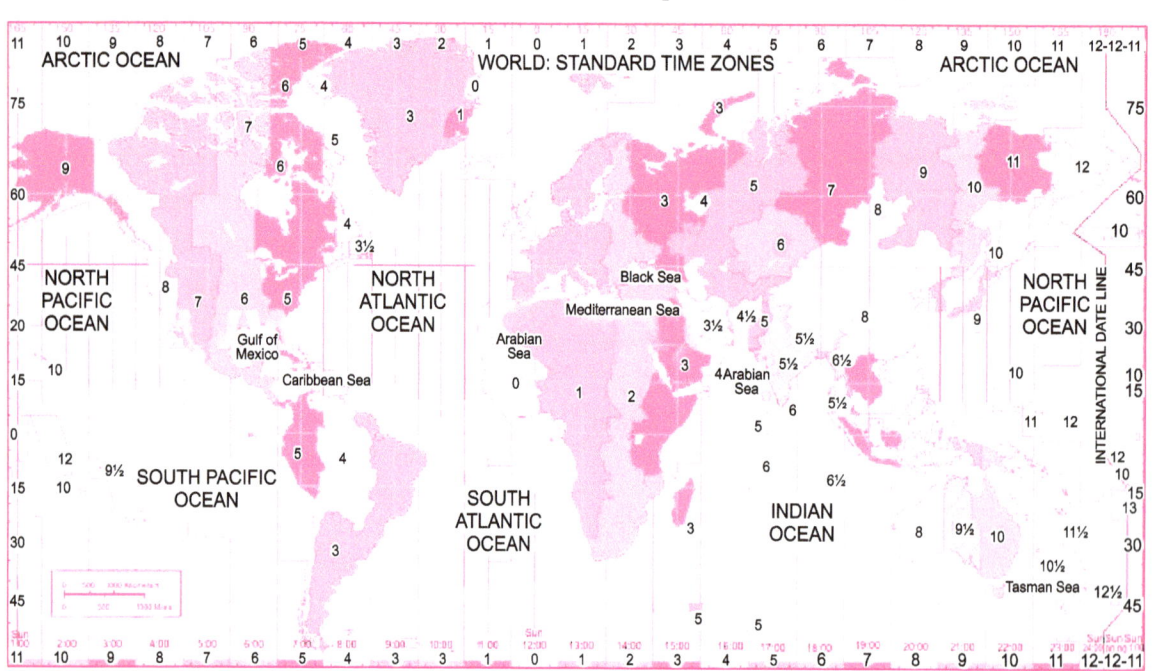

Fig. 2.9 : World Time Zones.

World Time Zones

A time zone is a region on Earth that has a uniform, legally mandated standard time. Each time zone in the world differs from the next by 15° in longitude or 1 hour in time. All the places within a particular time zone follow the fixed time as per central meridian, irrespective of their longitudes and local times. For example, in India the longitude of 82½° E (82° 30′) is selected as Standard Meridian, which passes through Allahabad. Since its local time is taken as Standard Time, the whole country follows it. It is called **Indian Standard Time (IST)**. The difference between the Indian Standard Time and the Greenwich Meridian Time (GMT) is 82½°, i.e., 5½ hours [0° to 82½° E = 82½° × 4 = 330 minutes or 5½ hours]. This means that when it is noon at England (0° longitude), it is 5.30 pm in India. Some countries such as USA, Canada, Australia, and Russia, which have a vast East to West extent, have several Time Zones. Canada has five time zones, Russia has as many as 11 time zones while, USA has five time zones: Atlantic, Eastern, Central, Mountain, and Pacific Time Zones from east to west *(Fig. 2.9)*.

International Date Line

The International Date Line (IDL) is generally a north-south imaginary line on the surface of the Earth, passing through the middle of the Pacific Ocean. It designates the place where each calendar day begins. IDL is a line concerned with the dates of the calendar and adopted internationally. It is roughly along the 180° longitude, opposite the Prime Meridian; but to avoid crossing nations internally, the line is drawn with diversion to pass around the far east of Russia and various island groups in the Pacific *(Fig. 2.10 & 2.11)*. The line is necessary in order to have a fixed, albeit arbitrary, boundary on the globe where the calendar date advances.

When we travel east of IDL it is referred to as 180°E and when we travel west of this, it is referred to as 180°W. On either side of IDL, a difference of one whole day is observed. This is because the Earth completes one rotation in 24 hrs on its axis as it moves from West to East. For example, suppose we start travelling from 0° meridian westward. On reaching 180°W, the time is decreased by 12 hrs. Hence, at 180°E, the time is increased by 12 hrs. Thus, at 180° meridian, there is a difference of exactly one day. Therefore, for the convenience of those travelling around the world, the IDL has been established.

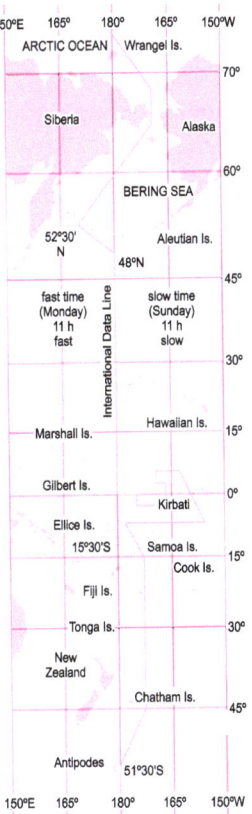

Fig. 2.10 : International Date Line (IDL)

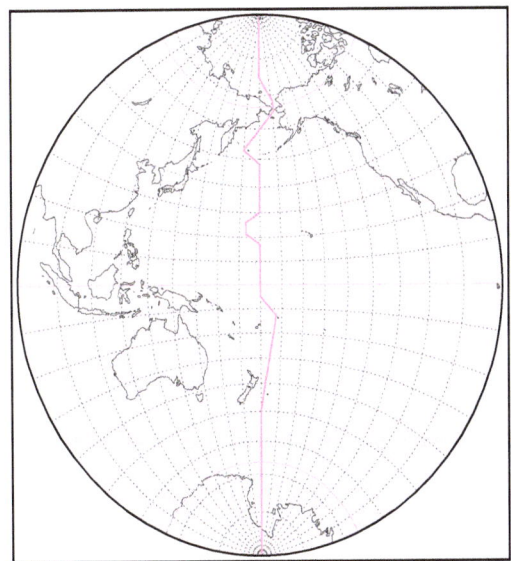

Fig. 2.11 : Closer view of IDL.

SUMMARY

- **Map :** It is a graphic representation of a portion of the Earth's surface (area of land or sea showing physical features, cities, roads, etc.) drawn to scale.
- **Equator :** It is 0° latitude that divides the Earth into Northen Hemisphere and Southern Hemisphere.
- **Arctic Circle :** It is the latitude, which is located 66½° north of the Equator.
- **Antarctic Circle :** It is the latitude, which is located 66½° south of the Equator.
- **Tropic of Cancer :** It is the latitude, which is located 23½° north of the Equator.
- **Tropic of Capricorn :** It is the latitude, which is located 23½° south of the Equator.
- **Torrid Zone :** The geographic region lying in between the Tropic of Cancer (23½°N) and the Tropic of Capricorn (23½°S).

- **Eastern Hemisphere :** The Eastern Hemisphere, also called the 'Oriental Hemisphere' refers to the half of the Earth that is east of the Prime Meridian (which crosses Greenwich, England, United Kingdom) and West of 180° longitude.
- **Western Hemisphere :** The geographical Western Hemisphere of Earth refers to the half of the Earth that lies west of the Prime Meridian.
- **Temperate Zones :** The North Temperate Zone extends from the Tropic of Cancer (23½°N) to the Arctic Circle (66½°N). The South Temperate Zone extends from the Tropic of Capricorn (23½°S)to the Antarctic Circle (66½°S).
- **Frigid Zones :** The region between the Arctic Circle (66½°N) and North Pole (90°N) in the northern hemisphere, and the Antarctic Circle (66½°S) and the South Pole (90°S) in the southern hemisphere.
- **Grid System :** It is a pattern of horizontal and vertical lines drawn on a map, which interesect at coordinates.
- **Latitude :** It is the angular distance (expressed in degrees, minutes and seconds) of a point north or south of the Equator.
- **Time Zones :** Zones or belts of given East-West (longitudinal) extent within which the standard time is applied according to a uniform system.
- **Longitude :** Longitude is a geographic coordinate that specifies the east-west position of a point on the Earth's surface. It is an angular measurement, usually expressed in degrees, minutes and seconds, and denoted by the Greek letter lambda (λ).
- **Greenwich Mean Time :** Greenwich Mean Time (GMT) is a term originally referring to mean solar time at the Royal Observatory in Greenwich, London (0° longitude).
- **Great Circle :** A Great Circle of a sphere is the intersection of the sphere and a plane, which passes through the center point of the sphere.
- **Meridian :** A meridian (or line of longitude) is an imaginary line on the Earth's surface from the North Pole to the South Pole that connects all locations along it with a given longitude.
- **Prime Meridian :** The Prime Meridian is the meridian (line of longitude) at which the longitude is defined to be 0°. It is line passing near the Royal Astronomical Observatory, Greenwich (near London in the UK).
- **International Date Line :** The International Date Line (IDL) is generally a north-south imaginary line on the surface of the Earth, passing through the middle of the Pacific Ocean.

EXERCISES

A. Answer the following questions

1. Why do we need to locate places on Earth?
2. What is a map?
3. What do you mean by grid system?
4. What is the difference between parallels and meridians?
5. How many main parallels of latitude are there in the globe and what are they?
6. Name the important climatic zones of the Earth.
7. Why are the places in the Torrid Zone hotter than the places of other zones?
8. Why are the places in the Frigid Zone colder than the places of other zones?
9. What do you mean by longitude?
10. What do you mean by Prime Meridian?
11. State the importance of Great Circle.
12. How is the local time of a place fixed?
13. What is the necessity of fixing a standard time?
14. What is Greenwich Mean Time?
15. What is Coordinated Universal Time?

B. Explain the following terms

1. Local time
2. Time Zone
3. Indian Standard Time

4. Prime Meridian
5. Latitude
6. Longitude
7. Grid System

C. Distinguish between the following

1. Latitude and Longitude.
2. Great Circle and Small Circle.
3. Parallels and Meridians.

D. Give reasons for the following

1. Equator is the only Great Circle.
2. The distance between two successive lines of latitudes remains constant.
3. Frigid Zones are very cold regions.
4. Radius of latitudinal circle diminishes from Equator to Poles.
5. The International Date Line is not a straight line like other longitudes.

E. Diagrams

1. Draw diagram to show meridians of longitude.
2. Draw diagram to show Earth's grid.
3. Draw diagrams to show the climatic zones of the Earth.

F. Board Questions

1. What is a Great Circle ?
   Name the latitude which is a Great Circle.

   Or

   Give a reason in support of your answer.
2. What do you understand by the Standard Meridian ?
3. Why it is practical to follow standard time rather than the local time ?
4. What is a time zone ? How many time zones are there in the world ?
5. (i) What is a latitude ?
   (ii) Name the latitudes which demarcate northern and southern limit of the torrid zone.

   Or

   Calculate the time of a place located at 30° E longitude, when it is 10 pm at 30° W longitude.
6. The distance between two consecutive latitudes is always the same, but it is not in case of longitudes. Explain why this is so ?

   Or

   Study the diagram given below and answer the questions :

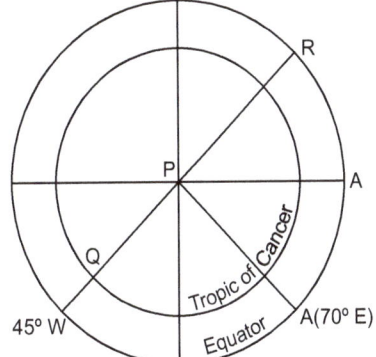

   (i) Calculate the time at Q when it is 7 am at A.
   (ii) What does IDL stand for ?
7. Give reason why pilots follow the Great Circle route.

CHAPTER 3
ROTATION AND REVOLUTION

Rotation : Direction, Speed and its Effects (Occurrence of Day and Night, the Sun rising in the East and setting in the West, Coriolis Effect).
Revolution of the Earth and its Inclined Axis-effects : The Variation in the length of the Day and Night and Seasonal Changes with Equinoxes and Solstices.

The solar system is made up of the Sun, the planets that orbit the Sun, their satellites, and many other small objects, like asteroids and comets. All these celestial bodies are constantly on the move, and we can observe their movements. We notice that the Sun rises in the east in the morning, and sets in the west in the evening. We observe different stars in the sky at different times in different places. Initially, it was believed that the Earth remained still, while all the other objects were constantly in motion. In 1543, Nicolaus Copernicus first proposed that the Earth and the other planets make regular revolutions around the Sun. In this lesson, we will look into the movements of the Earth and their significant effects.

MOVEMENTS OF THE EARTH

Two important movements of the Earth are :

- **Rotation :** It is the movement of the Earth around the axis of rotation.
- **Revolution :** It is the movement of the Earth around the Sun.

Together, these two movements create variations in the temperature, weather, and in the seasons.

Rotation

The Earth rotates on its axis from West to East. The axis of rotation is an imaginary line that passes through the North and South Poles of the Earth. Earth rotates about this axis once in 24 hours (23 hours 56 minutes, to be specific) at a speed of 1670 km/h. The Earth's axis is tilted with respect to the plane of its orbit at an angle of about 23.5°. Orbit is the path in space of an object as it goes around another body.

Effects of Rotation

- The primary effect of the Earth's rotation is the phenomenon of day and night *(Fig. 3.1)*. The varying length of day and night is directly related to rotation. The part facing the Sun has day, while the opposite part has night. At all times, half of the Earth is under Sunlight of varying intensities, half of it is in darkness, with in the great-circle boundary between night and day on Earth, known as the Circle of Illumination.

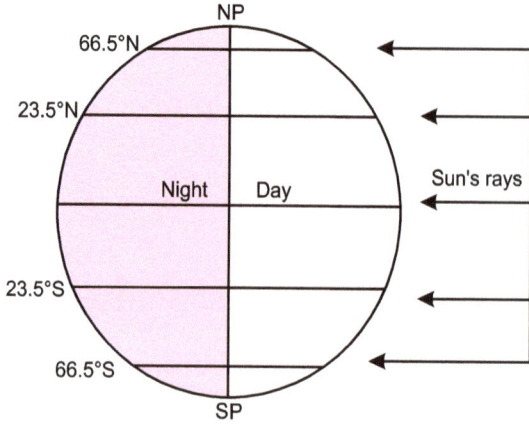

Fig. 3.1 : Occurrence of Day and Night.

- The rotation of the Earth about its axis in an anticlockwise direction (when viewed from over the North Pole), gives us the impression that the Sun rises in the east and sets in the west. Once the direction of the rising Sun is known, it is easier to find out the other directions.

- Another effect that is brought about by rotation and its varying speeds towards the Poles is the Coriolis Effect (Ferrell's Law). The ocean currents and winds are deflected towards the right in the Northern Hemisphere, and towards the left in the Southern Hemisphere due to the Coriolis force created due to Earth's rotation.
- The rotation of the Earth causes it to bulge in shape at the Equator. The Earth is not a perfect sphere, its shape has actually been modified by its rotation, and it is described as an 'oblate spheroid'.
- The rotation of the Earth contributes to the magnetic field around our planet that protects us against the Sun's harmful radiation and solar storms.
- Variation in temperatures is also caused by rotation. During daytime, there is a rise in temperature because of the Sun's rays, while at night the temperature comes down.
- The rotation also causes tides.

Revolution

The Earth revolves around the Sun in an elliptical orbit. It takes 365 days, 5 hours, 48 minutes, and 46 seconds (approx. 365.25 days) to make a full revolution around the Sun.

Revolution Period

The Earth orbits the Sun at a speed of 108,000 km/h. It takes 365.25 days to make a full revolution around the Sun. This explains the occurrence of Leap years. A leap year is a year in which an extra day is added to the calendar in order to synchronize it with the seasons. The one-fourth day gets added up and is counted as one full day every 4 years. A leap year has 366 days, the extra day being added as February 29.

Perihelion and Aphelion

The words 'Perihelion' and 'Aphelion' come from the Greek language. In Greek, *helios* means Sun, *peri* means near, and *apo* means away from *(Fig. 3.2)*. The mean distance between the Earth and the Sun is about 150 million km. The Earth's orbit around the Sun is not a circle, but slightly elliptical. Therefore, the distance between the Earth and the Sun keeps on varying throughout the year. When the Earth is closest to the Sun (about 91 million miles/147 million km), it is called Perihelion. It occurs on January 3rd. When the Earth is farthest away from the Sun (about 95 million miles/152 million km), it is called Aphelion. It occurs on July 4th.

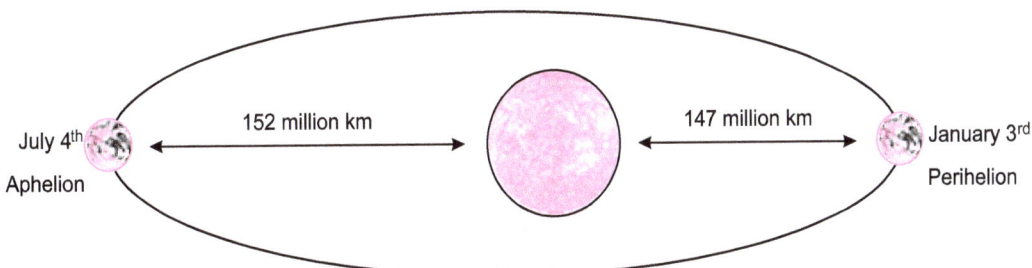

Fig. 3.2 : Perihelion and Aphelion.

Effects of Revolution

- **Changing Altitude of the Mid-Day Sun :** The Earth's revolution around the Sun changes the apparent altitude of the mid-day Sun. The Sun is directly overhead at the Equator on March 21st (Spring Equinox), and September 23rd (Autumn Equinox). After Spring Equinox, the Sun appears to move north and shines directly over the Tropic of Cancer on June 21st (Summer Solstice). On December 21st, the Sun shines overhead the Tropic of Capricorn (Winter Solstice). The Tropic of Cancer and Tropic of Capricorn marks the limit of the overhead Sun, as the Sun never shines vertically beyond the tropics *(Fig. 3.3)*.
- **Varying Lengths of Day and Night :** The length of day and night varies according to the seasons. On June 21st, the Sun is overhead at noon along the Tropic of Cancer and all parallels in the Northern Hemisphere experience the longest day of the year. Length of day increases with an increase in latitude towards north of Equator. On December 22nd, the Sun is overhead the Tropic of Capricorn and the conditions are reversed. Length of day increases with increasing latitude, south of the Equator. On March 21st and September 23rd, as the Sun is overhead at noon at the Equator, all places have 12 hours of day and 12 hours of night.

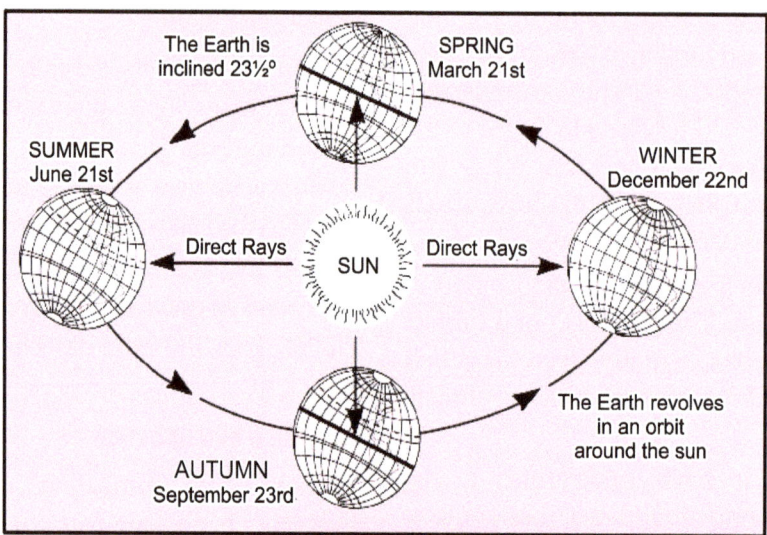

Fig. 3.3 : Inclination of the Earth's axis.

- **Variation of the Seasons :** Revolution causes different seasons, i.e., the changing weather condition due to differences in the heating of the Earth.
- **Inclination of the Earth's Axis and its Significance :** The Earth spins on an imaginary line called Axis. The North of this line is called North Pole (90°N of Equator) and the South of this line is called South Pole (90°S of Equator). Equator is an imaginary line on the Earth's surface equidistant from the North Pole and South Pole that divides the Earth into Northern Hemisphere and Southern Hemisphere. It is also known as the 0° latitude. The Sun appears to move around the Earth in a path, which is called the ecliptic *(Fig. 3.4)*.

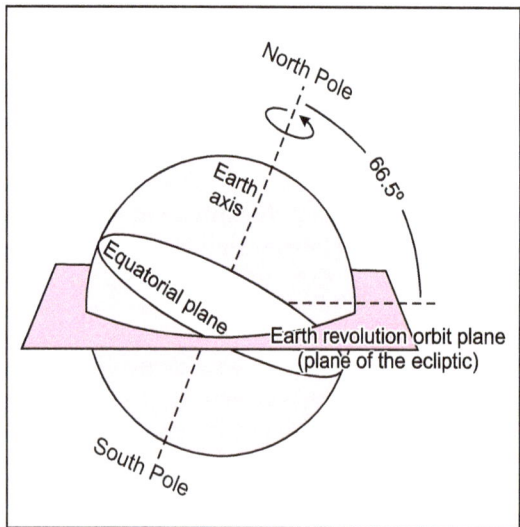

Fig. 3.4 : Different positions of the Earth around the Sun.

The Earth's axis is tilted 23½° from the perpendicular to the ecliptic. Also, Earth's axis points in the same direction. Currently, it is pointing in the direction of the North Star, also called Polaris. In other words, the ecliptic is tilted to the plane of the Earth's Equator by 23½°. Our orbital motion makes the Sun to move eastward among the stars. Our axial tilt also causes the Sun to move northward or southward with respect to the Equator. This change in the position on Earth over which the Sun is shining directly overhead results in the seasonal changes. Summer is warmer than winter (in each hemisphere), because the Sun's rays hit the Earth at a more direct angle during the summer than during winters, and because the days are much longer than the nights during the summers. During the winters, the Sun's rays hit the Earth at an extreme angle, and the days are very short. These effects are due to the tilt of the Earth's axis.

The hemisphere that is tilted towards the Sun is warmer because Sunlight travels more directly to the Earth's surface, so less of it gets scattered in the atmosphere. That means that when it is summer in the Northern Hemisphere, it is winter in the Southern Hemisphere. The hemisphere tilted towards the Sun has longer days and shorter nights. That is why days are longer during the summer than during the winter.

In general, the further you travel away from the Equator, the summer and winter temperatures become cooler. At the Equator, there are no seasons because each day the Sun strikes at about the same angle. Every day of the year, the Equator receives about 12 hours of Sunlight. The poles remain cool because they are never tilted in the direct path of Sunlight.

The Onset of Seasons

To understand why we have seasons, we need to look at the relations between the Earth and the Sun. The plane of the ecliptic is the plane of the Earth's orbit around the Sun. Most of the planets in the solar system also orbit on or near the plane of the ecliptic.

The Sun's rays are parallel to each other when they reach the Earth. Therefore, if the Earth's axis of rotation were perpendicular to the plane of the ecliptic, the direct rays of the Sun would always shine on the Equator (that is, the angle of incidence at the Equator would be 90°), and you would always see the Sun just on the horizon at the North and South Poles (i.e., the angle of incidence at the Poles would be zero). If it was to happen like this, we would have no seasons.

However, the Earth's axis is not perpendicular to the plane of the ecliptic. If you drew a line perpendicular to the plane of the ecliptic, the Earth's axis of rotation would be tilted, or inclined, at an angle of about 23½° with respect to the perpendicular line. It is this inclination of the Earth's axis that gives us the four seasons of the year – spring, summer, autumn (fall), and winter. Since the axis is tilted, different parts of the Earth are exposed towards the Sun at different times of the year.

SOLSTICES

The times when the Sun is at its furthest from the Equator are called the summer and winter solstices and these occur in mid-summer and mid-winter. The word 'solstice' comes from the Latin word 'solstitium' meaning Sun stands still because the apparent movement of the Sun's path north or south stops before changing direction.

Summer Solstice

On June 21st or 22nd, the Sun shines vertically over the Tropic of Cancer and the North Pole is tilted towards the Sun. It is termed as Summer Solstice *(Fig. 3.5)*.

Characteristics

- Tropic of Cancer receives the direct rays of the Sun and Northern Hemisphere experiences summer season.
- The Southern Hemisphere receives the minimum amount of heat, and thus experiences winter season.
- On this day, Northern Hemisphere experiences the longest day and shortest night.
- In the Southern Hemisphere, days are shorter and nights are longer.
- The Circle of Illumination touches the Arctic Circle on the far side of the Earth and the Antarctic Circle on the near side of the Earth.
- There is daylight for 24 hours north of the Arctic Circle (66.5° N of the Equator; also termed as the Land of the Midnight Sun as the Sun never sets that day) and 24 hours of darkness south of the Antarctic Circle (66.5° S of the Equator).
- The length of day increases with increasing latitude north of the Equator.
- The Sun's rays are directly overhead along the Tropic of Cancer (the latitudinal line at 23.5° N, passing through Mexico, Saharan Africa, and India).

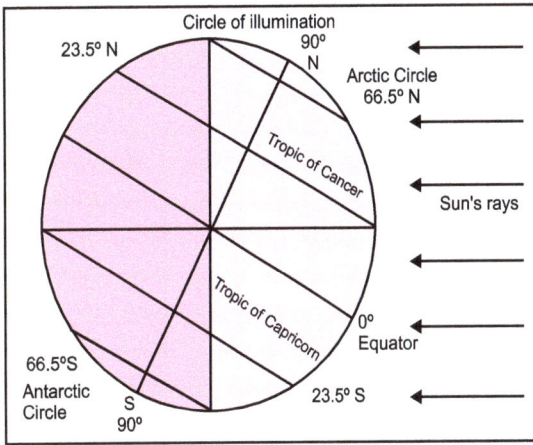

Fig. 3.5 : Summer Solstice.

Winter Solstice

On December 22nd, the Sun shines vertically over the Tropic of Capricorn and the South Pole is tilted towards the Sun. It is termed as Winter Solstice *(Fig. 3.6)*.

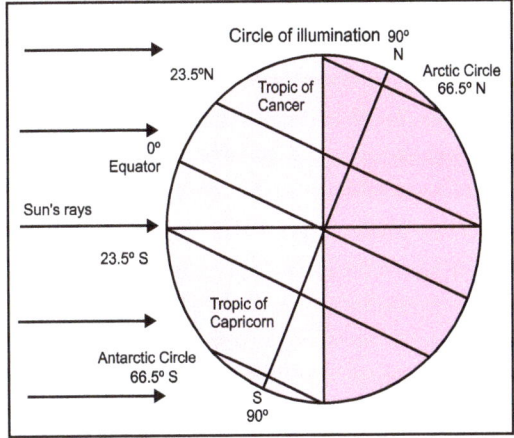

Fig. 3.6 : Winter Solstice.

Characteristics

- Tropic of Capricorn receives the direct rays of the Sun and Southern Hemisphere experiences summer season.
- The Northern Hemisphere receives the minimum amount of heat, and thus experiences winter season.
- On this day, Southern Hemisphere experiences the longest day and shortest night.
- In the Northern Hemisphere, days are shorter and nights are longer.
- The Circle of Illumination touches the Antarctic Circle on the far side of the Earth and the Arctic Circle on the near side of the Earth.
- There is daylight for 24 hours south of the Antarctic Circle (66.5°S of the Equator) and 24 hours of darkness north of the Arctic Circle (66.5°N of the Equator).
- The length of day increases with increasing latitude south of the Equator.
- The Sun's rays are directly overhead along the Tropic of Capricorn (the latitudinal line at 23.5° S, passing through Brazil, South Africa, and Australia).

Summer Solstice	Winter Solstice
1. It occurs on 21st June.	1. It occurs on 22nd December.
2. Sun is overhead at the Tropic of Cancer.	2. Sun is overhead at the Tropic of Capricorn.
3. It is the longest day in the Northern Hemisphere.	3. It is the longest day in the Southern Hemisphere.
4. Causes Summer in Northern Hemisphere.	4. Causes Summer in Southern Hemisphere.

EQUINOXES

Equinoxes occur when the axis of rotation of the Earth is exactly parallel to the direction of motion of the Earth around the Sun *(Fig. 3.7)*. The Sun's rays pass through both the poles. This happens on just two days of the year, the vernal and autumn equinoxes. This means that the length of the day is exactly the same (12 hours) at all points on the Earth's surface on this day (except the poles, where it will change from permanent light to dark, or vice versa). The name Equinox is derived from the Latin word *'aequus'* (equal) and *'nox'* (night), because the night and day are almost equally long.

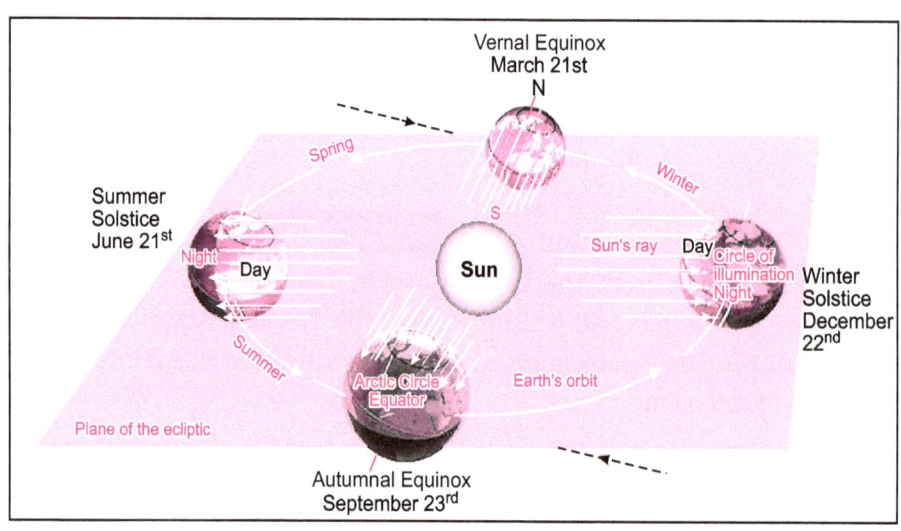

Fig. 3.7 : Equinox.

Vernal Equinox

It is the first day of the spring season and occurs when the Sun passes the Equator moving from the southern to the northern hemisphere. It is the beginning of a long period of sunlight at the Pole. In the northern hemisphere, the North Pole begins to lean toward the Sun. Day and night are of approximately the same length. It falls on March 20th or 21st. It is also called as Spring Equinox.

Autumnal Equinox

It is the first day of the autumn season and occurs when the Sun passes the Equator moving from the northern to the southern hemisphere. It is the beginning of a long period of darkness at the Pole. The North Pole begins to tilt away from the Sun.

Day and night are of approximately the same length. It falls on September 22nd or 23rd.

Twilight and Dawn

No place on earth has an abrupt change from day to night or vice versa. There is a transition period between day and night as well as night and day.

During this transition period, there is diffused light produced by the scattering of air molecules, minute particles of dust and moisture which reflects the Sun rays back to the earth surface. Long after the Sun has disappeared below the horizon, this occurs both before sunrise and after sunset.

The period of diffused light before sunset is called *Twilight* and the period of diffused light before sunrise is called *Dawn*. In low latitudes, the duration of dawn and twilight is short, in the middle and higher latitudes, there is long period of twilight lasting for many days during the Summer season especially beyond 50° latitude. At the Polar region, twilight or dawn continues nearly for 7 weeks during the winter season when the Sun is within 18° of the horizon.

Solstice	Equinox
1. This is the highest point of the Sun at the two Tropics.	1. This is the highest position of the Sun at the Equator.
2. Takes place on 21st June and 22nd December.	2. Takes place on 21st March and 23rd September.
3. Length of days and nights varies. On 21st June, days are longer and nights are shorter in the Northern Hemisphere. On 22nd December, days are longer and nights are shorter in the Southern Hemisphere.	3. The length of days and nights are equal in both the Hemispheres.

SUMMARY

- **Axis :** It is the imaginary line on which the Earth spins.
- **Aphelion :** When the Earth is farthest from the Sun, it is said to be in Aphelion.
- **Equinox:** Equinoxes (Vernal and Autumnal) are days on which the day and night are of equal duration.
- **Leap Year :** It is the year in which an extra day gets added to the calendar. It comes once in 4 years.
- **Orbit :** It is the path in space of an object as it goes around another body.
- **Perihelion :** When the Earth is closest to the Sun, it is said to be in Perihelion.
- **Rotation :** It is the movement of the Earth about its axis that passes through the North and South Poles of the Earth. Earth rotates once in 24 hours (23 hr 56 min).
- **Revolution :** It is the movement of the Earth around the Sun. Earth completes one revolution in 365.25 days.
- **Solstice :** Solstices (Summer and Winter Solstice) are the days when the Sun reaches its farthest northern and southern declinations.

EXERCISES

A. Answer the following questions

1. What do you mean by Solar System?
2. What are the two motions of the Earth?
3. What causes the occurrence of day and night?
4. What causes the slight flattening of the Earth at the poles?
5. How long does the Earth takes to move around its own axis?
6. What is an orbit?
7. What is Ferrell's Law?
8. Explain the meaning of the term 'Solstice'.
9. When and how do Vernal Equinox and Autumnal Equinox occur?
10. What are the effects of 'Inclination of the Earth'?

B. Explain the following terms

1. Axis
2. Leap Year
3. Perihelion
4. Plane of Ecliptic
5. Revolution
6. Geoid
7. Equinox
8. Solstice

C. Distinguish between the following

1. Perihelion and Aphelion
2. Solstice and Equinox
3. Summer Solstice and Winter Solstice

D. Give reasons for the following

1. The variation in the length of day and night goes on increasing towards poles.
2. Beyond the Tropics, the Sun is never overhead.
3. Norway is called "The Land of the Midnight Sun".
4. On 21st March, day and night are of equal duration at all places on Earth.

E. Diagrams

1. Draw a sketch to show the phenomenon of day and night.

F. Board Questions

1. (i) On which date will the North Pole have 24 hours of day light ?
   (ii) Give a reason for your answer.
2. Draw a neat, well labelled diagram to show Winter Solstice.
   (i) Mention two effects of the Earth's revolution.
   (ii) How much time does the earth take to make one revolution.

Or

Draw a fully labelled diagram of the position of the Earth on 22nd December.

3. Give reason for the speed of rotation of Earth is maximum at the Equator.
4. What do you mean by the term Equinox ?
   Give the dates on which this phenomenon takes place.

CHAPTER 4
STRUCTURE OF THE EARTH AND INTERNAL PROCESSES

Core, Mantle, Crust : Meaning, Extent and their Composition.

Our planet Earth is more than five thousands million years old and is still in the process of changing. The origin of the Earth plays an important role in determining its material make up and structure as well as temperature, pressure condition and density at various depths.

While the gaseous and liquid realms of the Earth are constituted by the Atmosphere and Hydrosphere, the Lithosphere remains as the solid inorganic realm. The surface of the Earth consists of mountains, plateaus, plains, valleys, etc., all of which vary in size and distribution. Some of these landforms are created by the external denudation processes taking place on the Earth's surface, while others originate due to the internal forces operating in the interior of the Earth.

Therefore, to understand the surface features of the Earth, it is necessary to have knowledge about the interior structure of the Earth.

Sources of Information About the Interior of the Earth

It is not possible to make for direct observation of the Earth interior, except by mining and drilling, that too for a few kilometers only. The deepest bore ever drilled at Kola in the Arctic Ocean extends only 13 kilometers below the surface of the Earth. Many such drilling operations have provided valuable information by the analysis of the extracted materials.

The indirect sources of information about the Earth interior are inferences drawn from a study and analysis of the properties of the matter – temperature, pressure, density, magnetic field, gravitation and response to seismic activities.

Temparature, Density and Pressure Inside the Earth

Temperature

The temperature inside the Earth's surface increases with depth. On an average, for every 32 m of descent from the surface, the temperature rises by 1°C. This rapid increase in temperature continues up to a great depth. Thereafter, the temperature increases slowly. At this rate, the temperature at the centre or core of the Earth can be calculated to be more than 4000°C. At a depth of 48 km, the temperature would be between 1200°C and 2000°C at which the rocks and materials cannot remain in solid state.

Pressure

The pressure inside the earth increases as we go deeper. The interior of the Earth is under tremendous pressure from the layers above. Taking one atmospheric unit equals to a pressure of about 14.7 lb per sq inch, the pressure, at a depth of 2500 km, is about one million atmospheres and at the core of the Earth, the pressure is estimated to be about 3.5 million atmospheres.

Density

The average density of the Earth is 5.5 gm per cubic centimeter. The densities of the rocks change with increasing temperatures inside the Earth.

LAYERS OF THE EARTH

Based on the study of physical property of the Earth's surface, behavioral pattern of seismic waves of Earthquakes and the lava erupted from volcanoes, the Earth is made up of three different and distinct layers, i.e., The Crust, The Mantle, and The Core *(Fig. 4.1)*.

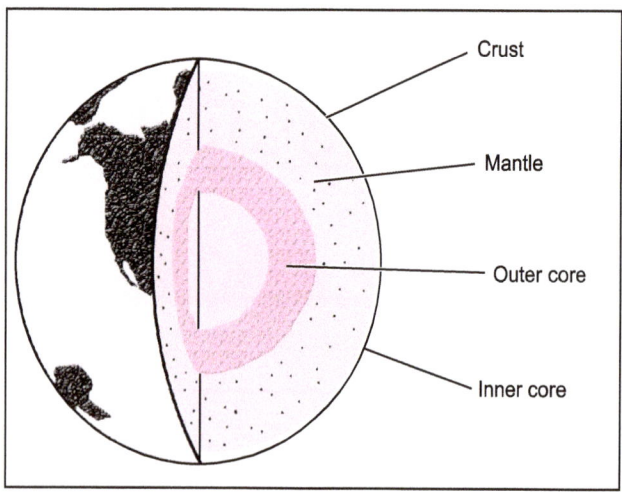

Fig. 4.1 : Concentric layers of the Earth

Each layer has its own specific properties. The deeper layers are composed of heavier materials; they are hotter, denser and under greater pressure than the outer layers. The density, temperature and pressure of these layers increase with depth. To study the landforms on the Earth's surface, it is essential to learn about the chemical composition and physical state of the matter inside the Earth.

The Crust or Lithosphere

The crust is the outermost layer, also known as Lithosphere, taken from the Greek word *'Lithos'* meaning rock. It is a thin layer of rock enveloping the interior of the Earth. The crust has an average thickness of about 60 km and forms less than 1% of the Earth's radius. The temperature of the crust varies from air temperature on top to about 1600°F (870°C) in the deepest parts of the crust. The thickness of the crust and density of the rocks increases with depth. There are two different types of crust *(Fig. 4.2)* :

SIAL Layer

It is the top most layer consisting of granitic rocks which on an average forms the first 25 km of the crust. The main mineral constituents are silica and aluminium, thus it is called SIAL (Si-silica; Al-aluminium). It is thicker over the continents but thin or absent on the ocean floor especially the Pacific Ocean. It has an average density of about 2.7 gm per cubic centimeter.

SIMA Layer

Below the SIAL layer is a denser layer, on an average 35 km, which consists of Silicate and Magnesium, Iron and other denser materials. It is a continuous zone of basaltic rocks forming the ocean floor. Its main mineral constituents are silica and magnesium, thus it is called as SIMA (Si-silica; Ma-magnesium). It has an average density of about 3.0 gm per cubic centimeter.

Though these two layers are in a solid state, the lighter SIAL is considered as 'floating' on the denser SIMA layer. The arrangement of SIAL floating on the SIMA layer forms the basis of Wegener Continental Drift Theory.

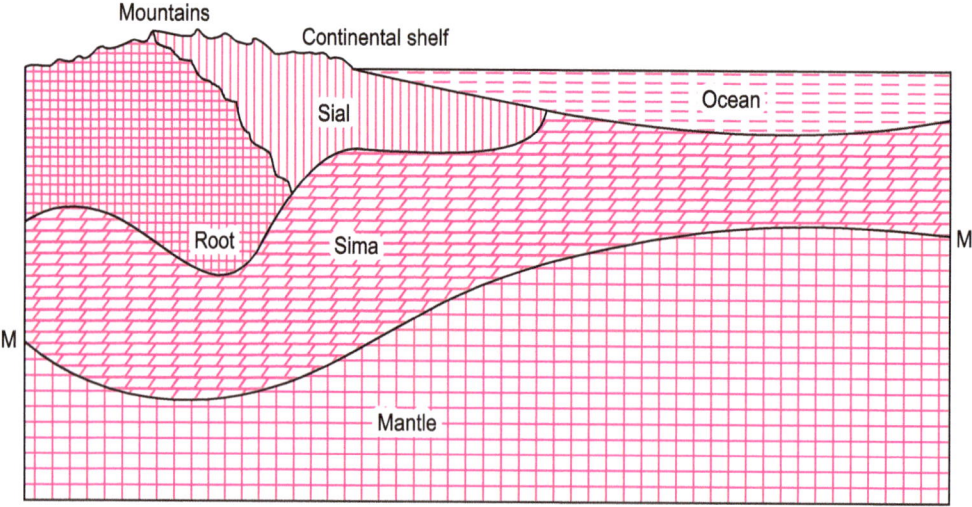

Fig. 4.2 : SIAL and SIMA layers

The composition of the Earth's crust is of great interest to us as it has the valuable soil layer that influences our lives in many ways. Soil, the medium for growing plants, supports our agricultural economy and the rocks that we use to construct our shelters and create materials or living.

The Mantle or Mesosphere

The mantle is the middle layer of the Earth's interior, also known as the Mesosphere. It extends to a depth of 2900 km, making it the thickest layer of the Earth. The boundary between the crust and the mantle is called the **Mohorovicic Discontinuity,** and has a density of 3.3 gm per cubic centimeter.

The mantle consists of mixed Silicates and Metals (Magnesium and Iron) and is rich in Olivine. The upper mantle or Asthenosphere is in a partially molten state. The velocity of the Earthquake waves decreases in it. It is also called 'lower velocity zone'. The lower mantle is called Mesosphere. The boundary between the mantle and the core is known as **Gutenberg Discontinuity.** The Gutenberg Discontinuity was named after the German Seismologist named Beno Gutenberg.

The temperature gets warmer with depth; the top of the mantle being about 1600°F (870°C), towards the bottom of the mantle, it is about 6700°F (3700° C). The density of the mantle varies between 3.3 and 5.7 gm per cubic centimeter.

The mantle contains most of the mass of the Earth. Due to great temperature differences from the bottom to the top of the mantle, this layer of rock even floats like oil floats on water. The movement of the mantle is the reason that the plates of the Earth move.

There are six large plates and about 12 to 15 are smaller ones. All these plates of the Lithosphere are continually on the move, float, ride and rotate like a giant raft on the Asthenosphere or the upper mantle.

The Core or Barysphere

The core is the innermost layer of the Earth, also known as Barysphere with a radius of about 3500 km, i.e., 7000 km in diameter, which is more than half the Earth's diameter. It abundantly comprises metals like nickel and iron. Therefore, the core can be called 'NiFe' (Ni-nickel: Fe-iron). The density of the core ranges from 12 to 15 gm per centimeter.

Due to high temperature, Nickel and Iron are found in molten stage and the liquid iron generates its own electricity and so under pressure, the core is the source of the Earth's magnetic field.

The core consists of two layers *(Fig. 4.3)* :

- **Outer Core** : The outer core is located about 1800 miles beneath the crust and is about 1400 miles (2250 km) thick. It is present in a liquid state, mainly composed of a nickel-iron alloy. The temperature ranges between 4000°F to 9000°F. Earth's magnetic field is believed to be control by the liquid outer core.

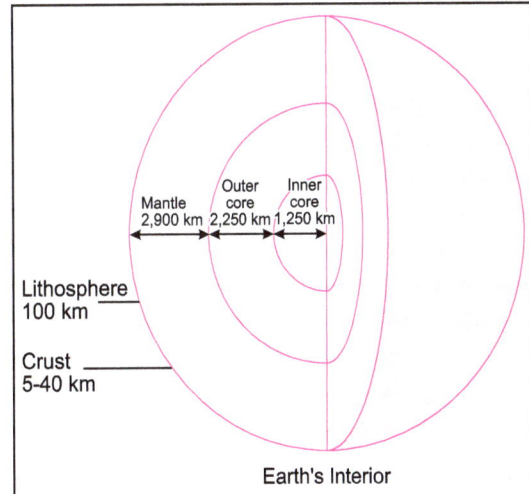

Fig. 4.3 : Interior layers of the Earth

- **Inner Core** : The inner core begins about 4000 miles beneath the crust and is about 800 miles (1250 km) thick. It exists in a solid state, almost entirely composed of iron. The temperature is about 13000°F (7200°C) and the pressures are 45,000,000 pounds per square inch.

Materials of the Earth's Crust : Rocks and Minerals

Earth's crust is composed of various types of rocks. The term 'rocks' refers to both hard materials like granite as well as soft and loose particles like sand, silt and clay. Rocks are built from minerals. Minerals, in turn, are formed from natural elements and compounds, which are chemical in nature, and give minerals a fixed or unchanging chemical composition and physical properties. Minerals are generally crystalline in appearance, and are homogeneous in form while rocks are heterogeneous in composition. Geologists have identified more than 2500 minerals in the Earth's crust, of which 250 are said to be plentiful on the Earth and only 25 minerals are found on the Earth's surface and in most surface rocks. Most of them are made of only eight elements.

Eight Major Elements of the Earth's Crust	
Element	Abundance (by weight)
Oxygen	47
Silicon	28

Potassium	25
Aluminium	8
Iron	5
Calcium	4
Sodium	3
Magnesium	2

Oxygen, the one element crucially needed to sustain life on Earth, is most abundantly found in the Earth's crust while the second most abundantly found element is silicon. Given the abundance of oxygen and silicon in the crust, it should not be surprising that the most abundant minerals in the Earth's crust are the silicates. Quartz, Feldspar and Mica are examples of silicate minerals while Calcite, Dolomite, Gypsum and rock salts are examples of other types of minerals.

TECTONIC PLATE MOVEMENT

In 1912, a German meteorologist, Alfred Wegener put forth his radical theory of continental drift. According to him, two hundred and fifty million years ago, all the land drifted together to form one supercontinent, called *Pangaea*, meaning all land. The massive area of land was surrounded by a single vast sea called *Panthalassa*. The northern part of Pangaea, called Laurasia, consisted of North America and most of Eurasia.

By 1968, this theory of the continental drift had been amalgamated with the more important Theory of Plate Tectonics. Tectonics comes from the Greek word *Tectonicos* meaning, building or constructing.

The Plate Tectonic theory holds that the solid lithosphere comprises of about 16 to 20 great slabs of rock called Plates. They average about 100 km thick and thousands of kilometers wide. As they move and grind against each other, they are constantly changing the face of the planet by pushing up mountains, spawning volcanoes, and causing earthquakes.

Major Plate Systems

Six major plates play a very important role because of their enormous size and weight.

The American Plate

It consists of the continental lithosphere of North and South America and the mid-Atlantic ridge which divides the Atlantic Ocean Basin.

The Pacific Plate

It consists mainly of oceanic lithosphere plus the coastal portion of the plate's boundary of the San Andreas fault.

The Eurasian Plate

It is mainly a continental lithosphere but it is fringed on the North and East of the Oceanic lithosphere.

The African Plate

It has a central core of the continental lithosphere nearly surrounded by the Oceanic lithosphere.

The Indo-Australian Plate

It is an elongated rectangle consisting of mainly oceanic lithosphere but with two main continental lithosphere. The plateau of peninsular India and the mainland of Australia.

The Antarctic Plate

It forms the central core of continental lithosphere, completely surrounded by oceanic lithosphere. The plate has an elliptical shape.

Reasons For Plate Movement

The plates move in response to convection in the upper mantle. There are two theories to explain the plate movement and its effects:

Gravity

In mid-ocean, the plates are higher than along the ocean borders and the plates could be sliding downhill under the force of gravity.

Convection

The plates may be driven apart by the convection currents set up by intense heat generated in the interior of the Earth when rising, thus building new crusts. When the currents sink, the plates are pulled down causing buckling of land and formation of mountain. For example, the Alps were formed when Europe collided with Africa, and the Himalayas were formed when Asia ran into India.

- The Earth's surface is divided into three parts : Crust (Lithosphere) : It is the upper layer of Earth's interior, made up of thin layer of rock. Mantle (Mesosphere) : It is the middle layer of Earth's interior, consisting of dense and rigid rocks.

STRUCTURE OF THE EARTH AND INTERNAL PROCESSES

- Core (Barysphere): It is the centre of the Earth, consisting mostly of metals like nickel (Ni) and iron (Fe). Therefore, it is also known as NiFe.
- When one moves from surface of the Earth towards its centre, the temperature, pressure and density, goes on increasing.
- The temperature of the Earth's interior keeps increasing at the rate of 1°C for every 32 meters.
- The density of the materials in the core of the Earth is much more than the density of rocks found in the uppermost layers.
- SIAL and SIMA form the outermost layer of the Earth's crust or lithosphere. SIAL is composed of silicon and aluminium while SIMA is composed of silica and magnesium. The density of SIAL is much higher than that of SIMA. Hence SIAL is a discontinuous layer floating over the continuous layer of SIMA.
- The one element Oxygen, crucially needed to sustain life on Earth, is most abundantly available on the Earth's crust. Silicon is the next element most abundantly available.
- The solid lithosphere comprises 16 to 20 great slabs of rock called Plates.
- There are six major Plates that play a very important role as they move and grind against each other, constantly changing the face of the planet by pushing up mountains, spawning volcanoes and causing earthquakes.
- The Plates move because of gravity and convection currents.

EXERCISES

A. Answer the following questions

1. State the names of the three different layers of the Earth.
2. What do you mean by the crust of the Earth? Give the names of its two layers.
3. State the composition and location of the SIAL and SIMA.
4. What is the importance of the Earth's crust?
5. What do you mean by the mantle? Name is main constituents.
6. Define the core of the Earth. State its properties.
7. What is meant by Mohorovicic and Gutenberg discontinuity?
8. What forms the basis of Wegener's 'Continental Drift Theory'?
9. Which part of the Earth's crust is responsible for the Earth's magnetism and why?
10. What are the major plates that play important role on Tectonic movement?
11. Define the factors that cause the plate movement.

B. Define the following terms

1. Crust
2. Mantle
3. Core
4. Tectonic Movement
5. Asthenosphere

C. Distinguish between the following

1. SIAL and SIMA.
2. Asthenosphere and Mesophere

D. Diagram

1. Draw a self-explanatory diagram showing the composition and structure of the Earth.

E. Board Questions

1. What is the Composition of the Earth's Crust?
2. Mention the differences between SIMA and SIAL.
3. (i) What is the composition of the core of the Earth?
   (ii) Why does it occur in a semi molten state?
4. Give a geographical reason of each of the following.
   (i) Although temperature is extremely high, yet the core of the Earth is not in motter state.

CHAPTER 5
LANDFORMS OF THE EARTH

Mountains, Plateaus, Plains (Definition, Types and their Formation) : Mountains–fold, residual and block. Plateaus–Intermont and Volcanic. Plains–Structural and Depositional. Examples from the world and India.

The Earth undergoes continuous changes due to internal and external forces, because of which the surface or the landscape of the Earth is very uneven, creating a number of landforms like mountains, valleys or river systems. Each landscape has its own geological structure and topographic relief. While landscapes are considered to be the product of geological events over thousands or millions of years, the topographic relief is the change of elevation between the highest and the lowest places.

CAUSES OF LANDFORM FORMATION ON THE EARTH'S SURFACE

The major causes for formation of the landforms on the Earth's surface are as follows :

Geological Factors

The geological structures of the rocks and their bedding planes, folds and faults and the direction of the slopes are the major influences on the origin and evolution of the landscape and landforms. There are three geological factors which are as follows :

Plate Tectonics

The several broken plates of the Lithosphere float on the semi-molten asthenosphere by pushing, colliding or sliding past each other. This creates a disturbance and compression of the sedimentary rocks lying between two or more plates, thus causing the folding of rocks. Almost all the fold mountain ranges of the world are formed by this process.

Uplift and Submergence

Epeirogenic movements are the vertically moving forces that operate inside the Earth acting along a radius from the Earth's centre to the surface. These movements cause fault or crack in the Earth's surface, thus forming block mountains, basins, and rift valleys.

Sudden Forces

Earthquakes and volcanic activities are described as sudden forces as they result in the formation of volcanic mountains, extensive plateaus, plains, lakes, etc. These sudden forces are also known as 'constructive forces' as they create relief features on the Earth's surface.

Climatic Factors or Exogenic Forces

The temperature, wind, rainfall and humidity in the air are the various agents of erosion of the existing landforms. These are the external forces that cause widespread destruction through weathering and erosion of existing landforms, thus forming new landforms. These include alluvial valleys, glacial valleys, erosional plains, etc.

Types of Landforms

Landforms are the natural physical features of the Earth's surface *(Fig. 5.1)*. There are many

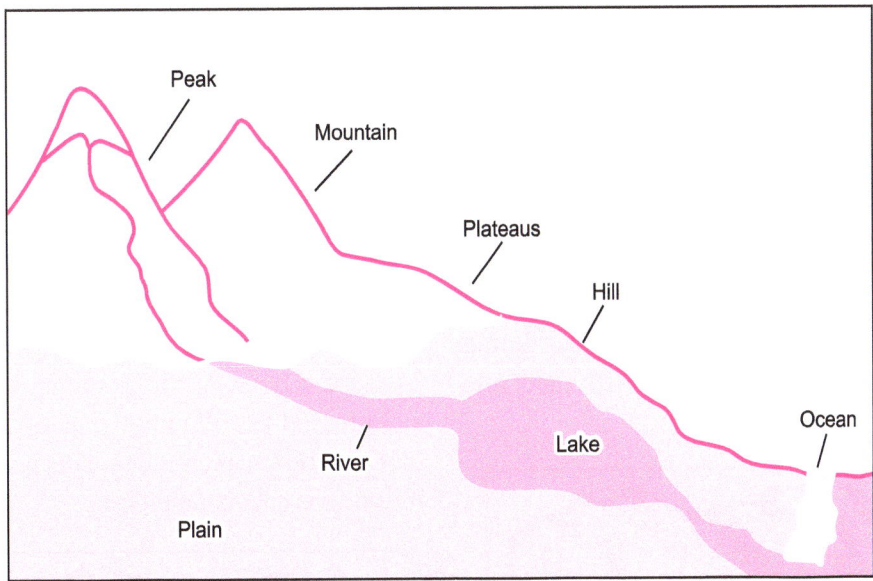

Fig. 5.1 : Landforms

landforms, which can be classified by different methods. Landforms are formed by the internal forces of the Earth, but they can be modified by the external forces. There are three types of major landforms : Mountains, Plateaus and Plains.

MOUNTAINS

Mountains are the major geological features on the Earth's surface. A mountain is a very steep land or hill rising to great heights above 600 m over the land surrounding it, usually existing, either as an individual mountain or as an extensive mountain chain. Some of these mountain-building periods occurred between 600 and 3500 million years ago. The three most recent orogenics or mountain building movements are the Alpine, Hercynian and Caledonian. While the Alpine period took place about 30 million years ago, the Hercynian period was about 240 million years ago and the Caledonian period covered 350 million years ago.

Mountains can be formed by a number of tremendous forces on the Earth, like :

- **Earth Movements :** Volcanism, erosion, and disturbances or uplift in the Earth's crust.
- **Plate Tectonics :** Geological forces like heat and pressure produce changes and movements under the Earth's crust, thus dividing it into a number of vast rigid plates that move about at the rate of a few centimeters a year. The uplift is caused by the collision of plates below the Earth's surface that triggers various geologic processes that produce this crustal uplift.
- **Horizontal Compression :** The deformation of crustal strata produces folds or wrinkles.

Eg.: The Himalayas were raised by the compression that accompanied collision of the Indian plate with the Eurasian plate, the European Alps and Jura mountains were also formed by horizontal compression due to collision of the African plate and the Eurasian plate *(Fig. 5.2)*.

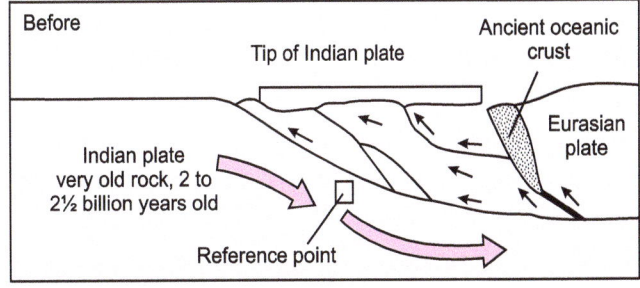
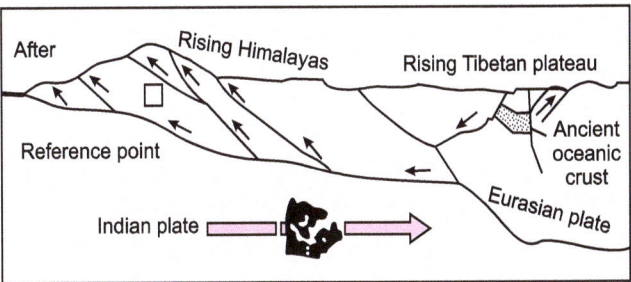

Fig. 5.2 : Horizontal Compression.

Classification of Mountains

Depending on the geological processes, mountains can be classified into the following five categories: Fold, Block, Volcanic, Dome, and Residual.

Fold Mountains

These include some of the highest mountains of the world. They are formed due to the folding of the Earth's crust, when two plates move together due to large-scale Earth movements caused by stresses in the Earth's crust. Such stress may be caused by weight of the overlying rocks, movements in the mantle, the expansion or contraction of some part of the Earth *(Fig. 5.3)*. This process of mountain building is called *Orogenesis*. These are further divided into two types, namely:

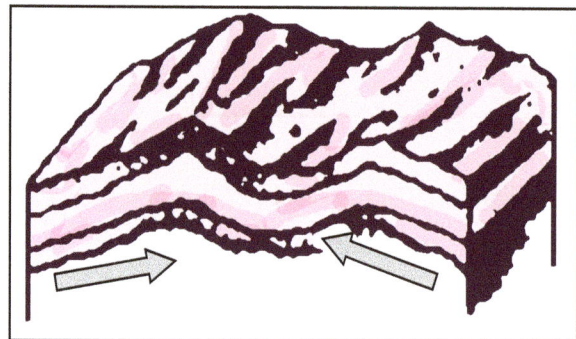

Fig. 5.3 : Fold Mountain.

Young Fold Mountains

These were formed during the last 10 to 25 million years – The Alpine period and are still growing. The main characteristics of these mountains are the complex folding of the rocks, faulting, volcanic activities, cordillera form, the erosion and weathering caused by running water, ice, winds, etc. They have deeper and steeper slopes with glacier-capped high peaks. These mountain regions are areas of crustal instability.

Eg. : Himalayan Mountains (Asia); Alps (Europe); Andes (South America); Rockies (North America); and the Circum-Pacific oceanic mountains.

Old Fold Mountains

These were formed over 240 million years ago in the Hercynian period–Eg. Urals in Russia, Pennines and Welsh Highlands of Britain, Harz Mountain in Germany and the Applachians in North America and Aravallis in India. The other orogenies that formed the Old Fold Mountains are the Caledonian (above 350 million years ago)– good examples are Scandinavian and Scottish Highlands. The main characteristics of these mountains are accordant summits, sculptured domes, the irregular forms of peaks, etc. They have rounded peaks with gentler slopes.

Block Mountains

These are formed by the Earth's crust being stretched and extended by tensional forces when large areas of bedrock are widely broken up by faults creating large vertical displacements of continental crust. (Fig. 5.4) Vertical motion of the resulting blocks, sometimes accompanied by tilting, can then lead to high slopes. If there are two parallel faults, the crustal block between them may either rise to produce a horst-block mountain or fall to produce a depressed portion known as rift valley. The fallen block is known as a graben. This process of mountain building is called *Taphrogeny*.

Fig. 5.4 : Block Mountain.

These mountains are characterized by massiveness, steep slopes, and comparatively smooth topography. They usually arise in folded zones that once had a mountain relief, but have lost their plasticity and have been smoothed by denudation.

Eg.: The Sierra Nevada Mountains (North America), Harz Mountains (Germany), Vosges Mountains (Rhine Valley).

Residual Mountains

These are the remnants of old mountains, which have been subjected to weathering and erosion for a long time by agents of denudation, such as rain, frost, running water and wind. These continuously erode away the soft rocks leaving behind the harder rocks.

Eg.: Mountain Monadnock (USA), Namuli Mountains (Northern Mozambique), Catskill Mountains (New York), Nilgiris and Rajmahal Hills (India), and Hombori Mountains (Mali).

Ten Highest Himalayan Peaks		
Name	Location	Height
Everest	Nepal	8848 m (29035 ft)

Godwin Austin (K-2)	India	8611 m (28251 ft)
Kanchenjunga	India	8586 m (28169 ft)
Makalu	Nepal	8462 m (27765 ft)
Dhaulagiri	Nepal	8167 m (26794 ft)
Nanga Parbat	India	8126 m (26660 ft)
Annapurna	Nepal	8091 m (26545 ft)
Nanda Devi	India	7824 m (25663 ft)
Kamet	India	7756 m (25446 ft)
Namcha Barwa	India	7754 m (25444 ft)
Gurla Mandhata	Nepal	7728 m (25355 ft)

Significance of Mountains

- Act as effective climatic barriers, climates of regions on either side of a high mountain range are very different.
- Its swift streams are frequent sources of hydroelectric power, especially in countries that have no coal.
- Provides minerals like gold, copper, lead, silver, platinum, tin, etc.
- The lumbering industry is highly benefited by the availability of soft woods, hard woods, teak and sal.
- The fertile land and pastures are used for agriculture, irrigation and cattle rearing.
- Snow capped mountains are rich sources of perennial rivers.

PLATEAUS

A Plateau, also known as 'tableland', is an area of highland consisting of a relatively flat surface, usually limited on at least one side by a steep slope falling abruptly to lower land.

Plateaus can be formed due to a number of processes, like :

- **Diastrophism :** It is the large-scale deformation of the Earth's crust that produces continents, ocean basins and mountain ranges, etc. All the highest plateaus of the Earth are the direct products of diastrophism.
- **Upwelling of volcanic magma :** Magma rises from the mantle causing the ground to swell upward, thus uplifting flat areas of rock.

Classification of Plateaus

According to their mode of formation or their physical aspects, plateaus can be classified into the following four categories :

Intermontane Plateau

These plateaus are the most high and extensive types of the world. These are surrounded by hills and mountains on all sides, and are formed along with Fold Mountains.

Eg. : The Tibetan plateau lying between the Himalayas and the Kunlun, the Bolivian plateau lying between two ranges of the Andes Mountains, and the Mexican plateau lying between eastern and western Sierra Madre Mountains.

Piedmont Plateau

These are plateaus, which lie at the foot of the mountains. These are surrounded by mountain ranges on one side and plains on the other side, with the part facing the plains having a steep slope.

Eg. : The Patagonian plateau of South America, the Appalachian Piedmont Plateau in the Atlantic Coastal Plains, the Ardennes and Middle Rhine Highland, and the Colorado mountains lying between the Rockies and the range province of USA.

Dissected Plateau

These are also known as 'domed' or 'uplifted' plateaus. These are dome-shaped tablelands that are formed due to the upliftment of the middle portion of the landmass. These are further divided into two types, namely :

- **Continental Plateaus :** These are the huge tablelands rising from lowlands or seas. They are mostly surrounded by sea on one side.

Eg. : The plateaus in the parts of Africa, Arabia and Greenland, etc.

- **Fault-Block Plateaus :** These are formed when Earth's movements in the mountains cause faults, hence dislocating rock strata, making one side to go up and the other side to go down along the fault line.

Eg. : Central Plateau of France.

Volcanic Plateaus

These are formed due to the cooling down of volcanic lava by enormous accumulation of basaltic rock *(Fig. 5.5)*.

Eg. : The Plateau of Peninsular India, Plateau of South Africa, Columbian Plateau, Ethiopian Plateau, and the Deccan Plateau.

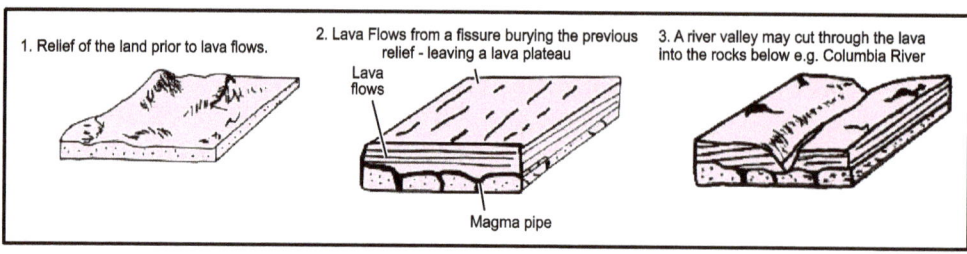

Fig. 5.5 : Lava Plateau Formation.

Significance of Plateaus

- Different plateau regions have different type of climatic condition and varied topography, thus creating a biodiversity of life on Earth.
- Agricultural development is made possible in certain plateau areas rich in basaltic soil.
- Mineral resources development is made possible by plateaus rich in iron ore, mica, manganese, copper, gold and diamonds.

PLAINS

A plain is an extensive area of land with relatively low relief, less than 150 m, and having a flat or gently rolling surface. A plain is often thought of as a grassland, but plains in their natural state may also be covered in shrub lands, woodland and forest, or vegetation may be absent in the case of sandy or stony plains in hot deserts. In a valley, a plain is enclosed on two sides, but in other cases, a plain may be distinguished by a complete or partial ring of hills, by mountains or cliffs.

Plains can be formed by a number of processes, like :

- A sudden heavy downpour may wash away a standing landform or fill up a depression to form a plain.
- They may be formed by flowing lava.
- By the process of deposition, denudation or erosion by water, ice or wind from hills and mountains.

Classification of Plains

According to their mode of origin and structure, plains can be classified into the following three categories :

Structural Plains

These plains lie near the coasts and are formed due to uplift or subsidence of land. If the coastal area is a flat land, then the newly formed area will be wide, which increases in width towards sea by the addition of sediments brought by the sea waves. Moreover, if there is a hilly region near the coast, then the newly formed area will be a narrow belt.

Eg. : The Great Plains (USA), Gulf Coast, Coromandel Plains (India), countries of Belgium, Netherlands and Germany.

Depositional Plains

These plains are formed by the deposition of sediments by various agents of transposition. The agents of erosion cut the rocks, transport the eroded material from the source and deposit them at some other place. Based on the agents of erosion and place of deposition, these plains can be further divided into the following types :

- **Alluvial Plains :** These are formed by the gradual accumulation of silt brought down by rivers. The fan-shaped deposits at the foot of the hills are called Piedmont alluvial fans.

  If the eroded material of a river is deposited in the form of a belt along the foot of the hills, it is called the Piedmont alluvial plain. Eg.: Khadar Plains and Bhangar in India.

  When the river widens its valley or overflows the bank during floods, the clay and sand is deposited over large area, such plains are called flood plains. They are the most fertile areas of the world.

  Eg. : Plains of China, Indo-Gangetic Plain (India), Mississippi Plains (USA).

- **Glacial Deposits :** These are formed when the continental glaciers melt and the debris is deposited. These have irregular and undulating surface made by existence of sand dunes and fallows.

  Eg. : Plain of Central North America and Western European Plain.

- **Loess Plains :** These are formed by the materials that are transported and deposited by the wind.

They are composed of very fine silt, rich in lime and yellowish in colour.

Eg. : The vast areas of North China.

- **Lacustrine Plains :** When the river enters a lake, the water is muddy, but when it comes out at the other end, the water is comparatively cleaner and free of silt. This silt settles and fills up the lake beds and later becomes a level land known as the Lacustrine Plain.

Eg. : The Plains of Hungary (Europe), Kolleru Lake (India), Plain of the River Po (Italy), and the Plains surrounded by the Great Lakes (North America).

Significance of Plains

- In many plain regions, the soils are deposited as sediments that are deep and fertile, thus facilitating irrigation and mechanization of crop production.

  The fertile soil provides rich grasslands for good grazing for livestock.

- Construction of settlements, rails, roads, etc., is easy on flat and soft surface.

- Fine climate and fertile lands of alluvial plains provide great chances for agricultural and industrial development.

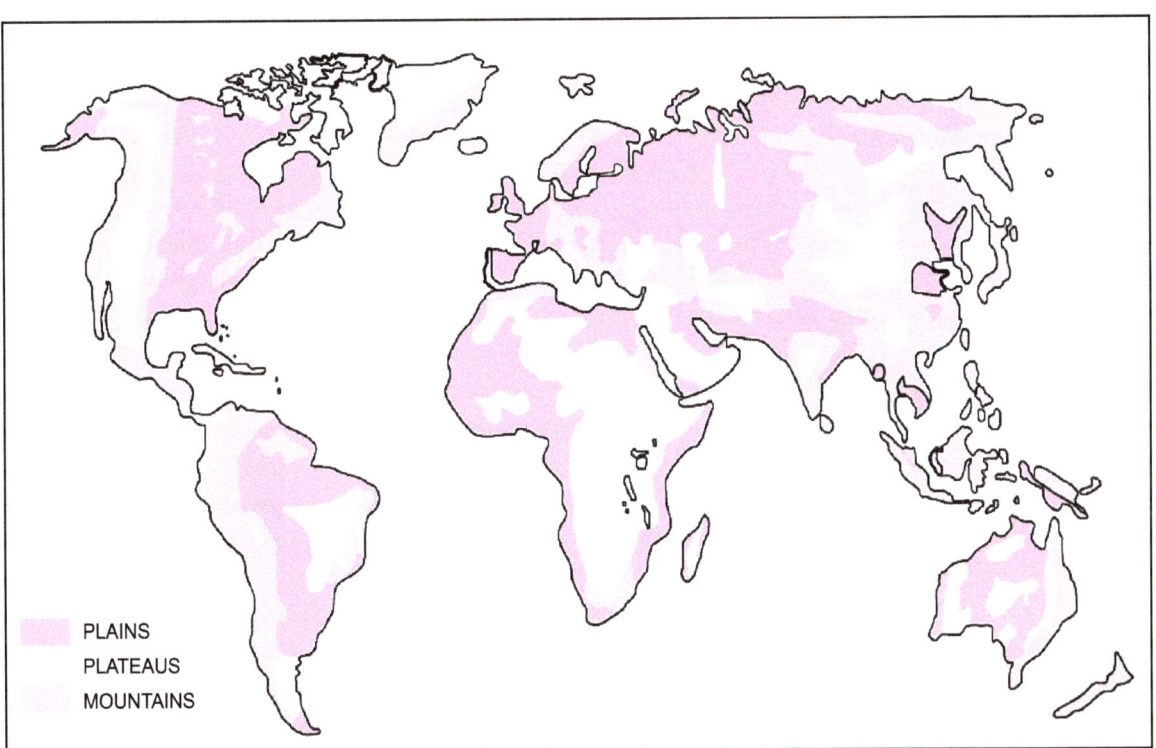

Fig. 5.6 : World map showing the distribution of Mountains, Plateaus and Plains

SUMMARY

- Landforms are created by the continuously acting internal and external forces inside the Earth's surface.
- Mountains are the steep-sided hills, which are more than 600 m high, existing either as a single eminence or as an extensive mountain chain.
- There are three types of mountains : (i) Fold mountains, (ii) Block mountains, and (iii) Residual mountains.
- Orogenesis is the process of large-scale mountain building. It is also known as the birth of mountain.
- Plateaus or 'tablelands' are highlands with relatively flat surface, usually limited on at least one side by a steep slope falling abruptly to lower land.
- There are four types of plateaus : (i) Intermontane plateaus, (ii) Piedmont plateaus, (iii) Dissected plateaus, and (iv) Volcanic plateaus.
- Diastrophism is the large-scale deformation of the Earth's crust that produces continents, ocean basins and mountain ranges, etc.
- Plains are extensively flat-leveled lands without prominent hills or depressions.
- There are two types of plains : (i) Structural plains, (ii) Depositional plains.

EXERCISES

A. Answer the following questions

1. What are landforms?
2. What are the causes for the development of landforms on the Earth's surface?
3. What are mountains? How are they formed?
4. Define briefly the different types of mountains. Give one example of each.
5. What is meant by Orogenesis?
6. What are plateaus? How are they formed?
7. Define briefly the different types of plateaus. Give one example of each.
8. State any two characteristics for each of the following :
   - (i) Young fold mountain
   - (ii) Old fold mountain
9. What are plains? How are they formed?
10. Explain the different types of plains by giving at least one example of each type.
11. Give any two significances for each of the following :
    - (i) Mountains
    - (ii) Plateaus
    - (iii) Plains
12. How is a rift valley formed?

B. Define the following terms

1. Mountains
2. Plateaus
3. Plains
4. Orogenesis
5. Rift valley
6. Diastrophism

C. Distinguish between the following

1. Young and Old mountain.
2. Fold and Block mountain.
3. Intermontane and Piedmont plateaus.
4. Dissected and Volcanic plateaus.
5. Continental and Fault-block plateaus.
6. Loess plains and Lacustrine plains.
7. Structural and Depositional plains.

D. Give reasons

1. Old fold mountains have low altitudes and gentle slopes.
2. Young fold mountains have rugged relief features.
3. Plains are thickly populated.

E. Map Work

1. On an outline map of the world, mark the major mountains, plateaus and plains with the help of different colours.

F. Board Questions

1. (i) How are fold mountains formed ?
   (ii) Give an example of a young fold mountain.
2. (i) Name two agents responsible for the formation of Depositional Plains.
   (ii) Give an example of each type.
3. Give an example of each of the following :
   (i) Block Mountain
   (ii) Structural Plain
   (iii) Volcanic Plateau
4. Give a geographical reason for the following :
   (i) Fold mountains are associated with Intermontane Plateau.

CHAPTER 6
ROCKS

> **Rocks :** Rocks–Differences between Minerals and Rocks. Type of Rocks–Igneous, Sedimentary, Mentamorphic, their Characteristics and Formation; Rock Cycle.

The Earth's surface is covered with a very thin layer of loose materials called soil, which are the products of rocks. Rocks are the chief components of the Earth's crust. They differ from one another in texture, structure, colour, permeability, mode of formation and degree of resistance to denudation. Therefore, it is essential to have a basic knowledge of the different types of rocks and their relationship with landforms to determine the types of natural vegetation and land use.

ROCKS

Rocks are the chief component of the Earth's crust, usually defined as a substance formed by the mixture of various elements or minerals. They can be hard as basalt or as soft as clay. Rock can be defined as, "an aggregate of minerals that forms a more or less definite unit of the Earth's crust". The minerals and metals we find in rocks are essential for the prosperity and cultural splendour of human civilization.

MINERALS

Minerals are different from rocks. They are the naturally occurring solid inorganic substances in the Earth's crust consisting of one or more elements. Each of the minerals has a definite chemical composition. They are extracted from the ore through various refining processes. An ore is a deposit that contains one or more minerals, usually metals in quantities that makes mining profitable.

Distinction Between Rocks and Minerals

A mineral is a naturally occurring solid composed of formation while a rock is a naturally occurring solid combination of more than one mineral. A mineral has a unique chemical composition and is necessarily defined by its crystalline structure and shape. On the other hand, since a rock can be composed of several minerals it is classified according to the process of its formation. Rocks are subjected to undergo changes by certain transformation processes while no such process is applicable to minerals.

The differences between the two can be summarized as follows :

Rocks	Minerals
1. Rocks are solid aggregates of mineral elements, which make up the Earth's crust.	1. Minerals are naturally occurring solid inorganic substances consisting of one or more elements.
2. Rocks are heterogeneous in their composition.	2. Minerals are homogeneous in their composition.
3. Rocks have no definite chemical composition.	3. Minerals have a definite chemical composition.
4. Minerals are organized to form rocks.	4. Elements are organized to form compounds known as minerals.

5. Three chief types of rocks are igneous, sedimentary and metamorphic.	5. Two chief mineral types are metallic and non-metallic.
6. Example : basalt, granite, sandstone, slate, quartz, etc.	6. Example : iron, silicon, nickel, calcium, sodium, etc.

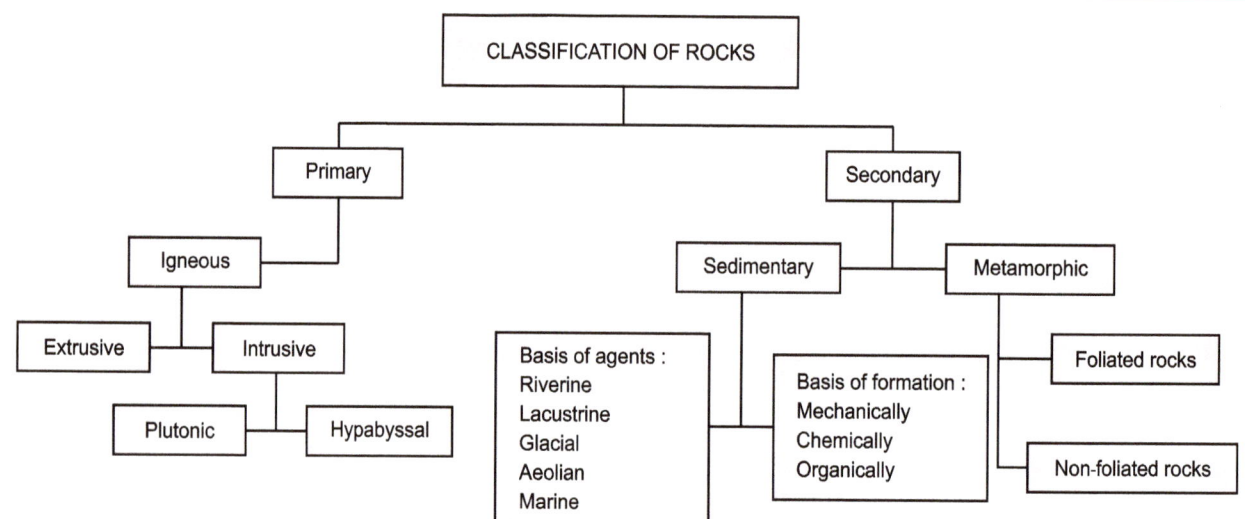

Fig. 6.1 : Classification of Rocks.

CLASSIFICATION OF ROCKS

Rocks are generally classified by mineral and chemical composition, by the texture of the constituent particles and by the processes that formed them. However, geologists classify rocks based on their formation. The three classes are : *(Fig. 6.1)*

- Igneous rocks (formed directly from liquid rock).
- Sedimentary rocks (formed by eroded materials from other rocks).
- Metamorphic rocks (formed by direct alteration of existing rocks).

Each of these types is further sub-divided based on their physical and chemical characteristics and forms of their occurrence.

Igneous Rocks

The word 'igneous' comes from the Greek word, meaning fire. These rocks are formed by the hardening and crystallization of molten material (magma), that originates deep within the Earth near active plate boundaries or hot spots, and then rises toward the surface. They may form with or without crystallization, either below the surface as intrusive (plutonic) rocks, or above the surface as extrusive (volcanic) rocks. Typically, the melting is caused by one or more of three processes: an increase in temperature, a decrease in pressure, or a change in composition. Even today, the process is repeated now and then. Therefore, the formation of igneous rocks goes deep down into history and is also a feature of today.

Characteristics of Igneous Rocks

- They are generally hard, resistant to erosion, and water percolates with great difficulty.
- They are generally weathered by mechanical weathering.
- Most of the igneous rocks consist of silicate.
- They do not contain fossils as they are formed from cooling and solidification of very hot and molten magma.
- They are grained, smooth and compact or may have large crystals with coarse texture. They are the primary rocks, meaning thereby that they were formed first in the process of rock formation.
- They are associated with volcanic activities and are thus found in volcanic regions.

Types of Igneous Rocks

Igneous rocks are classified by the geologic environment where they are formed by two pro-cesses namely by cooling and by solidification of molten material *(Fig. 6.2)*.

On the Basis of Origin

- **Extrusive Igneous Rocks :** These are also known as volcanic rocks. These are formed when the magma, called lava, flows onto the Earth's surface through deep cracks or fissures, cools and solidifies almost instantly due to the exposure to the relatively cooler temperatures of the atmosphere. Quick cooling means that mineral crystals do not have much time to grow, so these rocks have a very fine-grained or even glassy texture and small crystals. Hot gas bubbles are often trapped in the quenched lava, forming a bubbly, vesicular texture. They are generally dark coloured and are mainly made up of silicates like quartz, feldspar and mica.

  Eg. : Pumice, Obsidian and Basalt.

- **Intrusive Igneous Rocks:** These are formed when magma cools and solidifies deep beneath the Earth's surface. The insulating effect of the surrounding rock allows the magma to solidify very slowly. This gives the individual mineral grains a long time to grow, so they grow to a relatively large and irregular mass, and are characteristically coarse-grained. Intrusive rocks can also be classified according to the shape and size of the intrusive body and its relation to the other formations into which it intrudes.

  Intrusive rocks are again grouped into several subtypes according to their position below the Earth's surface *(Fig. 6.3).*

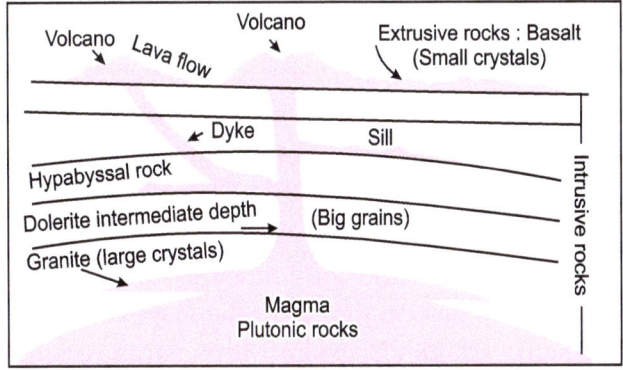

Fig. 6.3 : Igneous Rocks.

- **Plutonic :** These are the igneous rocks of deep-seated origin. These rocks are coarse-grained, which result from their having been formed at depth where cooling and crystallization have occurred very slowly.

  Eg. : Laccoliths and batholiths.

- **Hypabyssal :** These are small-scale igneous intrusions, formed due to cooling and solidification of rising magma during volcanic activity in the cracks, just beneath the Earth's surface.

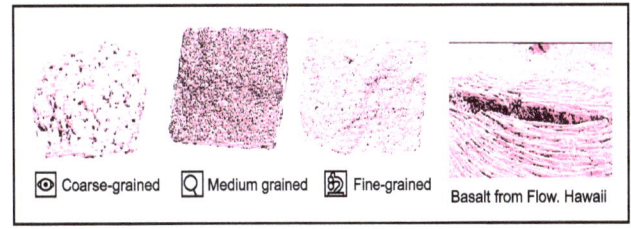

Fig. 6.4 : Texture of Igneous Rocks.

  Eg. : Sills and Dykes.

On the Basis of Chemical Composition

- **Acid Igneous Rocks :** These rocks are formed in the hot interior. They are coarse-grained, less dense, light in colour and are homogeneous. They contain high percentage of silica and lack in iron and magnesium.

  Eg. : Granite.

- **Basic Igneous Rocks :** These rocks are darker in colour, have large and dense grains. They contain less percentage of silica and high percentage of basic oxides like iron and magnesium. Eg. : Gabbros.
- **Ultra-Basic Rocks :** These rocks do not have silicates. They consist of Ferrous and Magnesium. Eg. : Carbonatites

Sedimentary Rocks

Sedimentary rocks are made of rock particles deposited on the Earth's surface by water, wind or ice. These rocks cover about three-fourths of the land area, and most of the ocean floor. Where the Earth's crust is deformed or eroded, large areas of buried sedimentary rock may be exposed.

Sedimentary rocks are formed by Lithification, which is the process that turns the loose sediments into hard rock (lith). Rocks are weathered and eroded into tiny particles, which are then transported and deposited along with other pieces of rock called sediments. Lithification involves three processes, namely :

- **Evaporation :** Water from loose materials evaporates as in the case of rock salt. The accumulation of rock salt mainly takes place through evaporation before being compacted and cemented.
- **Compaction :** After the sediments are piled up, they are gradually squeezed by the weight of overlaying layers and hardness of underlying layers. In this way, sand is compacted to sandstone.
- **Cementation :** The compacted sediments are bonded together by natural bonding materials like calcium compounds, silica and iron.

Eg. : Sandstone, clay, shale, conglomerates and loess.

Characteristics of Sedimentary Rocks

- They are formed from materials derived from other rocks. Hence, they contain fossils, the remnant parts of the plants and animals. By studying the fossils found in a rock, one can determine the age of the rock.
- They contain layers or strata, and are therefore also known as stratified rocks.
- The layers of these rocks are sometimes horizontal and at times tilted due to lateral compressive and tension forces.
- They are generally not crystalline, but most of these rocks are permeable and porous.
- They are characterized by different sizes of joints, which are generally perpendicular to the bedding plane.
- They may be well consolidated, poorly consolidated and even unconsolidated.
- They are the most widespread on the Earth's surface, i.e., about 75%. They, however, constitute only 5% of the Earth's crust. Thus, they are more important for extent and not for depth in the Earth's crust.

Types of Sedimentary Rocks

On the Basis of Formation

- **Mechanically Formed Rocks :** Rocks build up fragments of pre-existing rocks, which have been produced by the process of weathering and erosion. Various agents of denudation like, river, sea, wind, ice and glacier, accomplish the tasks of erosion, transportation and deposition of sediments mechanically. In this process, the sediments are gradually squeezed by the weight of overlying sediments, while the lower layers harden to form rocks *(Fig. 6.5)*.

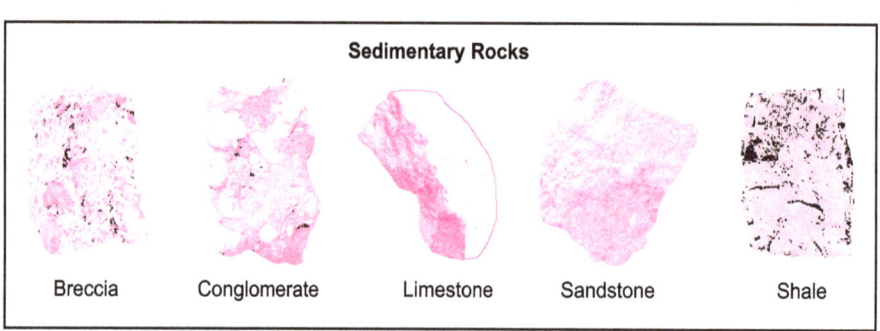

Fig. 6.5 : Types of Sedimentary Rocks.

- Rounded pebbles found in the river bed get consolidated to form a rock called Conglomerate.

- Angular fragments of gravel, accumulated at the bottom of the cliff, may get compacted to form a rock called Breccia.
- Deposits of clay get hardened to form rock called Shale or Mudstone.
- Sandstone is formed when deposits of sand get consolidated and it consists of mainly quartz of various colours.
- **Chemically Formed Rocks :** These rocks are formed by direct inorganic mineral compounds precipitated from a salt water solution or as hard parts of organisms. They are compacted through evaporation and the accumulation takes place in lakes and lagoons. Hot deserts are favourite areas for it. Dead Sea is a storehouse of chemically formed rocks because the salty water of this shallow lake contains several types of salts and the rate of evaporation is also very rapid there.

    Eg. : Rock Salt, Gypsum, Potash, Limestone, Magnesium Nitrates, Calcite, Dolomite, etc.
- **Organically Formed Rocks :** These are also called Calcareous rocks. These organic rocks consist of the remains of the marine plants and animals, which have been buried and preserved in these rocks for a long time. These types of rocks are called fossils. Various kinds of decayed vegetation matter consisting of plants, twigs, etc., are buried in swamps and accumulated in great thickness. In the course of time, because of pressure and heat, they lose most of their elements except carbon, which in stages becomes peat, lignite or coal.

    Eg. : Limestone, Chalk, Petroleum (rock oil), Coal, etc.

On the Basis of Agents of Formation

- **Riverine Rocks :** These are formed as a result of deposition of sediments by flowing water streams. Therefore, the regions of these rocks are the river basins.
- **Lacustrine Rocks :** These are found on the bed of a lake corresponding to successive periods of deposition.
- **Glacial Rocks :** These are formed by the glacial deposits in the form of debris or tills. The glaciers erode the surface and the sides of a valley and transport the eroded material further. When the glacier melts due to heat, the debris brought by it is left behind in the form of moraines that forms glacial rocks like, boulders, gravels, sand, etc. *(Fig. 6.6)*.
- **Aeolian Rocks :** These are formed by the wind deposits of sand particles. The process goes on and layer after layer of sediments get deposited and become consolidated to form sedimentary rocks.

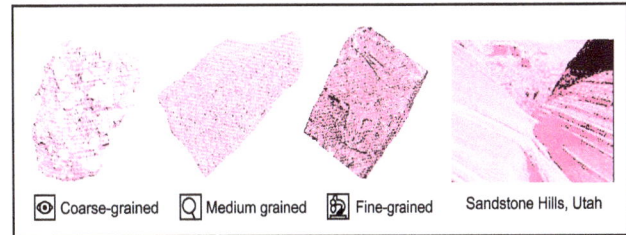

Fig. 6.6 : Texture of Sedimentary Rocks.

- **Marine Rocks :** These are formed by deposition of sediments on the ocean bed. The rivers flowing into the sea, drop loads of sediment into it. These get scattered on the continentshelf and thus very thick layers of sediments are deposited on the ocean floor. These rocks are further classified into two types :
- **Calcareous Sedimentary Marine Rocks :** These are formed by the deposition of shells and skeletons of sea organisms like corals, clams, oysters, etc. They live on ocean floor and extract calcium carbonate from the ocean water.
- **Carbonaceous Sedimentary Marine Rocks :** These are formed by the fossils of sea plants and animals by converting them into coal, lignite and peat due to pressure of overlying rocks on them.

Metamorphic Rocks

Metamorphic rocks are formed due to the effects of heat, pressure and the weight of the overlaying rocks. Igneous and sedimentary rocks when subjected to these factors, they are metamorphosed to Metamorphic rocks with completely change in character and appearance. During this changing process, there is an essential solid-state change in mineralogy and textures too.

Metamorphism

The word 'Metamorphism' comes from the Greek words '*meta*', meaning change and '*morph*', meaning form. Thus, we get metamorphism, which means '*a change in form*'. In geology, this refers to the changes in mineral contents and texture that result from subjecting a rock to conditions such as pressure, temperature, and chemical environment different from those under which the rock is originally formed.

Metamorphism occurs at high temperature and pressure where rocks are buried deeper in the Earth.

The original rocks melt and get solidifies again, thus changing the nature and composition of the rocks to a great extent *(Fig. 6.7)*.

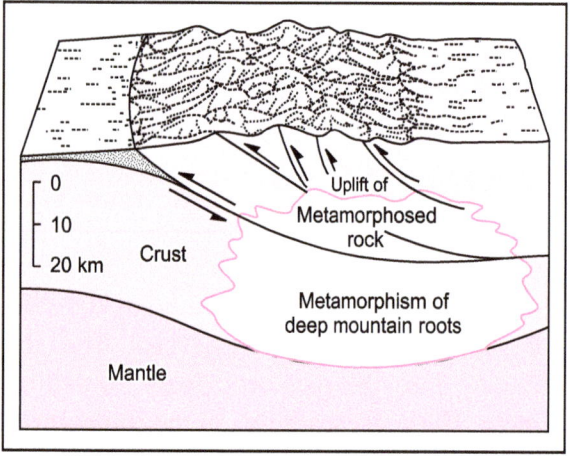

Fig. 6.7 : Metamorphism.

Types of Metamorphism

On the basis of agency involved, we have thermal and dynamic metamorphisms; and on the basis of the extent of the area, we have contact and regional metamorphisms.

- **Thermal Metamorphism :** This occurs when the changes are caused due to high temperature, thus forming a new rock. Eg. : Graphite.
- **Dynamic Metamorphism :** This occurs when the changes are caused due to tremendous pressure, thus forming a new rock.
- **Contact Metamorphism :** This occurs when magma forces its way into the original rock. The heat of the magma bakes the surrounding rocks causing them to change. This type of metamorphism is subjected to relatively small areas and are said to be low-grade metamorphism. Eg. : Marble created from Limestone that has been subjected to heat.
- **Regional Metamorphism :** This occurs during a mountainbuilding movement, when a large area is subjected to great pressure. This type of metamorphism is said to be highgrade metamorphism, usually resulting in the formation of strongly foliated metamorphic rocks. Eg. : Slate, Schist and Gneiss.

Characteristics of Metamorphic Rocks

- The temperature and pressure must be sufficiently high so as to change the original minerals into other mineral types or else into other forms of the same minerals.
- Metamorphic rocks being harder than other types of rock are more resistant to weathering and erosion. Eg. : Marble from Limestone, Quartzite from Sandstone and Diamond from Carbon.
- A rock always converts into the same type of metamorphic rock. For example, the sedimentary rocks Limestone and Shale become Marble and Slate, respectively, when metamorphosed.
- The fossils of the original sedimentary rocks are destroyed and, therefore, metamorphosed sedimentary rocks do not contain fossils.
- Many of the metamorphic rocks may split along the bedding planes, e.g., micaschist.
- Most gneiss metamorphic rocks comprise bands of regular quartz and feldspar.

Original rock	Turns into	Metamorphic rock
Limestone/dolomite	→	Marble
Sandstone	→	Quartzite
Shale	→	Slate
Coal	→	Graphite
Basalt	→	Schist
Granite	→	Gneiss

Types of Metamorphic Rocks

- **Foliated Rocks :** These types of rocks are formed when pressure squeezes the flat or elongated minerals within a rock until they are aligned. These rocks develop a platy or sheet-like structure that reflects the direction in which the pressure was applied. Eg. : Shale, Slate, Schist and Gneiss *(Fig. 6.8)*.

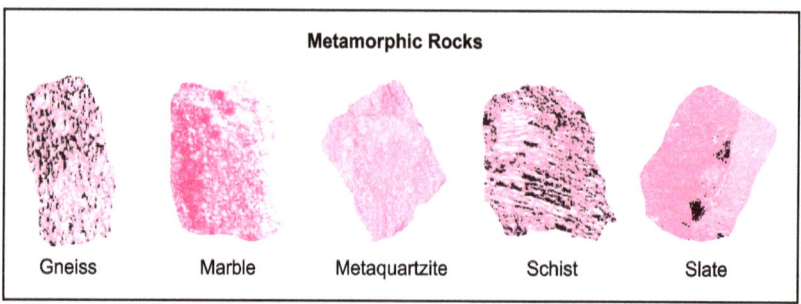

Fig. 6.8 : Types of Metamorphic Rocks.

- **Non-Foliated Rocks :** These types of rocks are formed by several ways and do not have a platy or sheet-like structure. They are not necessarily made of minerals that are flat or elongated. No matter how much pressure is applied, the grains do not align *(Fig. 6.9)*. Eg. : Quartz, Marble, etc.

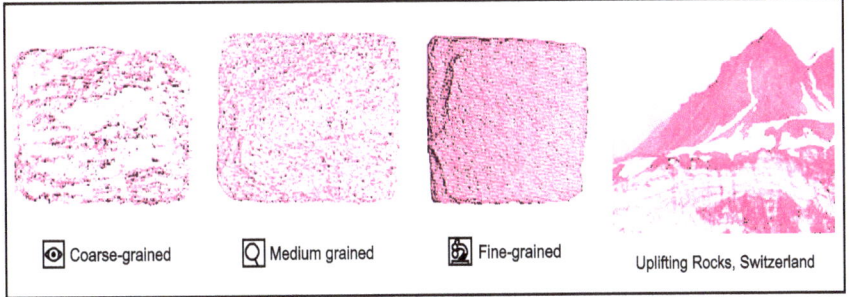

Fig. 6.9 : Texture of Metamorphic Rocks.

Rock Cycle

The Rock Cycle is a continuous process that transforms old rocks into new rocks. By this process, igneous rock can change into sedimentary rock or into metamorphic rock, sedimentary rock can change into metamorphic rock or into igneous rock, metamorphic rock can change into igneous or sedimentary rock *(Fig. 6.10)*.

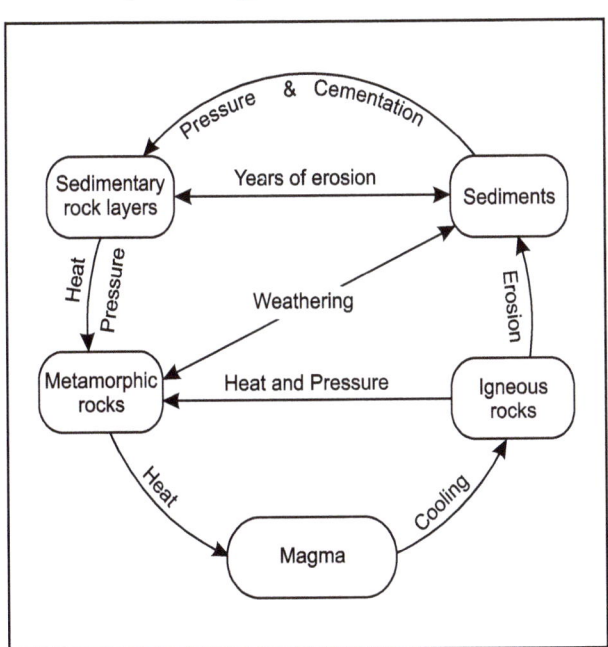

Fig. 6.10 : Rock Cycle.

- It is a gradual change of rocks that begins when the rocks are pushed up by tectonic forces, and eroded by climatic factors.
- As soon as the igneous rock, which is the parent material of all rocks, comes out of the Earth's surface, they are disintegrated by different agents of denudation into sediments.
- These sediments deposit in layers at some place forming sedimentary rocks, which are again buried into the Earth due to forces of the Earth.
- In case these sedimentary rocks go deep in the Earth, they get buried in melting form, magma, which comes out to the Earth's surface through volcanic activities and solidifies to form igneous rocks.
- In case these sedimentary rocks do not go deep, they neither disintegrate nor melt but only change their form by intense heat and pressure. They may change into metamorphic rocks or igneous rocks, again converting into sediments whenever they come out of the Earth's surface.
- Metamorphic, sedimentary and igneous rocks may then be pushed up by tectonic forces, starting the rock cycle again.

In this way, the rock cycle goes on and continuously transforms one type of rock to another.

Importance of Rocks

- Rocks disintegrate into smaller particles forming soil that is valuable for farming and agricultural purposes. The alluvial soil regions found on river basins are rich in fertile soil, hence supporting big population and civilizations. Black soil is a product of lava-flow rocks, rich in several minerals that are useful for cultivation of several crops, mainly cotton.
- Rocks provide several important mineral resources like coal and petroleum, which are very essential for the development of a country. The modern transport system including rail-ways, airplanes, automobiles and shipping vessels are sustained by coal and petroleum.
- Rocks supply a wide variety of minerals that are used as raw materials in modern manufacturing industries. Limestone and gypsum for cement

industries. Iron ore, dolomite, manganese, chromium, etc., for iron and steel industries. Bauxite for aluminium industries. Coal and petroleum for various types of chemical industries.

- The fossils and layers in rocks provide important facts to the life forms that existed in the environment millions of years ago.
- Rocks are widely used for building purposes by human beings throughout the world. Hard rocks such as granite, sandstone or limestone are used for construction of roads, houses and buildings. Heating clay or shale with crushed limestone produces cement for making concrete and laying bricks.
- Rocks also supply precious metals like gold, silver, diamond, platinum, which are used for making jewellery.
- Rocks and stones have been used to make tools and implements since early civilization.

Environmental Concern

There is a growing environmental concern because of extensive mining being undertaken. Mining is the process of extracting and processing the minerals present in the earth's crust.

A large number of minerals including metals like gold, silver, iron, copper, aluminium and non-ferrous metals such as stone, sand and shale are mined almost every day. Coal and petroleum are the other minerals, which are mined extensively. Such extensive underground mining can cause subsidence, pollution of aquifers and mine accidents. Surface mining destroys the vegetation of the area and pollutes the landscape with dust. A large number of craters are created post mining.

When hills that act as watersheds are mined, water level goes down, for example the case of Aravallis in Rajasthan.

SUMMARY

- Rocks are the chief component of the Earth's crust. They are generally hard substances formed by the mixture of various elements or minerals.
- Minerals are solid inorganic substances found in nature.
- Lithification is the process that turns loose sediments into rocks.
- Types of rocks : (i) Igneous rocks, (ii) Sedimentary rocks and (iii) Metamorphic rocks.
- Igneous rocks are formed by cooling and solidification of magma on or below the Earth surface.
- Types of igneous rocks : (i) Extrusive rocks, and (ii) Intrusive rocks.
- Sedimentary rocks are made of rock particles deposited on the Earth surface by water, wind or ice.
- Types of sedimentary rocks : (i) Riverine rocks, (ii) Lacustrine rocks, (iii) Glacial rocks, (iv) Marine rocks, and (v) Aeolian rocks.
- Metamorphic rocks are formed by the change in the form of igneous or sedimentary rocks under the Earth's crust by temperature and pressure.
- Types of metamorphic rocks : (i) Foliated rocks, and (ii) Non-foliated rocks.
- Metamorphism is the process that changes the natural structure and composition of the original rocks to a great extent. It occurs when the original rocks are subjected to extremely high pressure and temperature generated under the Earth's surface.
- Types of metamorphism : (i) Thermal, (ii) Dynamic, (iii) Contact, and (iv) Regional.
- Types of minerals : (i) Metallic, and (ii) Non-metallic.
- Rock cycle is the continuous process that transforms old rocks into new rocks.

EXERCISES

A. Answer the following questions

1. What is a rock? How is it formed?
2. What are minerals?
3. Name and define the chief types of rocks.
4. What is meant by igneous rocks? How are they formed?

5. What are the characteristics of :
    (i) Acid igneous rocks
    (ii) Basic igneous rocks
    (iii) Ultra-basic rocks
6. What are sedimentary rocks? How are they formed?
7. Name the agents involved in the formation of sedimentary rocks.
8. Name the different types of sedimentary rocks. Give examples for each type.
9. What are metamorphic rocks?
10. Define the process of metamorphism.
11. What are the types of metamorphism?
12. Name the metamorphic rocks that are formed from igneous and sedimentary rocks.
13. What are the stages involved in the process of Lithification in the formation of sedimentary rocks?
14. What is the significance of fossils?
15. Give examples for each of the following types of rocks :
    (i) Formed by the deposition of shells and skeletons of organisms.
    (ii) Containing a low percentage of silica and a high percentage of basic oxides.
    (iii) Covering a wide area of Peninsular India.
    (iv) Wind-deposited stratified rock.
16. What is the importance of rocks?

B. Define the following terms
1. Rocks
2. Minerals
3. Plutonic
4. Hypabyssal
5. Lithification
6. Metamorphism
7. Fossils
8. Rock cycle

C. Distinguish between the following
1. Rocks and Minerals.
2. Extrusive and Intrusive rocks.
3. Plutonic and Hypabyssal intrusive rocks.
4. Thermal and Dynamic metamorphism.
5. Contact and Regional metamorphism.
6. Foliated and Non-foliated rocks.

D. Give reasons
1. Igneous rocks are also called primary rocks.
2. Extrusive igneous rocks have generally small crystals.
3. Sedimentary rocks are also called stratified rocks.
4. The water of Dead Sea is very salty.
5. Silicates are the most common rock forming minerals.
6. Rocks provide a wide variety of minerals.

E. Board Questions
1. State two ways is which Igneous Rocks differ from Sedimentary Rocks.
2. (i) What are fossils ? In which type of rocks do we find fossils ?
   (ii) What do you understand by 'ROCK CYCLE' ?
3. (i) How is metamorphic rock formed ?
   (ii) Classify the following rocks into igneous, sedimentary and metamorphic rocks :
        1. Granite   2. Limestone   3. Basalt   4. Marble
4. Give a geographical reason for the following :
    (i) Plutonic Igneous rocks have large crystals.

CHAPTER 7
VOLCANOES

Meaning and Types : Active, Dormant and Extinct.
Effects—Constructive and Destructive. Important Volcanic Zones of the World.

According to the observations made by Geologists, when one goes down into the interior of the Earth, the temperature keeps increasing. It increases at the rate of 1°C per 32 metres of descent. This increase in temperature is due to the radioactive elements deep within the Earth. When the temperature and pressure are favourable, the rocks are found in a molten state. These molten rocks or magma pour out when the pressure is released through a deep fissure or joints of the surface.

Volcanicity is the process that involves the intrusion of magma in the Earth's crust or the extrusion of such molten material into the Earth's surface, hence giving rise to volcanic eruptions, which are the Earth's most destructive and violent agents of change.

The word volcano is derived from *'Vulcan'*, the nature of the Roman God of Fire. The science of study of volcanic phenomena is called Volcanology.

VOLCANO

A volcano is an opening on the Earth's surface or crust, connected by a conduit to the underlying magma chamber, through which allows hot magma, volcanic ash and gases to erupt, often with powerful force. *(Fig. 7.1)* It is like a mountain that opens inward to molten rocks below the Earth's surface. The opening is called a vent. A vent is the weak spot or opening in the Earth through which magma comes out, while the hollow shape of the opening is called a crater.

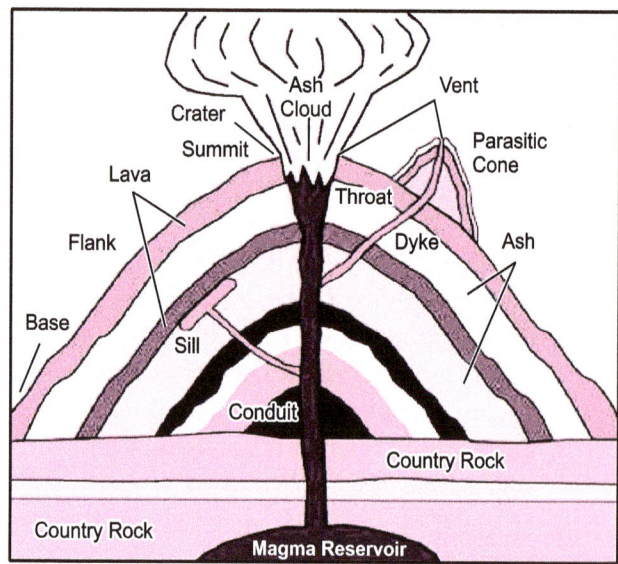

Fig. 7.1 : Parts of a Volcano.

Magma is a mixture of molten or semi-molten rocks found beneath the Earth's surface. When there is extremely high pressure, the magma is forced onto the Earth's surface, where it is known as lava. As it escapes from a confined space, a lot of energy is released with it. This is the reason why many eruptions also produce huge quantities of gases and dust. Due to the enormous pressure, it not only finds cracks in the Earth's crust, but also creates them.

Products of a Volcano

- **Volcanic Gases :** Magma contains dissolved gases that are released during and between eruptions. These gases are mainly steam, carbon dioxide and compounds of sulphur and chlorine.
- **Lava Flows :** These are streams of molten rock.

- **Pyroclasts :** These are high-speed avalanches of hot ash, rock fragments and gases, which move down the sides of a volcano. These flows occur when the vent area collapses.

Types of Volcanoes

On the Basis of Types of Eruptions

- **Central Volcano :** When the rock material comes out and mounds, hills or cones are formed, and then the volcanoes so formed are known as central type of volcanoes. E.g. : Fujiyama (Japan).
- **Conical Volcano :** A conical volcano is one, which has a conical shape and steep slope. It erupts with explosive force and the material accumulates round the vent creating a cone. E.g. : Deccan Plateau (India), Northern Ireland, Iceland.
- **Fissure Volcano :** It erupts from narrow cracks (fissures) several kilometers in length. The vast quantities of extremely fluid lava (basalt) that spreads far and wide forming layers of lava sheets. *(Fig. 7.2)* Eruptions at intervals lead to the piling up of lava sheets one over the other forming a series of steps. E.g. : Deccan trap region of peninsular India has several lava sheets having a maximum thickness of 2000 meters, Idaho Plateau of USA, etc.

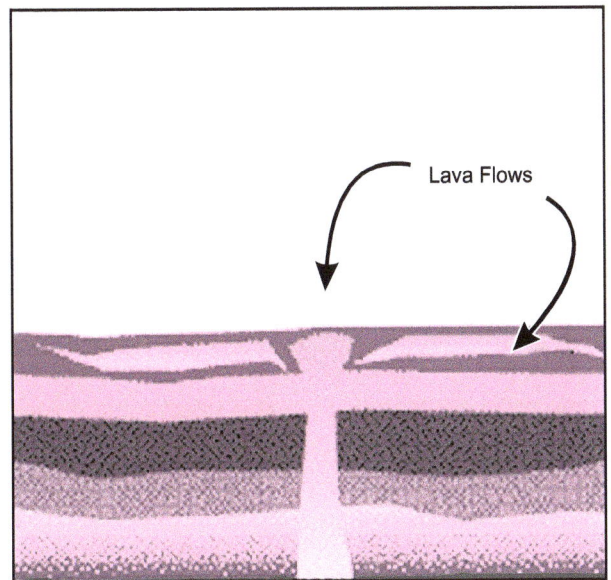

Fig. 7.2 : Fissure Volcano.

- **Shield Volcano :** This type of volcano can be across hundreds of miles and many tens of thousands feet high. It has low slopes and consists almost entirely of frozen lava. *(Fig. 7.3)* It usually has a large crater at its summit. Eg. : The individual islands of the state of Hawaii are large shield volcanoes. Mauna Loa, a shield volcano in Hawaii, is the largest single mountain in the world, rising over 30,000 feet above the ocean floor and reaching almost 100 miles across at its base.

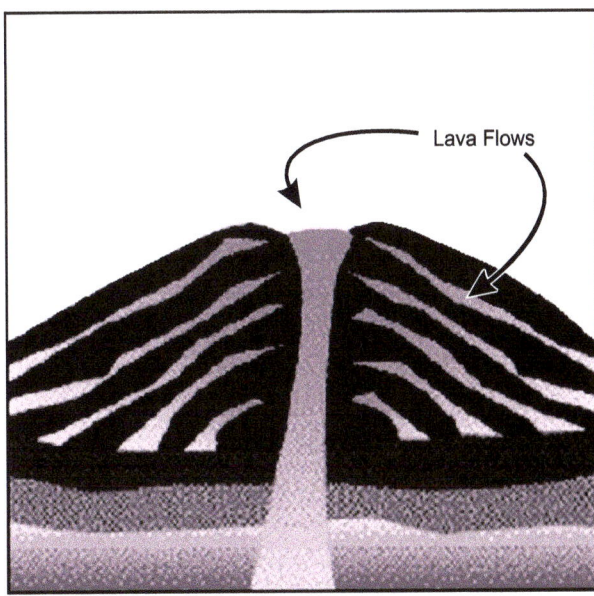

Fig. 7.3 : Shield Volcano.

On the Basis of Composition of Lava

- **Acid Lava Dome :** This is formed when volcanoes are erupted with very slow moving acidic, viscous lava that solidifies quickly and gives rise to dome shaped, steeply sloping cone, whose sides are convex and it is comparatively higher than the other cones. This is known as spines or plugs. Acid lava is rich in silica and poor in iron and magnesium. E.g. : Mt. Pelee (Martinique, West Indies).
- **Basic Lava Shield :** These are built of fluid lava, commonly basic, which flows far out from the central vent before hardening and thus builds a mountain, broad and gently sloping in proportion to its height. It is not so high but it is more extensive. Basic lava is poor in silica, and rich in iron and magnesium. E.g. : Kilauea (Hawaii).

On the Basis of Frequency of Eruption

- **Active Volcanoes :** These are the ones, which are presently in active state and have erupted lava, gases, ashes, cinder, pumice, etc., in the recent past. There are more than 500 potentially active volcanoes on the Earth. E.g. : Mauna Loa (Hawaii) is considered as the world's biggest active volcano. Mt. Stromboli (Mediterranean Sea, north of Sicily) erupts frequently, making the summit glow. Thus also known as 'Lighthouse of the Mediterranean'. The Krakatoa (Indonesia) is also an active volcano. Its terrible explosion in 1883 made history by causing the entire mountain to disappear. Other notable examples are Mt. Etna (Italy), Pinatubo (Philippines), Paricutin (Mexico), etc.

- **Dormant Volcanoes :** These volcanoes are those which have remained inactive for a long period of time (at least 2000 years) or which have a possibility of eruption in the future. These are 'sleeping' volcanoes, which may become active once again. Such volcanoes are often found in the regions of recent fold mountains. E.g. : Fujiyama (Japan), Vesuvius (Italy) – It had erupted first in AD 79. It remained dormant for over 1700 years and then suddenly erupted in AD 1631, subsequent eruptions occurred in 1803, 1872, 1906, 1927, 1928 and 1929.

- **Extinct Volcanoes :** These are the volcanoes, which have not erupted for a very long period of time (at least 10,000 years) or which have no probability of erupting in the future. E.g. : Mt. Kilimanjaro, Mt. Kenya, etc.

Landforms in Volcanic Regions

Landforms in volcanic regions can be classified into two types : Intrusive and Extrusive.

Intrusive Landform

It occurs when lava solidifies within the Earth's crust and gives rise to various shapes and forms. Some of the common intrusive landforms are discussed below *(Fig. 7.4)* :

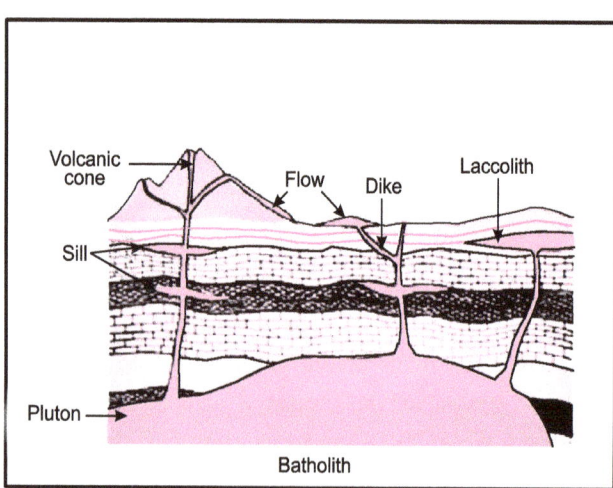

Fig. 7.4 : Intrusive Landforms

- **Sill :** It is the molten magma, which solidifies horizontally between the layers of sedimentary rocks. The sills may be of any thickness, and can stretch for several kilometers.

- **Dykes :** These are formed when lava makes its way out through cracks and fissures developed on land. It solidifies vertically as a narrow wall and can spread over several kilometers in length. E.g. Cleveland Dyke of Yorkshire (UK) is a good example.

- **Batholiths :** These are huge masses of magmatic materials that occur at a considerable depth to develop large domes or the core of old mountains. They appear on the Earth's surface only after denudation of the overlying material.

- **Laccoliths :** It is a large sill of acid lava, which has solidified gradually, giving it a dome shape. It varies in thickness and extent. It forces the overlying strata to bulge upwards, which is prone to erosion and denudation.

- **Lopoliths :** The lava that solidifies in the shape of a saucer is called lopolith. These are formed between the layers of sedimentary rocks. E.g. The uplands of Brittany (France).

- **Phacoliths :** It is a dome-shaped mass of igneous rock, which is formed when acid lava solidifies on an anticline or on the base of a syncline.

Extrusive Landform

It is formed when lava comes out of the Earth's crust and solidifies into magma, in various shapes and forms.

- **Ash and Cinder Cones :** These are formed when lava is thrown upwards from a central vent and solidifies at the surface. When lava is ejected from a central vent, its pieces and fragments solidify around the vent forming a conical structure known as cinder cone.

- **Composite Cones :** These are formed when volcano ejects both lava and fragments of rocks from a number of vents. The cones are built of layers of cinders and ash, alternating with layers of lava.

- **Crater :** The funnel-shaped basin around the vent is called a crater.

- **Caldera :** When a tremendous eruption takes place, the entire central portion or the summit of the volcano is blown out. This creates a massive depression, which is called a caldera. E.g. Crater Lake in Oregon, USA (has a diameter of over 9 km). *(Fig. 7.5).*

- **Lava Shield :** This is formed when basic fluid lava flows far away from the central vent and solidifies into a broad and gently sloping summit.
- **Lava Plateau :** These result from fissure eruptions in which basaltic lava flows out of a crack in the Earth's surface. This lava spreads over a large area, solidifies in layers and takes the shape of a plateau. It is a very thick deposit of volcanic material. E.g. : Deccan Plateau, Columbia Plateau, Antrim Plateau, etc.

Fig. 7.5 : Caldera.

Ten Deadliest Volcanic Eruptions			
Volcano	Year	Death Toll	Effects
Tambora, Indonesia	1815	92,000	The concussion from the explosion was felt as far as a thousand miles away. Mt. Tambora, which was more than 13,000 feet tall before the explosion was reduced to 9,000 feet after ejecting more than 93 cubic miles of debris into the atmosphere.
Krakatau, Indonesia	1883	36,417	Destroyed 2/3rds of the island, ejecting more than six cubic miles of debris into the atmosphere. The sound of the explosion was the loudest ever documented, and was heard as far away as Australia.
Mt. Pelee, Martinique	1902	29,025	Thought to be dormant, Mt. Pelee began a series of eruptions on April 25th, 1902. The primary eruption on May 8th destroyed the city of St. Pierre completely.
Ruiz, Colombia	1985	25,000	A small eruption melted part of the volcano's ice cap creating an enormous mudslide that buried the city of Armero.
Unzen, Japan	1792	14,300	The eruption was followed by an earthquake, which collapsed the east flank of the dome. The resulting avalanche created a tsunami.
Laki, Iceland	1783	9,350	Nearly a year of constant eruptions created a dusty volcanic haze that created massive food shortages.
Kelut, Indonesia	1919	5,110	Most of the casualties were the result of mudslides.
Galunggung, Indonesia	1882	4,011	Dormant for almost 10 years, it erupted in 1882. It blanketed all the surrounding areas with ash. This violent activity continued for about 2 years.
Vesuvius, Italy	AD 1631	3,500	The lava flow consumed many of the surrounding towns.
Vesuvius, Italy	AD 79	3,360	Completely destroyed the Roman towns of Pompeii and Herculaneum. The eruption, which lasted 19 hours, buried Pompeii in ten feet of volcanic ash.

Source : Volcano World, University of North Dakota.

Other Forms of Volcanic Activity

Geysers

The word geyser is taken from the language spoken in Iceland and it means springing water. These are natural fountains that throw up jets of hot water and steam at regular intervals through a vent in the Earth's surface. They may spout to a height of over 150 ft. In some areas, rainwater seeps through cracks in the rocks and drains into a crevice or a large cave-like chamber so deep that it reaches the hot rocks. *(Fig. 7.6)* Eventually, the intense heat boils the water, which then turns into steam. This increases the pressure inside the crevice as bubbles of steam build up. Finally, the pressure is strong enough to shoot the water and steam upwards and out through a vent, high into the air. When the jet has died down, the crevice fills with new water and the process is repeated. Eg. : Old Faithful Geyser (Yellowstone National Park, USA) is the most famous geyser. (Fig. 7.7) It erupts every 60-70 minutes spewing jets of hot water nearly 60 meters highand attracts numerable tourists, Valley of Geysers (Russia), El Tatio (Chile), are a few other popular geysers.

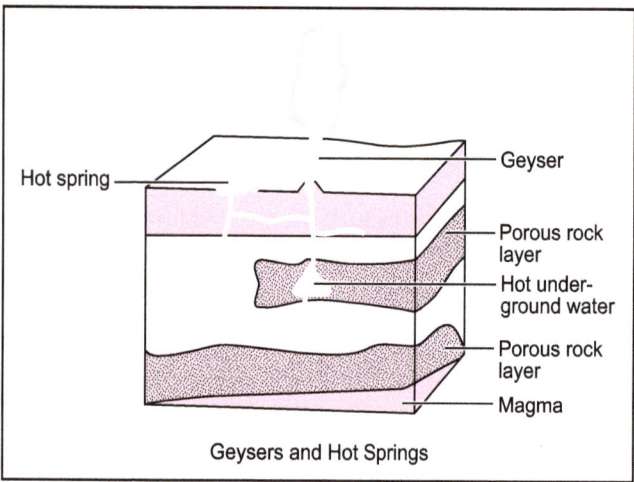

Fig. 7.6 : Formation of Geysers and Hot Springs.

Fig. 7.7 : Old Faithful Geyser (Yellowstone National Park, USA).

Hot Springs

Hot springs are called thermal springs. These are the fountains of hot water rising from underground continuously without any eruptive forces. They are usually associated with the areas where groundwater has sunk and is heated underground by the internal forces. Usually such water rises without any explosion or noise. They are sometimes medicinal as they contain certain minerals in solution. These spots have become sources of recreation. In countries like Iceland, these are harnessed to produce energy, which in turn is utilized in heating homes, swimming pools or for other domestic purposes. *(Fig. 7.8)*

Fig. 7.8 : Hot Spring.

Eg. : Beppu (Japan), Lava Hot Springs (Idaho), Glenwood Springs (Colorado), Sohna Town (Gurgaon, India), etc.

Distribution of Volcanoes

Volcanoes are not randomly distributed on the surface of the Earth, rather they are found in certain well-defined belts. *(Fig. 7.9)* These belts coincide with major lines of weakness in the Earth's crust. However, there are also many other volcanoes, which are found scattered outside these belts. The three volcanic belts are discussed below :

The Circum-Pacific Belt

This is the most important belt of volcanoes, which is also called as the 'Ring of Fire' *(Fig. 7.10)*. This belt extends through the Andes of South America, Central America, Mexico, the Cascade Mountains of western United States, the Aleutian Islands, Kamchatka, the Kuril Isles, Japan, the Philippines, Celebes, New Guinea, the Solomon Islands, New Caledonia and New Zealand. It has 452 volcanoes and is home to over 75% of the world's active and dormant volcanoes. The Ring of Fire encapsulates several tectonic plates including the vast Pacific Plate and the smaller Philippine, Juan de Fuca, Cocos, and Nazca plates. Some of the major volcanoes found in this belt are Mt. Tambora, Krakatoa, Novarupta, Mt. St. Helens, Mt. Ruiz, Mt. Pinatubo, etc.

The Mid-Continental Belt

It includes the volcanoes of Alpine mountain chain, the Mediterranean Sea and the fault zone of eastern Africa. The volcanic eruptions are caused due to the convergence and collision of the Eurasian Plates and the African and Indian Plates. Some famous volcanoes found in this belt are Stromboli, Vesuvius, Etna, Kilimanjaro, Meru, Elgon, Rungwe, etc.

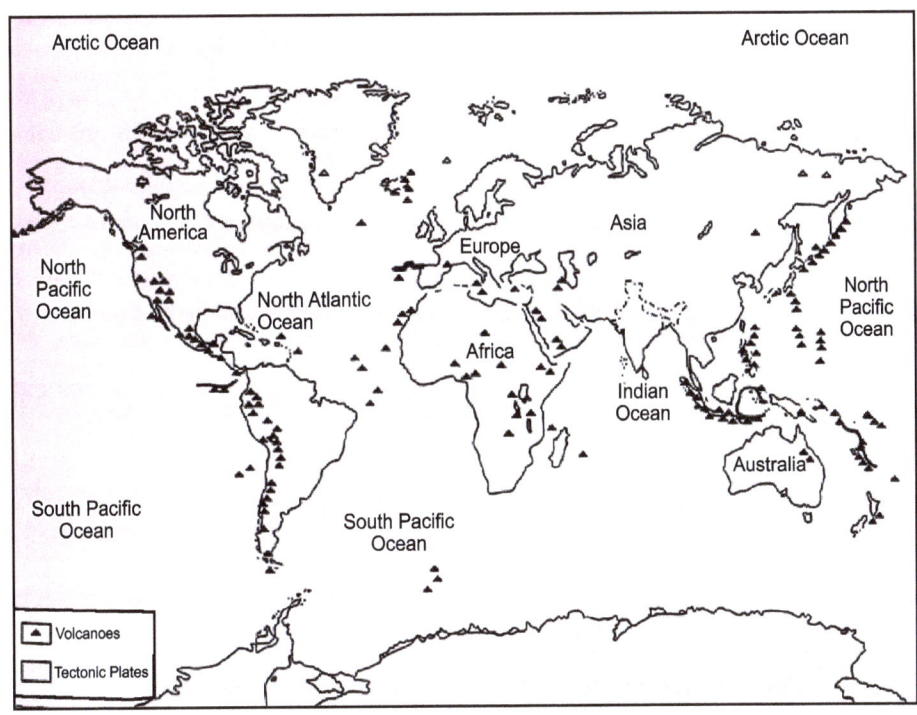

Fig. 7.9 : Distribution of Volcanoes in the World.

The Mid-Atlantic Belt

It includes the volcanoes lying along the mid-Atlantic ridge, which is a divergent plate zone (American plate moving westwards and Eurasian plate moving eastwards). Volcanoes in this belt are generally of fissure-eruption type. Eg. Iceland, Canary Islands, Cape Verde, Azores, etc.

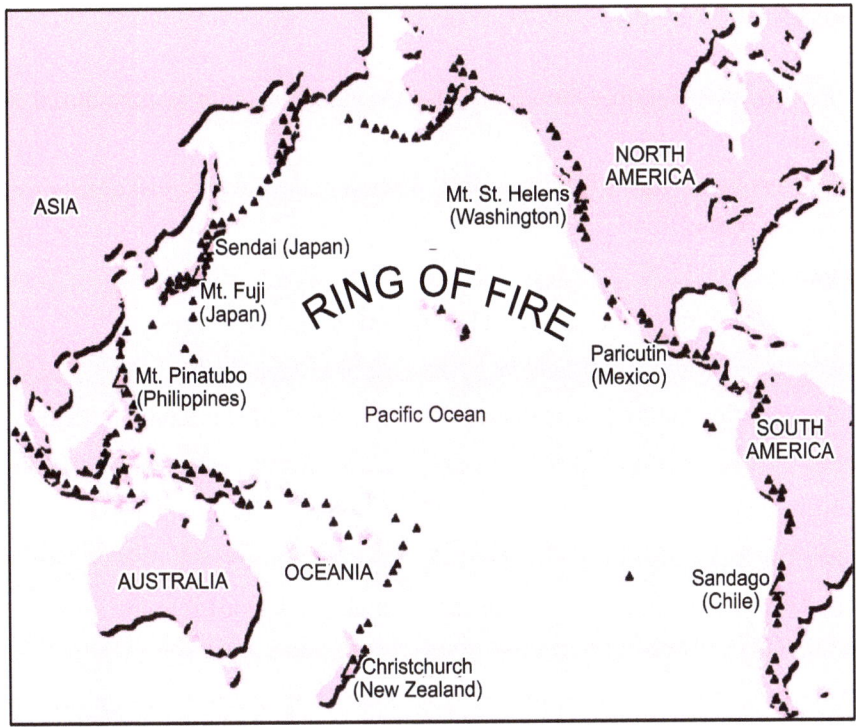

Fig. 7.10 : Ring of Fire

The **"Ring of Fire"** lies in the basin of the Pacific Ocean. It is a horseshoe-shaped arc stretching from New Zealand, along the eastern edge of Asia, north across the Aleutian Islands of Alaska, and south along the coast of North and South America. It is the home of many of the most famous and well-known fault zones and volcanoes on the planet. Over 75% of the world's active and dormant volcanoes lie in this area. This huge ring of volcanic and seismic (earthquake) activity was noticed and described before the invention of the plate tectonics theory.

Effects of Volcanoes

Constructive

- Volcanic ash blown over thousands of square kilometers of land increase the soil fertility for forests and agriculture by adding nutrients.
- Geothermal energy can be harnessed from the Earth's natural heat associated with active volcanoes or geologically young inactive volcanoes. Steam from hightemperature geothermal fluids can be used to drive turbines and generate electrical power, while lower temperature fluids provide hot water for space-heating purposes, heat for greenhouses and industrial uses, and hot or warm springs at resort spas. For example, geothermal heat warms more than 70% of the homes in Iceland, and The Geysers geothermal field near Santa Rosa, in Northern California produces enough electricity to meet the power demands of San Francisco.
- Physical breakdown and chemical weathering of volcanic rocks have formed some of the most fertile soils on Earth. Some of the best rice-growing regions of Indonesia lie in the shadow of active volcanoes. Similarly, many prime agricultural regions in the western USA have fertile soils wholly or largely of volcanic origin.
- Volcanic rocks, when exposed to the surface, are a storehouse of metals and minerals.
- Volcanic areas (crater lakes, geysers, hot springs) are places of tourist attraction.

Destructive

- There is widespread loss of life and property. Hot, flowing lava can bury buildings, kill people, animals, destroy farmlands, lakes, forests, etc.
- Large quantities of cinders, dust, ash, smoke, etc. can pose health hazards due to poisonous gases emitted during eruption.
- Explosive eruptions can result in earthquakes, which can further cause avalanches, mudslides and tsunamis. All of these are capable of causing devastating damages.
- It can change the heat balance of the Earth and atmosphere, causing climatic changes.

SUMMARY

- A volcano is an opening on the Earth's surface or crust, through which hot magma mixed with gases and steam erupts forcefully.
- Volcanicity is the process that involves the intrusion of magma in the Earth's crust or the extrusion of such molten material into the Earth's surface.
- **Types of Volcanoes :**
    - (i) According to Eruptions : (i) Conical, (ii) Fissure, (iii) Shield, (iv) Central.
    - (ii) According to Composition : (i) Acid lava dome (ii) Basic lava shield.
    - (iii) According to activity of frequency of eruption : (i) Active, (ii) Dormant, (iii) Extinct.
- **Volcanic Belts :**
    - (i) The Circum-Pacific Belt, (ii) Mid-Continental Belt, and (iii) Mid-Atlantic Belt.
- **Effects of Volcanoes :**

    Constructive : (i) They bring changes in landscape which are favourable for farming, (ii) Lava contains important minerals, (iii) Volcanic activity has given rise to lakes at places.

    Destructive : (i) They disturb peaceful routine of life. (ii) They bring wide-ranging catastrophes to man and bring a wide-ranging devastation. (iii) The lava flow destroys the crops over an extensive area.

EXERCISES

A. Answer the following questions

1. What are volcanoes?
2. How are volcanoes formed?
3. Name some products of a volcano.
4. Name the types of volcanoes based on their frequency of eruption. Give an example of each.
5. How does the fissure volcano erupt?
6. Which type of lava is more viscous?
7. Name any four types of landforms associated with volcanoes.
8. How is a crater formed?
9. What are geysers?
10. How are hot springs formed?
11. Describe the three volcanic belts.
12. What is "Ring of Fire"?
13. State three advantages of volcanoes.
14. Mention three adverse effects of volcanoes.

B. Define the following

1. Caldera
2. Batholiths
3. Sills
4. Lava
5. Crater
6. Magma
7. Active volcano
8. Cinder cone
9. Volcanology
10. Ring of Fire

C. Distinguish between the following

1. Cinder and Composite cone
2. Dormant and Extinct Volcano
3. Geysers and Hot Springs
4. Intrusive and Extrusive landforms.
5. Acid and Basic lava.

D. Give reasons for the following

1. Some volcanoes erupt explosively.
2. Hot springs are common in volcanic regions.
3. The belt of volcanic activities and earthquakes are the same.
4. Most of the volcanoes lie in the "Ring of Fire".

E. Map work

1. On an outline map of the world, mark the volcanic belts of the world.

F. Board Questions

1. (i) Draw a labelled diagram of the structure of a volcano.
   (ii) State any two positive effects of volcanoes.

CHAPTER 8
EARTHQUAKES

Meaning, Causes and Measurement. Effects : Destructive and Constructive. Earthquake Zones of the World.

Earthquake, in simple words, means shaking of the Earth. When there are intense Earth tremors, we experience an Earthquake. Earthquakes are one of the most destructive natural phenomena because of the extent of damage to life and property they cause. They have been a source of apprehension and dismay. Hence, these have aroused great curiosity in mankind. And he has applied his action and thought to explore the secret behind them.

EARTHQUAKE

Earthquakes are tremors or convulsions of the Earth's crust. They are caused by a rapid release of stress along a fault line or by volcanic activity.

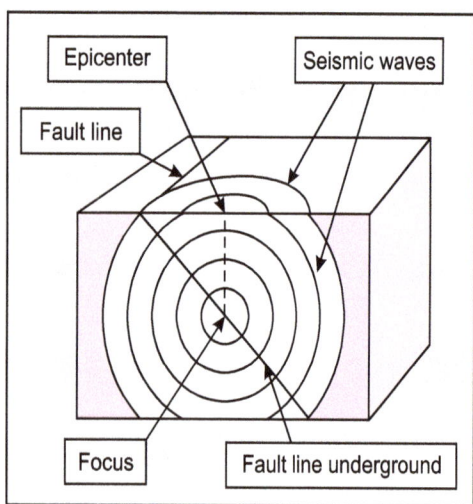

Fig. 8.1 : Earthquake

An Earthquake is a sudden movement within the crust or mantle, occurring when two blocks of the Earth suddenly slip past one another due to tectonic forces. The surface where they slip is called the fault or fault plane. The center from which the Earthquake waves originate is called the seismic focus. Most of the Earthquakes have seismic focus at depths less than 60 km. Since this is often deep below the surface and difficult to map, the location of the Earthquake is often referred to the point on the Earth's surface directly above the focus, known as the epicenter. (Fig. 8.1) The intensity of the tremors is highest near the epicenter and decreases with the increasing distance. The path of the seismic (Earthquake) waves through a point on the Earth's surface is recorded by an instrument called Seismograph. The study of Earthquakes is known as Seismology.

Causes of Earthquakes

The Earthquakes are caused by the tension in the Earth's crust, which in turn is caused by several factors. When the Earth's crust is unable to accommodate itself to the tension, it results in a sudden release of tremendous energy in the form of a sudden violent shock. There are several reasons contributing to the occurrence of Earthquakes :

Volcanic Activities

A place where there is an active volcano, is often prone to Earthquakes too, because the pressure that is exerted by the magma exceeds the limit of the plate movement and causes Earthquakes. Earthquakes are also caused after a volcanic eruption since the eruption also leads to a disturbance in the position of plates, which either move further or resettle and can result in severe tremors. When extraordinary levels of pressure develops, the resultant explosion can be devastating, producing an Earthquake of considerable magnitude. Eg.: Krakatoa volcano's (between Java and Sumatra) explosion in 1883 was heard over 5000 km away in Australia. Its impact was even experienced in Cape Horn (12,800 km away). The shock waves produced a series of tsunamis (large sea waves), one of which was over 36 m high; that is the same as four, two-storey houses stacked on top of each other. These swept over the coastal areas of Java and Sumatra killing over 36,000 people.

Plate Tectonics

The outer layer of the Earth is divided into many sections known as plates, which are floating on the molten magma beneath the Earth's crust.

Now the movement of these plates is determined by the convection current in the molten magma. The tectonic processes include the upwelling of magma, plate movement, folds and faults, etc. These movements disrupt the balance and position of all plates leading to Earthquake tremors. The relation of interplate movements is defined by the type of plate margin. Constructive plate movement is well illustrated in the Atlantic Ocean. At the mid-ocean ridges, new ocean floor is continuously being produced as America moves further apart from Europe and Africa.

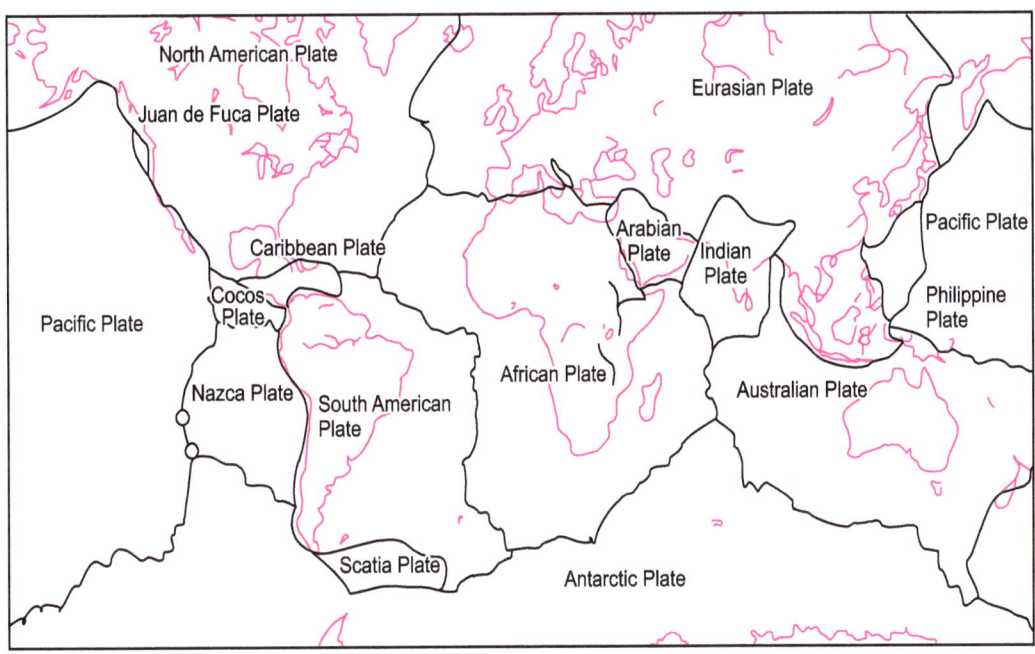

Fig. 8.2 : Distribution of Plates.

Destructive or conservative plate movement can cause the most destructive Earthquakes. It arises where adjacent plates slide on one another along transform faults. Eg.: The 'Ring of Fire' surrounding the Pacific Basin. *(Fig. 8.2).*

Folding and Faulting

These can be found in rocks of all ages, but the likelihood of movement occurring is minimal unless the fault is located in an active area of plate motion, i.e., in a zone where one plate moves against another. Eg.: The San Andreas Fault of California Earthquake, 1906.

Isostatic Disturbances

These are produced by the deposition of sediments by rivers and glaciers on the ocean floor. Since the asthenosphere below is in a semi-molten state, the disturbances in the equilibrium between oceans and continents also produce movements

causing Earthquakes. Eg.: Earthquake in Hindu Kush Region (4th March, 1949), tremors were experienced up to Lahore in Pakistan.

Anthropogenic Factors

These are the man-made causes. The extraction of minerals, deep underground mining, blasting of rocks by dynamites for the construction of large dams, roads and reservoirs, nuclear explosions, etc., near fault zones can also produce Earthquakes of various intensity and magnitudes. E.g.: Koyna Earthquake in Maharashtra, caused by construction of Koyna dam in seismically active region.

Measurement of Earthquakes

Earthquakes can be measured in following ways :

Intensity

Intensity of earthquake wave is measured by Richter scale ranging from 0 to 9. A strong earthquake can have intensity value of more than 5. The Richter is named after the American seismologist Charles Francis Richter. The intensity of earthquake is the destructive power of earthquake and evaluation of its severity of the ground motion at a given location when it occurs.

The intensity of earthquake that measures 5 or more is alarming and it may measure up to 11 when there is total destruction of life and people. Intensity of 8.1 was experienced on 26th Jan, 2001, at Bhuj in the State of Gujarat of India.

Intensity is also measured by another system using the Mercalli scale which grades the intensity of the earthquakes on the basis of observed effects on a 12-point scale.

Instruments

The **Seismograph** is used for measuring the intensity of Earthquakes. The recordings are known as seismograms. The seismograph has a base that sets firmly in the ground, and a heavy weight that hangs free. When an Earthquake causes the ground to shake, the base of the seismograph shakes too, but the hanging weight does not. Instead, the spring or string that it is hanging absorbs all the movement. The difference in position between the shaking part of the seismograph and the motionless part is what is recorded. *(Fig. 8.3)*

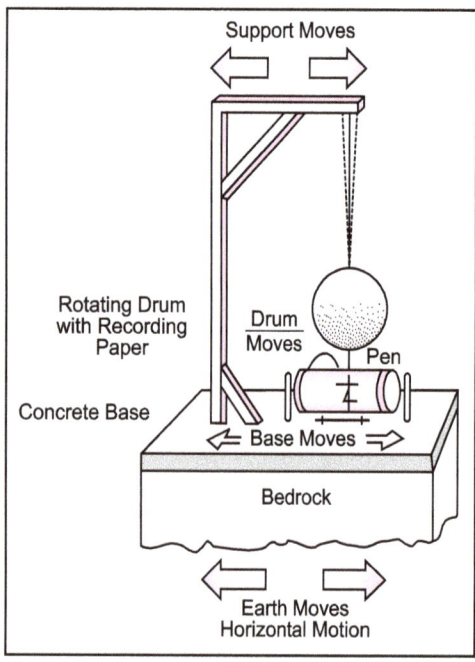

Fig. 8.3 : Seismograph

Types of Seismic Waves

The tension caused by the movement of the Earth's plates builds up until it is released in the form of powerful vibrations. These vibrations travel in three types of waves, namely: P-waves, S-waves and L-waves. These waves move outwards from the focus, but can travel in both the horizontal and vertical plains.

Let us study a detailed classification of the three types of waves. *(Fig. 8.4)*

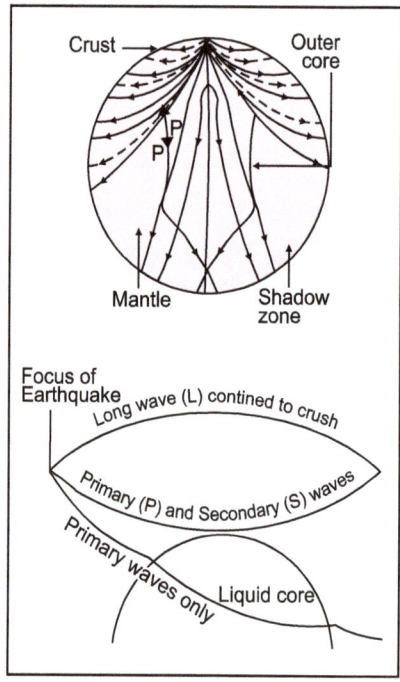

Fig. 8.4 : Seismic Waves

P (Primary or Push) Waves

These are identical in character to sound waves. They are high frequency, short wavelength, longitudinal waves, which can pass through both solids and liquids. The ground is forced to move forwards and backwards as it is compressed and decompressed. This produces relatively small displacements of the ground. They can be reflected and refracted, and under certain circumstances can change into S-waves.

S (Secondary or Shake) Waves

These travel more slowly than P-waves and arrive at any given point after them. They are high frequency, shortwavelength, but instead of being longitudinal, they are transverse waves. They move in all directions away from their source at speeds, which depend upon the density of the rocks through which they are moving. They cannot move through liquids. On the surface of the Earth, they are responsible for the sideways displacement of walls and fences, leaving them 'S' shaped.

L (Surface or Long) Waves

These are low frequency transverse vibrations with a long wavelength. They are created close to the epicenter and can only travel through the outer part of the crust. They are responsible for the majority of the building damage caused by Earthquakes, as they have a motion similar to that of sea waves. The ground is made to move in a circular motion, causing it to rise and fall as visible waves move across the ground.

Distribution of Earthquakes

Most Earthquakes originate from plate boundaries. The Earthquakes have a definite pattern of distribution *(Fig. 8.5)*. There are three major belts in the world. They are as follows:

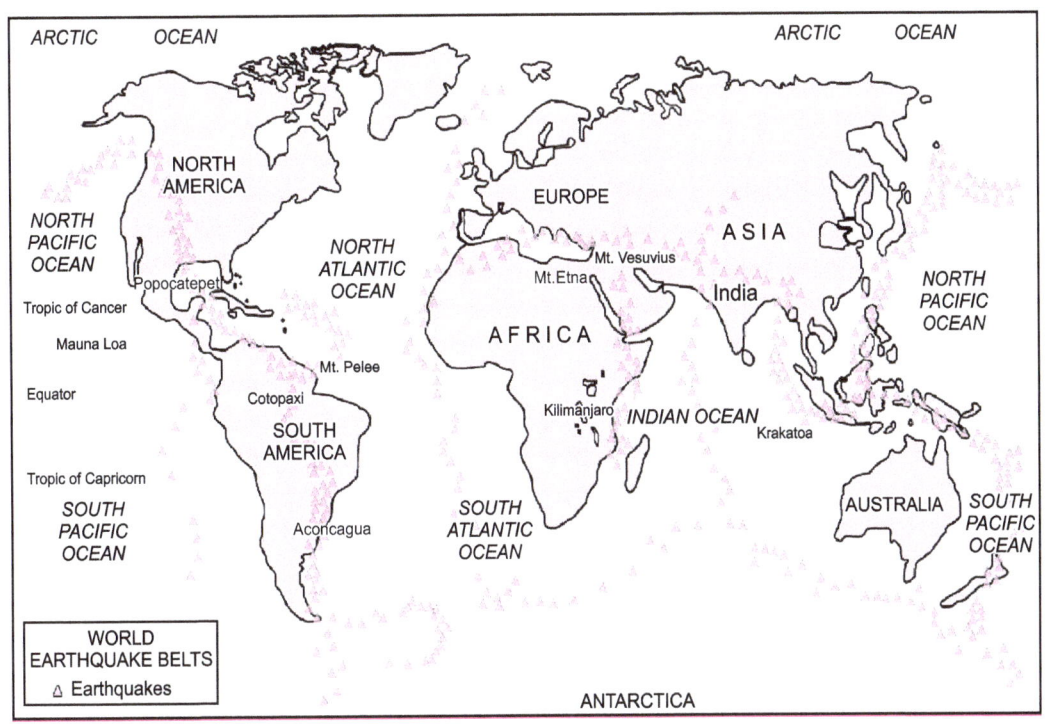

Fig. 8.5 : World Map Showing Earthquake Belts

- **The Circum-Pacific Belt :** This zone is prone to severe Earthquakes having their focus more than 25 km deep. It comprises about 66% of the total Earthquakes of the world. This belt extends in the west from Alaska to Kurile, Japan, Mariana and the Philippine trenches. On the eastern side of the Pacific, it follows the west coast of North America and continues southward along Peru and Chile trench on the west coast of the South America. Most of the Earthquakes that occur here are volcanic Earthquakes; therefore, this belt is called as the Fiery Ring of the Pacific.

- **The Mid-Atlantic Belt :** This belt of Earthquakes extends along the mid-oceanic ridges and several islands near the ridges of the Atlantic Ocean. The sea-floor spreading is the main cause for the moderate-to-mild intensity with shallow focus Earthquakes in this belt. E.g.: The Rift Valley of East Africa and the Red Sea.

- **The Mid-Continental Belt :** This zone is characterized by larger Earthquakes of shallow origin and some of intermediate origin. Deep focus Earthquakes are almost absent in this belt. It comprises about 21% of the total Earthquakes of the world. It stretches east-west along the fold ranges of Asia and Europe right across the Atlantic up to the Appalachians of North America.

Effects of Earthquake

In geological terminology, Earthquakes are a part of endogenic forces. From the human point of view, they are regarded to have destructive as well as constructive effects on the environment. Some of the effects are discussed below.

Constructive

- Earthquakes help the Earth to release its stored up energy. The majority of the Earthquakes occur around the plate margins. This energy release helps to keep Earth in good shape.

- On account of both vertical and lateral displacement of the Earth's crust, coastal areas

are lifted by Earthquakes creating new coastal plains, which can be utilized for farming.
- **Isostatic** Earthquakes may lift up fold ranges, which can be of great advantage to the area in influencing climate. Eg.: The Himalayas.
- As a result of subsidence of land along the fault planes, lakes are created. These lakes may be useful to man in many ways.
- Fissures open up on the Earth's surface. Through these fissures, springs may be created.
- The displacement of rocks with the folding and faulting helps in the formation of soil used for farming.
- Coastal submergence of land may cause inlets, bays and gulfs on the coast, which may favour the development of ports in that region.

Destructive
- **Loss of Human Life :** Human beings have settlements in active Earthquake zones. Most often, these lives and property collapse resulting in huge losses.
- **Loss of Agricultural Land :** Earthquakes have changed the course of rivers in the past. They have thus rendered many areas unsuitable for irrigation and agriculture.
- **Loss of Crops :** They cause floods in the rivers by creating physical barriers in the shape of uplift of land. Such floods prove disastrous for crops.
- **Disruption of Rail and Road Networks :** Transportation is hampered due to the big openings and extensive fissures in the surface of the Earth. Railway tracks may be bent and roads may be breached.
- **Damage to Bridges and Hydroelectric Power Stations :** Demolishment of big dams across the rivers damages the hydroelectric stations and breaks the bridges.
- **Fire :** Due to dislocation of electric wiring, fires break out causing a great loss of life and property.
- **Tsunami :** They bring havoc to the coastal areas causing tidal waves to surge skyward (known as tsunami), causing huge damage to ships and coastal establishments.

Major Earthquakes of the World			
Location	Date	Estimated Deaths	Magnitude on Richter Scale
Valdivia, Chile	22nd May, 1960	6,000	9.5
West Coast of Sumatra, Indonesia	26th December, 2004	230,210	9.3
Lisbon, Portugal	1st November, 1755	100,000	9.0
North Coast of Japan	11th March, 2011	28,000	9.0
Kamchatka, Russia	4th November, 1952	10,000	9.0
Bihar, India	15th January, 1934	8,100	8.7
Shaanxi, China	23rd January, 1556	830,000	8.0
Sichuan, China	12th May, 2008	85,000	8.0
Kwanto, Japan	1st September, 1923	142,800	7.9
Tangshan, China	28th July, 1976	655,000	7.8
Gansu, China	16th December, 1920	235,502	7.8
Kangra, Himachal Pradesh, India	4th April, 1905	20,000	7.8
Bhuj, Gujarat, India	26th January, 2001	13,805	7.7
Haiti	12th January, 2010	316,000	7.0

TSUNAMI

The name 'Tsunami' is taken from two Japanese words, *'tsu'* and *'nami'* meaning 'harbour' and 'waves', respectively. Tsunamis are formed as a result of Earthquakes, volcanic eruptions, or landslides that occur under the sea. When these events occur under the water, huge amounts of energy are released as a result of quick upward movement. For example, if a volcanic eruption occurs, the ocean floor may very quickly move upward several hundred feet. When this happens, huge volumes of ocean water are pushed upwards and a wave is formed. A large Earthquake can lift thousands of square kilometers of the sea floor, which causes the formation of huge waves.

In India, the most devastating tsunami occurred in 2004. The 9.3 magnitude Earthquake of Indonesia (2004) generated the disastrous tsunami that wiped out entire coastal areas across southeastern Asia, Sri Lanka, India, Thailand, Myanmar and islands in the Andaman Sea, and Maldives in the Indian Ocean. Scientists estimated that during the deep thrust faulting that generated the Earthquake, in which rock on one side of the fault moved up and over rock on the other side, the sea floor above the fault was uplifted by several meters. The displacement of overlying seawater triggered the massive tsunami, in which the waves reached as high as 15 meters.

Tsunamis can be generated when the sea floor abruptly deforms and vertically displaces the overlying water. Tectonic Earthquakes are particularly associated with the Earth's crustal deformation; when these Earthquakes occur beneath the sea, the water above the deformed area is displaced from its equilibrium position. Waves are formed as the displaced water mass, which acts under the influence of gravity, attempts to regain its equilibrium. When large areas of the seafloor elevate or subside, a tsunami can be created. Large vertical movements of the Earth's crust can occur at plate boundaries. Around the margins of the Pacific Ocean, for example, denser oceanic plates slip under continental plates in a process known as subduction, which are particularly effective in generating tsunamis. *(Fig. 8.6)*

Characteristics of Tsunami

- Tsunamis can savagely attack coastlines, devastating property and life.
- In the open ocean tsunamis may appear very small with a height of less than 1 meter (3 feet).
- Tsunamis will sometimes go undetected until they approach shallow waters along a coast. These waves have a very large wavelength (up to several hundred miles) that is a function of the depth of the water where they were formed.
- Although these waves have a small height, there is a tremendous amount of energy associated with them. As a result of this huge amount of energy, these waves can become gigantic as they approach shallow water.
- Their height, as they crash upon the shore, depends on the underwater surface features. They can be as high as 30 m (100 feet) or more.
- In the deep open sea, tsunamis move at speeds approaching a jet aircraft (500 mph or more). As they approach the shore, they slow down. When a tsunami arrives at the shore, it usually does so as a rapidly rising tide moving at about 70 km/hour (45 mph).
- A tsunami is not a single wave, but a set that may last for several hours, and the first wave is not always the largest. In 1737, a huge wave estimated to be 64 m (210 feet) in height hit Cape Lopatka, Kamchatka (Russia).
- The largest tsunami ever recorded occurred in July, 1958 in Lituya Bay, Alaska. A huge rock and ice fall sent water surging up to a high water mark of 500 m (1,640 feet).

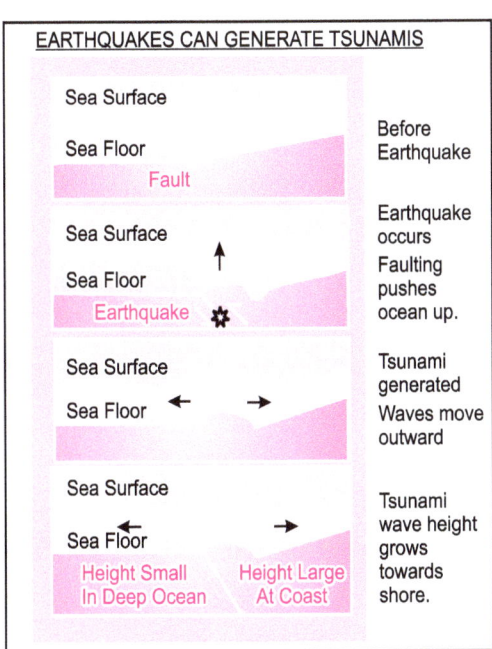

Fig. 8.6 : Propagation of Tsunami.

○ Earthquake is the sudden displacement of a part of the Earth's crust, occurring when two blocks of the Earth suddenly slip past one another due to tectonic forces.

- Causes of Earthquakes: (i) Volcanic activities, (ii) Plate tectonics, (iii) Folding and faulting, (iv) Isostatic disturbances, and (v) Anthropogenic factors.
- Distribution of Earthquakes: (i) Circum-Pacific Belt; (ii) Mid-Atlantic Belt, and (iii) Mid-Continental Belt.
- Seismic focus is the point of origin of seismic waves.
- Epicenter is the point on the Earth's surface exactly above the seismic focus.
- Seismograph is the instrument that measures the movement of Earthquake waves.
- Richter scale is the device that measures the intensity of an Earthquake.
- Tsunamis are the fatal harbour waves caused by oceanic Earthquakes.

EXERCISES

A. Answer the following questions

1. What is an Earthquake?
2. What are the natural causes of Earthquakes on the Earth surface?
3. What are the man-made causes of Earthquakes?
4. How is the intensity of Earthquakes measured? What instruments are used?
5. Give some examples of the Earthquakes of the world.
6. Name two belts where most Earthquakes originate.
7. Describe the distribution of Earthquakes in the world.
8. Explain the different types of Earthquake waves.
9. Explain in detail what is meant by tsunami.
10. Define the causes and effects of tsunamis.
11. How do Earthquakes generate tsunamis?

B. Define the following terms

1. Epicenter
2. Richter scale
3. Seismic focus
4. Seismograph
5. L-waves
6. Tsunami

C. Distinguish between the following

1. Mid-Atlantic Belt and Mid-Continental Belt.
2. Destructive and Constructive Effects of Earthquakes.
3. S-waves and P-waves.

D. Give reasons

1. Earthquakes are common in the young fold mountains belt.
2. Earthquakes are associated with volcanic belts.

E. Map Work

1. On an outline map of the world, mark and show the distribution of Earthquake belts.

F. Board Questions

1. (i) What is the term used to describe the point on the Earth's surface where the intensity of Earthquakes is maximum?
   (ii) Name the point of origin of an Earthquake.
2. Explain the following:
   (i) Epicentre
   (ii) Richter scale

CHAPTER 9
WEATHERING AND DENUDATION

Meaning, Types and Effects of Weathering :
Types : *Physical Weathering–Block and Granular Disintegration, Exfoliation; Chemical Weathering–Oxidation, Carbonation, Hydration and Solution; Biological Weathering–Caused by Humans, plants and animals. Meaning and agents of Denudation, work of river and wind, Stages of a river course and associated land forms V-shaped valley, waterfall, Meander and delta, Wind-deflation hollows and Sand dunes.*

Our Earth's crust is undergoing constant changes caused by various processes. The internal forces like tectonic movements operate in the interior of the Earth, leading to the formation of landforms, while the external forces act on the surface of the Earth through several processes like weathering, mass movement, erosion, transportation, deposition and soil formation. The agents involved in both the forces are similar, but not the same. When air, water, ice and sun rays act locally on a rock, they are known as Agents of Weathering. However, when the same agents are moving in the form of wind, streams, waves, glaciers, etc., and acting on rock surface, they are known as Agents of Denudation. These moving agents are aided in their task by weathering. The agents of denudation pick up the material produced by weathering and transport it from the original place to other convenient places ultimately to deposit them there. Thus to know about these processes more clearly, we will discuss about the external processes, weathering, mass movement, etc. in the following chapter.

EXTERNAL PROCESSES

The external processes operating on the surface of the Earth bring about the great diversity in the present day landforms.

They can be categorized into two groups:

Denudation

It is a twofold process, i.e., both constructive and destructive. It is constructive as it deposits the weathered material. It is destructive as it wears and tears away the rock and then transports the weathered material. Thus, denudation is a dynamic process that includes the disintegration and decomposition of rocks, as well as the wearing away of the land surface. Water, wind and glaciers act as the agents of denudation.

Gradation

It is the general leveling of land due to the dual process of erosion and deposition. Rivers, glaciers, wind, sea waves and underground water act as the agents of gradation. This process has two main components:

- Degradation

It is the general wearing away or lowering of a land surface by erosion, followed by degradation of the landform projecting above the surrounding ground.

- Aggradation

It is the process of deposition in which a landform of lower level is upgraded to a higher level.

All the external processes are interactive and interdependent, i.e., one process gives rise to another. For gradation, aggradation or degradation to occur, a rock must first have been disintegrated in the course of weathering. Erosion in turn leads to degradation of a surface area. Unless the agents of gradation have a load to carry, aggradation cannot occur. Hence, this disintegration of the rock, removal of the rock debris, wearing down the land surface and deposition of the load in lowlands are all interactive and interdependent processes.

WEATHERING

Weathering is the process of disintegration of rocks, or breaking of rocks and decomposition of rocks, or decay caused by the action of rain, frost, heat, cold and other associated features. It is thus described as the breakdown of rocks and minerals at or near the Earth's surface.

Weathering also contributes to the formation of soil by providing mineral particles like sand, silt, and clay. Elements and compounds extracted from the rocks and minerals by weathering processes supply nutrients for plant uptake. The fact that the oceans are saline, in the result of the release of ion salts from rocks and minerals on the continents. In conclusion, weathering is a process that is fundamental to many other aspects of the hydrosphere, lithosphere and biosphere.

Products of Weathering

Weathering is the alteration of rocks to more stable material from their exposure to the agents of air, water and organic fluids. No rock is stable or immune to weathering.

The residue of weathering consists of chemically altered and unaltered materials. The most common unaltered residue is quartz. Many of the chemically altered products of weathering become very simple, small compounds, or nutrient ions. These residues can then be dissolved or transported by water, released to the atmosphere as a gas, or taken up by plants for nutrition. Some of the products of weathering, less resistant alumino-silicate minerals, becomes clay particles. Other altered materials are reconstituted by sedimentary or metamorphic processes to become new rocks and minerals.

Characteristics of Weathering

- It involves disintegration or decay of solid rock.
- It depends on climatic conditions.
- It is affected by the chemical composition, hardness, texture and permeability of rocks.
- It affects the surface of the Earth.
- It helps in the formation of soil.
- It changes hard massive rocks into finer material.
- It prepares rock material for transportation by agents of gradation.

Types of Weathering

Weathering is a static process. The disintegration of rocks may occur through physical or chemical forces or by plants, animals, insects, etc. There are basically three types of weathering— physical or mechanical weathering, chemical weathering and biological weathering.

Physical Weathering

It is also known as mechanical weathering. It involves the disintegration of rocks by various agents of weathering without changing the chemical composition of the material. It is more rapid in desert areas as the temperature changes are sharpest in these hot and dry regions. The factors responsible for this type of weathering are as follows :

- **Block Disintegration :** Changes in temperature influence weathering to a great extent. The sudden rise and fall of temperature causes expansion and contraction of rocks. The repeated action causes their breakdown. The sandy and semi-arid regions are heated intensely during the day and lose heat rapidly at night. Hence, the diurnal range of temperature is very high. This causes expansion of the rocks during the day and contraction during the night. This leads to the rocks getting broken up along the joints or fissures into rectangular blocks.

- **Granular Disintegration :** Since rocks are made up of different minerals, weathering may also reduce rocks to pieces and fragments. Different minerals present in the rocks may have different rates of expansion and contraction. For example, dark coloured minerals will absorb more heat and expand to a greater extent than light colour minerals. Such alternating expansion and contraction between day and night leads to a break-up of the rock into different minerals. This is called granular disintegration.

- **Slope of Land :** Weathering also depends on the gradient of slope. The steep slopes of the rock are eroded more rapidly by the agents of weathering as compared to gentler slopes.

- **Exfoliation:** The changes in temperature during day and night of summer and winter, causes expansion and contraction in the rock surfaces. In the arid regions when the rock consists of homogeneous minerals, the mineral grains of bed rock expand or contract at different rates as a result of heating or cooling. The expansion and contraction of the outer rock layers may loosen the outermost layers completely and cause the scaling off of outer curved shells of rocks. This is known as exfoliation. Exfoliated dome-shaped rocks are found largely in the Australian Desert and the Kalahari Desert.

- **Frost Action:** In the middle latitudes or in the higher altitudes, when water enters the rocks and turns into ice, the volume increases. During the day, the ice thaw and water enters deep into the rocks. When temperature drops during the night, the water again freezes, thus widening the crack. This repeated freezing and thawing results in the disintegration of rocks. Where this process occurs on steep slopes, rock fragments collect at the base of the slope due to gravity in the form of a scree slope.

- **Wind:** The windblown particles attack the rocks and erode them. The rocks have different composition and structures. Hence, some particles of the soft rocks are easily eroded by action of wind, whereas the hard rocks remain exposed. This type of weathering commonly occurs in desert areas.

Chemical Weathering

In this type of weathering, the rocks are decomposed by chemical reaction between elements of the weather and rock minerals, resulting in either the alteration of a rock's internal mineral structure or the formation of new minerals. Weakened rock or the consequent deposits are then more easily removed by erosion processes. Water plays a key role in most chemical reactions and also provides a transport mechanism for other elements that carry out weathering. Chemical weathering is mostly dominant in hot and humid areas, such as equatorial zones and least effective where there is little rain, such as in desert or polar regions (where most water is held as ice). The susceptibility of rocks for chemical weathering is determined by the types of minerals they contain and their mineral structure. There are a number of different types of chemical weathering.

- **Oxidation:** It is the reaction that occurs between the compounds and oxygen. The exposure of rocks to oxygen in air or water can result in a reaction between the oxygen and iron-based minerals in the rocks. Iron readily oxidizes and during oxidation, blue grey ferrous iron (Fe^{2+}) is transformed to red ferric iron (Fe^{3+}). This causes a weakening of the rock structure enabling them to crumble easily and making them more susceptible to other weathering processes. The net result of this reaction is the removal of one or more electrons from a compound, which causes the structure to be less rigid and increasingly unstable. The most common oxides are those of iron and aluminum, and their respective red and yellow staining of soils is quite common in tropical regions which have high temperatures and precipitation.

- **Hydration:** In this process, expansion of minerals occurs on coming into contact with rainwater and gets converts into a powdery mass. Feldspar is a common rock forming crystalline minerals, which turns to clay minerals known as kaolin because of hydration. The other minerals present along with feldspar got separated into loosely arranged particles and the rock eventually breaks up.

- **Carbonation:** It is the reaction of carbonate and bicarbonate ions with minerals. The formation of carbonates usually takes place as a result of other chemical processes. Carbonation is especially active when the reaction of environment is abundant with carbon dioxide. When rain falls, the atmospheric carbon dioxide combines with it and turns it into a weak acid (Carbonic acid). The action of this acid on limestone produces a salt, calcium carbonate, which is readily carried off in the flow of groundwater and streams. This causes weathering of limestone regions where the limestone rocks are commonly seen pitted and grooved.

- **Solution:** In this process, water acts as a solvent by breaking down chemical bonds in minerals causing them to dissolve. Solution rates tend to increase with an increased acidity of water. It also entails the effects of a number of other dissolved compounds on a mineral or rock surface. Molecules can mix in solution to form a great variety of basic and acidic decomposition compounds. The extent, however, of rock being subjected to solution is determined primarily by climatic conditions. Solution tends to be most effective in areas that have humid and hot climates.

Biological Weathering

It is also known as organic weathering. It involves the disintegration of rock and mineral due to the chemical and/or physical agents of an organism. The types of organisms that can cause weathering ranges from bacteria to plants, to animals, and humans as well. Biological weathering involves processes that can be either chemical or physical in character. This is because all biological matter is made up of oxygen and water, the two substances that set off reactions of minerals in rocks.

- **Plants :** The roots of plants grow deep into the cracks and crevices in search of water or nourishment. As they grow, they exert great pressure on the rocks and break them. Sometimes the roots of plants produce carbonic acid that changes the composition of certain minerals in the rocks.
- **Animals :** Burrowing animals and insects help to loosen the surface materials around the rocks facilitating their physical disintegration. Upon death, the decaying animals also provide many chemicals and acids for rock disintegration.
- **Man :** Human activities such as construction of roads, mining, farming, deforestation, excavations, etc., promotes biological weathering of rocks.

Distribution of Weathering in Different Climatic Regions

Climate is one of the important factors that affect the process of weathering. For example, physical weathering is more rapid in desert climate, while chemical weathering occurs in moist and cold climate.

- **Equatorial Climates :** Humidity and temperature are constantly high. Especially chemical weathering is more active in these regions.
- **Tropical Climates :** There is a marked dry season and wet season. Difference in heating leads to consistently high rate of evaporation. During wet season, precipitation of oxides of iron and aluminium takes place from rocks. This promotes formation of laterite soils.
- **Dry Climates or Deserts :** Due to high diurnal range of temperature, mechanical weathering is most dominant in these regions.
- **Temperate Climates or Mid-Latitudes :** Frost action is the most powerful agent of weathering. In limestone areas, chemical weathering operates on a large scale.
- **Polar Climates :** Recent studies have shown that the melting water of polar regions contains more carbonic acid content because carbon dioxide is more soluble at low temperatures than high temperatures. This suggests that chemical weathering is more active in these regions.

Constructive Effects of Weathering

Weathering is a process of breaking up of rock materials under the influence of air and water. It designs the Earth's surface by shaping it through different physical and chemical processes. Each of these processes has a different effect on rocks and their minerals, and different rocks react differently to weathering, depending on their structure. Some effects are as follows :

- Formation of soil for agricultural activities.
- New minerals are formed due to chemical weathering, which benefit economic activities.
- Minerals are exposed and mining them becomes easier.
- Building materials like limestone for making cement are available.

MASS MOVEMENT

Mass movement, also known as mass wasting, refers to the large scale movement of loose material and rock debris formed due to weathering. It is called mass wasting for two reasons. Firstly, the loose material is actually rock waste. Secondly, the total movement down the slope on account of gravity causes waste of rock debris in higher slopes. The speed of the mass movement depends on the weight of the debris, presence of any lubricating moisture such as rainwater and gradient of the slope i.e. the steeper the slope, the more rapid is the movement.

Classification of Mass Movements

The process of mass movement of rock debris is affected by the slope of the land and presence of agents like water. there are various processes involved in this movement, which can be classified into two broad categories. These are also the destructive effects of weathering.

Slow Movements

- **Soil Creep :** This is a very slow process, the movement of soil is hardly noticeable, but it can be seen in the gradual tilting of the trees or falling of a wall.
- **Soil Flow :** This is also known as Solifluction. In this case, the water is mixed with soil particles that move easily over the underlying rocks. The soil flows like liquid and a soil flow occurs.

Rapid Movements

Almost all rapid movements except landslides involve water. This movements can be further divided into four types. These are also destructive.

- **Landslides :** It is the most common and significant of all types of mass movements. Some of its chief characteristics are as follows :
- They are rapid and sudden movements that occur when a large mass of soil or rock falls suddenly.
- It usually occurs in mountainous areas, on the steep slopes or on cliffs where man has artificially steepened a slope.
- It may also occur when a steep slope is under-cut by a river or the sea so that it falls by gravity.
- Earthquakes and volcanic eruptions can also start a landslide.
- It generally occurs after heavy rainfall on steep slopes. As rainwater seeps through the weathered particles, it reduces the friction between them. Also, the weight of the weathered particles increases, making it easier for the surface layer of the Earth to slide down the slope by the action of gravity.
- Human activities like deforestation, removal of plant cover over a rock for agriculture or housing can also lead to landslides.
- **Earth Flow :** It is the movement of water logged material down a slope. It is similar to mud flow, but the water content is less. It is common in areas having rich alluvial soil and on hill sides.
- **Mud Flow :** It is the flow of weathered material with water down a hill side. In mud flow, the water content is more than in Earth flow. It is most common in arid regions with steep slopes.

When such a region receives heavy rainfall, large amounts of weathered particles are washed down the slopes, which usually have very little vegetation to hold the loose material. Thus the final result is a rapidly moving mass of mud having the consistency of wet concrete. Because of its high density, a mud flow can easily carry large rocks and boulders along with it.

- **Sheet Wash :** It is a rapid movement of rock debris saturated with water, viscous like fluid similar to mud flow but in the form of long sheets or layers of soil. There is sometimes accelerated soil erosion on account of natural or human activity. Under such conditions large sheets or layers of soil are removed by agents of gradation like water, wind or ice. It has till date affected many parts of the world on account of removal of vegetation.

Landforms of Mass Wasting

Mass wasting of rocks or soils results in the creation of different landforms. The landslides on Himalayan hill slopes have created many lakes. Because of the wide range of variation in mass wasting, the topographic features also vary in size and shape. Some important landforms include meanders, scars, ripples, terraces, escarpments, mesas, etc.

WORK OF THE RIVER

The chief agents that shape the landforms on the surface of the Earth are running water, wind and ice. The action of running water is considered to be the most important agent of denudation that shapes landforms over a large part of the Earth surface. In rivers, erosion, and transportation go on simultaneously, comprising the following interaction processes:

- **Corrasion or Abrasion :** This is the mechanical grinding of the river's traction load against the banks and bed of the river. The rock fragments are hurled against the side of the river and roll along the bottom of the river.
- **Hydraulic action :** This is the mechanical loosening and sweeping away the materials by the river water itself.
- **Attrition :** This is the wear and tear of the transported materials themselves when they roll and collide into one another.

- **Solution :** This is the chemical action of the water on soluble or partly soluble rocks.

THE COURSE OF THE RIVER

The course of a river may be divided into three distinct part and a ideal river will have all these three courses, e.g., The River Ganga in India.
- The Upper or the Mountain course
- The Middle or Valley course
- The Lower or the Plain course.

Upper Course

The river originates in the mountain and flows very swiftly as it descends the deep slope. The predominant action is erosion. The most common landforms formed during the upper course of the river are as follows :

Gorge :

When the river flows through a region of hard and resistant rock bed, the rapid down cutting may cause steep-walled valleys called Gorges. Such a deep Gorge has been cut by the River Indus in Gilgit (Kashmir) and at Attock in Pakistan. When a Gorge is very deep and long, it is called Canyon. Example : Grand Canyon of River Colorado in USA. The Grand Canyon is about 320 km long and in places reaches a depth of over 1500 m.

V-shaped Valley :

When the river flows through a region of not so hard and resistant rocks, it forms a deep and wide valley forming a V-Shaped valley.

Waterfalls :

When the river water falls down almost vertically from a sufficient height along the course of the river, it forms a waterfall. The great force usually wears out a plunge-pool beneath. When the water plunges down the edge of a plateau, it forms a waterfall. Example : Livingstone Falls on river Zaire (Congo).

Some of important waterfalls in India are : Jog waterfalls on the Sharavati River, Shivasamudram falls on the Cauvery River in Karnataka state.

Middle Course

In the middle course, the river leaves the mountain and joins the plain. Here the volume of water increases because of the confluence of several tributaries. At this stage, the vertical erosion decreases while the lateral erosion becomes active. This causes widening of the valley building up its bed and forming extensive flood plains. The important features formed at this are :

Flood Plains :

The load of the river at this stage increases but the load carrying capacity of the river depends upon the rate of flow. During the rainy season, the volume of water increases, the water overflows causing flood. The water then spreads over the low lying lands along side the banks and deposits its loads (mainly silt) there. Thus extensive flood plains are formed.

Meanders :

The term Meander has been derived from the widening river Meanderez of Turkey. The irregularities of the ground force the river to swing from side to side in wide bends and form Meanders.

Oxbow lake :

In the middle course of the river, the Meanders become very much pronounced. The outside bend or the concave bank is so rapidly eroded that the river becomes a complete circle. There will come a time when the river cuts through the narrow neck of the loop, abandoning an Oxbow lake. The river then flows straight.

Lower Course

In the lower course, the main work of the river is deposition. The important features are :

- **Delta :** Delta means a fan-shaped alluvial area caused by the deposition of silt. The name Delta has been given to these triangular alluvial areas as they resemble the Greek letter *Delta*. When the deposits of the river are not removed by tidal currents, the formation of Delta takes place. The river may discharge its water through several channels called distributaries and the alluvial deposits between distributaries are known as Delta. Example – Ganga – Brahmaputra Delta, Nile River Delta

- **Estuary :** When the river flows through a hilly terrain, the mouth of the river is submerged in the sea. It forms a narrow opening at its mouth which gradually widens out into the sea. This funnel-shaped opening at the mouth of the river is called an Estuary. Example – Deltas of the Amazon and Ob rivers.

WORK OF THE WIND

Wind action, as an agent of gradation, is different from that of rivers. Wind may transport large quantities fine particles of sand and dust even against the general slope of the land over hundreds of kilometers. Wind action is dominant in the arid and semi-arid regions.

The absence of vegetation cover enables the winds to blow freely near the surface of the land and remove easily the dry particles of sand and dust.

Erosion by the Wind

The wind causes erosion in three ways :

- **Deflation :** This involves lifting and blowing away of loose materials from the ground. Deflation thus lowers the desert surfaces and causes extensive depression.
- **Abrasion :** Abrasion is most effective at or near the base of the rock where the amount of materials the wind is able to carry is greatest. The wind drives sand and dust particles against an exposed rock causing the rock surfaces being scratched, polished or worn away.
- **Attrition :** When the wind borne particles roll against one another and their sizes are greatly reduced. The grains are rounded into tiny particles of sand and the process is called attrition.

Features Produced by Wind Erosion

- **Sandy Deserts :** These are called Erg in the Sahara Desert and Koum in Turkestan. This is an undulating plain of sand produced by the wind action.
- **Stony Desert :** They are Reg in Algeria and Serir in Libya and Egypt. The surface is covered with boulders and angular pebbles and gravels which have been produced by the wind erosion.
- **Rocky Desert :** These are called Hamada in the Sahara. The bare rock surface is formed by the deflation which removes all the small loose particles. The best example of such a Hamada is found Libya in the Sahara Desert. It stretches over an area of more than 50,000 sq km.
- **Rock Pedestals or Mushrooms Rock :** The sand blast action against a projected rock mass produces pits, grooves and hollows in it. Thus irregular surfaces are formed because of the alternate band of hard and soft rocks. The undercutting is more near the base and the softer rocks are eroded more than the hard rocks and sculptures them into fantastic shapes. Some of these balance delicately upon a thin stems and are called Rock Pedestals or Mushroom Rocks. They are commonly seen in the Sahara Desert.
- **Depression or Hollows :** Sometimes the wind deflation in the desert region causes the blowing away of the loose rock materials to such an extent that it reaches down to the water bearing rocks. Then the water seeps out of the aquifer and forms an Oasis. The Qattar depression in Egypt is 122 m below sea level and a good example of Depression or Deflated Hollows.

FEATURES FORMED BY WIND DEPOSITION

Strong wind occasionally blow across the desert surfaces and they carry vast amount of sand and dust particles. This movement produces dust storm and in time, it results in the transport of enormous quantities of fine materials from one part to another part of a desert. Slight movement of air, called wind Eddies, bounce grains of sand forward, which, when deposited may form Sandy Ridges called Dunes.

Sand Dunes

A Sand dune is an accumulation of wind blown sand. It may be a mound or a ridge of sand. A Sand Dune is built up when the wind faces some obstruction in its path such as a boulder, a irregular surface, a large rock or a bush. Dune ranges in height from a few metres to about 150 m. They often move in the direction of the wind. There two types of Dunes :

- **Seif Dune (Sword in Arabic) :** A Seif dune forms when a cross wind develops to the prevailing wind and the corridors between the dunes are swept clear of sand by this wind. They are often several hundreds meter high and many kilometer long and are found in the desert of Western Australia.
- **Barkhans :** These are typical crescent shaped sand dunes, They develop in large number when the wind is constant in direction. The windward slope of a Barkhan is gentle and convex and the leeward slope is steep and concave, the Barkhan moves slowly at the rate of 1 meter per year in the direction of the prevailing wind. They are found in Persian and Atacama desert.

Loess

Loess is a yellowish-grey friable, fine grain and homogenous dust deposit which occurs in areas surrounding the desert. When the wind blows strongly, these particles are carried away for hundreds of kilometers and often beyond the limits of desert region. These dust particles are deposited in regions receiving rainfall with abundant vegetation. The Loess deposits of northern China covers an area of about 65,000 sq km.

SUMMARY

- Weathering is the process of rock breaking and rock decay caused by the action of rain, frost, heat, cold and other associated features.
- Denudation refers to all processes that cause degradation of landscape, weathering mass movement, erosion and transport.
- Gradation is the leveling of land due to erosion by such agents as river systems, groundwater, glaciers, wind and waves.
- Types of weathering: (i) Physical, (ii) Chemical, and (iii) Biological.
- Physical weathering is the disintegration due to mechanical or physical processes.
- Factors affecting physical weathering: (i) Block disintegration, (ii) Granular disintegration, (iii) Slope of land, (iv) Exfoliation, (v) Frost action, (vi) Wind, and (vii) Vegetation.
- Chemical weathering is the breaking down of rocks by altering or dissolving the component rock minerals due to chemical changes.
- The processes of chemical weathering are: (i) Oxidation, (ii) Hydration, (iii) Carbonation, and (iv) Solution.
- Biological weathering is the disintegration of bed rocks due to plants and animals.
- Exfoliation is a weathering process by which concentric shells, slabs, sheets or flakes are successively broken loose and stripped away from a rock mass.
- Mass Movement or Mass Wasting is the downward movement of loose material, rock debris formed due to weathering.
- There are three stages of development of a river valley which complete the life cycle of a river.
- The first stage or the stage of youth of the river is through the mountainous region. The river flows very swiftly and its main work is erosion.
- The second stage or the maturity stage of the river corresponds to the middle course. Here the river moves slowly and its main work is transportation.
- The old stage of the river corresponds to its lower course when the river flows sluggishly. The main work is deposition.
- The wind is an important agent of denudation in the arid and semi arid region.
- Its erosive action is greatest because of absence of moisture and vegetation.
- The erosive action proceeds unchecked because large areas remain free of obstacles.
- A strong wind has a tremendous power to carry smaller particles over hundreds of miles at a high level in the atmosphere.
- The materials picked up by the wind are dropped into some sheltered hollow or get piled against an obstacle.

EXERCISES

A. Answer the following questions

1. Describe the characteristics of weathering.
2. Name different types of weathering?
3. Describe the characteristics of weathering in different climates.
4. Explain the two processes involved in external processes.
5. What are the factors responsible for physical weathering?
6. Describe in brief the processes involved in chemical weathering.
7. What is meant by biological weathering?

8. Briefly describe what causes biological weathering.
9. What is meant by mass wasting?
10. What are the constructive effects of weathering?
11. Name the three stages of a river.
12. Describe the upper course of a river.
13. Describe the three ways in which wind erosion is caused.
14. Explain the features formed by wind deposition.

B. Define the following terms

1. Frost action
2. Exfoliation
3. Mass movement
4. Carbonation
5. Sheet wash
6. Gorge
7. Estuary
8. Attrition
9. Barkhans
10. Oxbow lake
11. V-Shaped valley

C. Distinguish between the following

1. Physical and Chemical weathering.
2. Denudation and Gradation.
3. Aggradation and Degradation.
4. Oxidation and Hydration.
5. Block and Granular disintegration.
6. Meander and Oxbow lake.
7. Stony desert and Rocky desert.
8. Gorge and Canyon.
9. Tributaries and Distributaries.
10. Seifs and Barkhan sand dunes.

D. Give reasons

1. Physical weathering is caused by change in temperature.
2. Block disintegration is caused due to frost action.
3. Chemical weathering is aided by presence of water.
4. Weathering is encouraged by human activities.
5. Frost cause weathering of rocks.
6. Many rivers do not form deltas.

E. Board Questions

1. Name a feature which is formed as a result of deposition by wind in desert area.
2. Briefly explain the meaning of the following :
    (i) Weathering
    (ii) Denudation
3. Distinguish between the following :
    (i) Oxidation and Corbonation.
    (ii) Young stage and Mature stage of a river.

CHAPTER 10
HYDROSPHERE

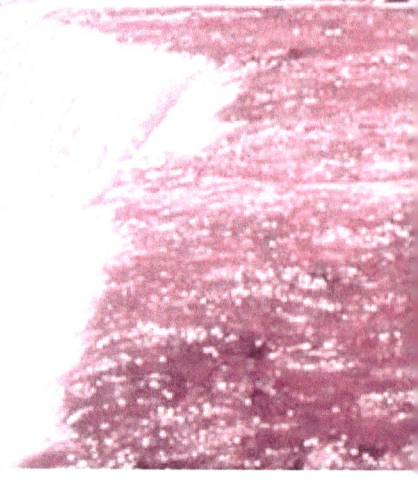

Meaning of Hydrosphere; Tides — Formation and Pattern. Ocean Currents–Their Circulation Pattern and Effects. (Specifically of Gulf Streams, North Atlantic Drift, Labrador Current, Kuroshio and Oyashio Current.)

Our Earth has abundant water in the form of oceans. A glance at a world map will show that land areas do not stretch continuously on the globe, but the oceans completely encircle the continents and islands. More than 70% of the Earth's surface is covered by oceans and seas. This layer of water on the surface of the Earth is called the hydrosphere. Thus, in this chapter, we will discuss in detail about the hydrosphere and its features.

HYDROSPHERE

Hydrosphere refers to the total water realm of the Earth's surface zone including the oceans, surface water of the land, groundwater and water held in the atmosphere. In physical geography, hydrosphere is described as the combined mass of water found on, under and over the surface of a planet.

The world's oceans contain 97% of the water in the hydrosphere, most of which is salt water. Ice caps, like that found covering Antarctica, and glaciers that occupy high alpine locations, compose a little less than 2% of all water found on Earth.

OCEANS

A deep study of the Earth shows that three-fourths of the surface of the Earth is covered with water and the rest one-fourth is land. There is twice more water (71%) than land (29%). In the Northern Hemisphere, the areas of land and water are nearly equal, while in the Southern Hemisphere, there is nearly fifteen times more water than land. This fact that three-fourths of the Earth's surface is covered with water is of a great advantage as the ocean waters help to store heat and provide warmth to the Earth. The ocean waters absorb the heat of the sun and hold it for a long time because water has an extremely high heat capacity, so it takes more sunlight to warm it up.

There is a balance on opposite sides, antipodal arrangement to be precise, between the continents and oceans in both the Northern and Southern Hemisphere. E.g., the North Pole lies in the midst of the Arctic Ocean while the South Pole is surrounded by the continent of Antarctica.

Physical Properties of Ocean Water

The oceans of the Earth serve many functions. The combination of temperature, salinity and density has a profound effect on the circulation of the oceans.

Temperature

The oceans affect the weather and temperature by absorbing incoming solar radiation, and distributing this heat energy around the globe. The temperature of the ocean water in the Tropical zone varies between 23°C and 27°C. It goes on gradually decreasing towards the poles where the temperature is about 2.2°C. Water becomes colder with an increase in depth. Hence, at greater depths, the water is very cold and in the Polar regions, the temperature is near the freezing point.

Salinity

It is the amount of salt dissolved in the ocean water. It varies from place to place. The salinity of ocean water varies between 3.0 and 3.7%, the average being about 3.5%. Salinity is primarily determined by the balance between evaporation and precipitation. In regions with high evaporation, the seawater becomes saltier, whereas salinity drops in the cooler regions, due to melting ice masses. Normal seawater has about 35 gm of dissolved salt per liter.

Density

It is the weight of ocean water. It mainly depends on temperature and salinity of the ocean water. The density of ocean water ranges from 1.026 to 1.028 gm/cm. High-salinity seawater is denser than low-salinity seawater. Thus, cold seawater is denser than warm seawater. Water density also depends on the amount of pressure, since pressure compresses water slightly, making it heavier.

Importance of Oceans

Oceans are significant in various ways for the people:

Global Significance

Covering 71% of Earth's surface, oceans provide vital, life-sustaining services to the global population. The world's oceans generate half of the oxygen on Earth, are the primary regulator of global climate, and provide economic and environmental services to billions around the globe. The oceans also act as an important sink, absorbing over 80% of the excess heat and approximately one-third of all anthropogenic carbon dioxide (CO_2) since the onset of the industrial revolution. Marine biodiversity and ecosystem resources and services provide basic life necessities, including food, freshwater, genetic resources, medicines and cultural products. Half of the world's population lives within 100 km of the sea, and three-quarters of all large cities are located on the coast; and coastal zones yield 9% of the global fisheries on which the livelihoods of 400 million fishers rely. 90% of world trade is carried by ship, and marine ecosystem provides huge economic benefits.

Seafood and Fishing Resources

Oceans provide variety of fishes, molluscs and other edible forms of animal life. It is estimated that about 10% of human protein intake comes from the oceans. Fishes provide 20% of the total animal protein intake to over 2.6 billion people. Some of the most important fishing areas around the globe are found on and along continental shelves, which are less than 200 meters in depth and within 100 km of the coast.

OCEAN CURRENTS

Ocean currents are defined as the general movement of large masses of oceanic water circulating in regular patterns. Land surface heats more rapidly than the ocean water, thus causing variations in the density and temperature of the oceans leading to the formation of ocean currents. These currents help in maintaining the Earth's heat balance by transferring heat from lower to higher latitudes.

Types of Ocean Currents

Ocean currents can be divided into two categories based on temperature.

Warm Currents

These currents bring warm water into cold water areas. They flow from the low latitudes in Tropical zones towards the high latitudes in the Temperate and Sub-polar zones.

Cold Currents

These currents bring cold water into warm water areas. They flow from the high latitudes in the Polar regions towards the low latitudes in the warm Equatorial regions.

Ocean currents can be divided into two categories based on their depth.

Surface Currents

These currents are the water movements that take place on the top layer of the ocean and make up about 10% of the ocean currents. They are mostly found in the upper 400 meters of the ocean, though this can vary due to tides, wind and weather conditions. They are caused primarily by winds, which create a friction as they move over the water. This friction then forces the water to move in a spiral pattern, creating gyres. In the northern hemisphere, gyres move clockwise and in the southern hemisphere, they spin counterclockwise. The speed of surface currents is greatest closer to the ocean's surface and decreases at about 100 meters below the surface. Gravity also plays a role in the movement of surface currents because the top of the ocean is uneven. Mounds in the water form in areas where the water meets land, where water is warmer, or where two currents converge. Gravity then pushes this water downwards on the mounds and creates currents.

Deep water Currents

These are also called Thermohaline circulation. They are found below 400 meters and make up about 90% of the ocean currents. These waters move around the ocean basins due to variations in the density and gravity. Gravity plays a role in the creation of deep water currents, but these are mainly caused by density differences in the water. Density differences are a function of temperature and salinity. Cold water has higher salt density than warm water, so as currents flow through cool areas, the warmer water in that region rises and the cool water flowing into the area sinks. By contrast, when cold water rises, it too leaves a void and the rising warm water is then forced, through downwelling, to descend and fill this empty space, creating deep water currents.

Causes of Ocean Currents

The ocean currents circulate in a regular pattern around the oceans. The origin and nature of the movement of the currents depends on some important factors mentioned below :

Planetary Winds

Winds play an important role in the origin and development of ocean currents. Most of the energy of the Earth's surface is concentrated in each hemisphere's Trade Winds and Westerlies.

- **Trade Winds :** These winds blow between the Equator and the Tropics. They warm the eastern coasts of continents. E.g. The Northeast Trade Winds move the North Equatorial Current to warm the eastern coasts of Japan as the Kuroshio Current; similarly, the Southeast Trade Winds drive the South Equatorial Current which warms the eastern coast of Australia as the warm East Australian Current.
- **Westerlies :** These winds blow in the temperate latitudes, resulting in a north-easterly flow of water in the Northern Hemisphere and vice versa in the Southern Hemisphere. E.g. the warm Gulf Stream is forced towards the western coast of Europe as the North Atlantic Drift, while the cold West Wind Drift flows towards the Equator as the Peru Current along South America and the Benguela Current along South Africa. *(Fig. 10.1)*

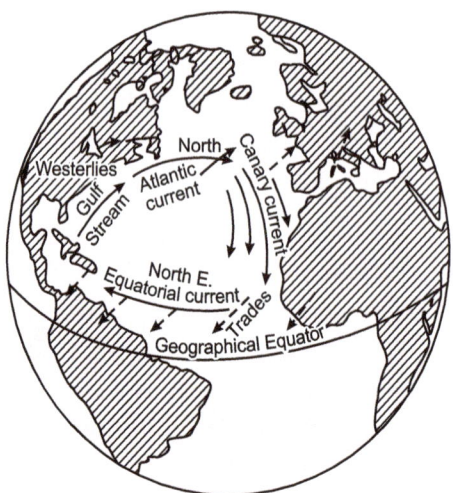

Fig. 10.1 : Formation of Gyres

- **Monsoon Winds :** The strongest influence of the prevailing winds on the flow of ocean currents is seen in the Northern Indian Ocean. Due to these winds, the direction of the currents changes from Southwest in summer to the Northeast in winter.

Rotation of the Earth

The rotation of the Earth brings about a change in the direction of currents. As the Earth rotates with the maximum speed at the Equator, the winds and ocean currents move in a clockwise direction in the Northern Hemisphere and anticlockwise direction in the Southern Hemisphere. This is known as the 'Coriolis Effect'. E.g. : Canary current and Gulf stream in Northern Hemisphere and Peruvian and West Wind Drift in Southern Hemisphere. *(Fig. 10.2)*

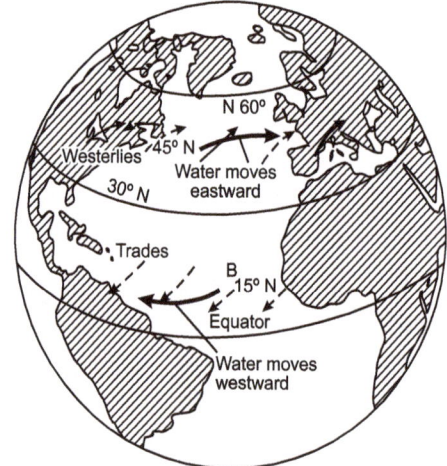

Fig. 10.2 : Coriolis Effect.

Variations in Temperature

Ocean currents are caused by the variations in temperature. The oceans near the Tropics and Equator are much warmer than the ocean water in the polar or temperate regions. This unequal heating sets up convection currents in the ocean. In Equatorial regions, due to high temperature, there occurs a decrease in the density of water. As a result, the warm water from this region moves towards the colder and denser waters of the polar areas. Contrary to this, there exists a movement of ocean water below the surface in the form of sub-surface current from the colder polar areas to warmer equatorial areas. E.g. Gulf Stream and Kuroshio currents move from Equator towards North Pole, Labrador and Kurile currents move from polar areas toward the Equator.

Variations in Salinity

The level of salinity of the ocean water affects its density. Water of high salinity is denser than water of low salinity. Thus, water of low salinity flows into the water of high salinity flowing at the bottom. E.g. the Mediterranean Sea is more saline, hence denser as compared to the less saline, less dense Atlantic Ocean. Therefore, the Atlantic water flows into Mediterranean Sea's surface.

Shape of the Land

The direction of the currents is greatly affected by the shape of the land masses and the coasts. A land mass diverts the movement of the ocean current by obstructing the flow of its water. E.g. At Cape Sao Roque, the South Equatorial Current divides into two branches, one joins the North Equatorial current, and the other becomes the Brazil current. Thus, the shape of Brazil deflects the south and west flowing Equatorial Current northwards to form the Gulf Stream and Cayenne Current and the Brazil Current flows southwest.

CIRCULATION PATTERN OF OCEAN CURRENTS

The circulation pattern of ocean currents roughly corresponds to the Earth's atmospheric circulation pattern. The air circulation over the oceans in the middle latitudes is mainly anti-cyclonic. The oceanic circulation follows this pattern at higher latitudes, where the wind flow is mostly cyclonic. In regions of pronounced monsoonal flow, the current movements are influenced by the monsoon winds. Due to the Coriolis force, the warm currents flow from low latitudes to move to the right in the Northern Hemisphere and to the left in the Southern Hemisphere. The cold waters of the Arctic and Antarctic circles move towards the warmer waters in tropical and equatorial regions, while the warm waters of the lower latitudes move towards the pole. *(Fig. 10.3)*

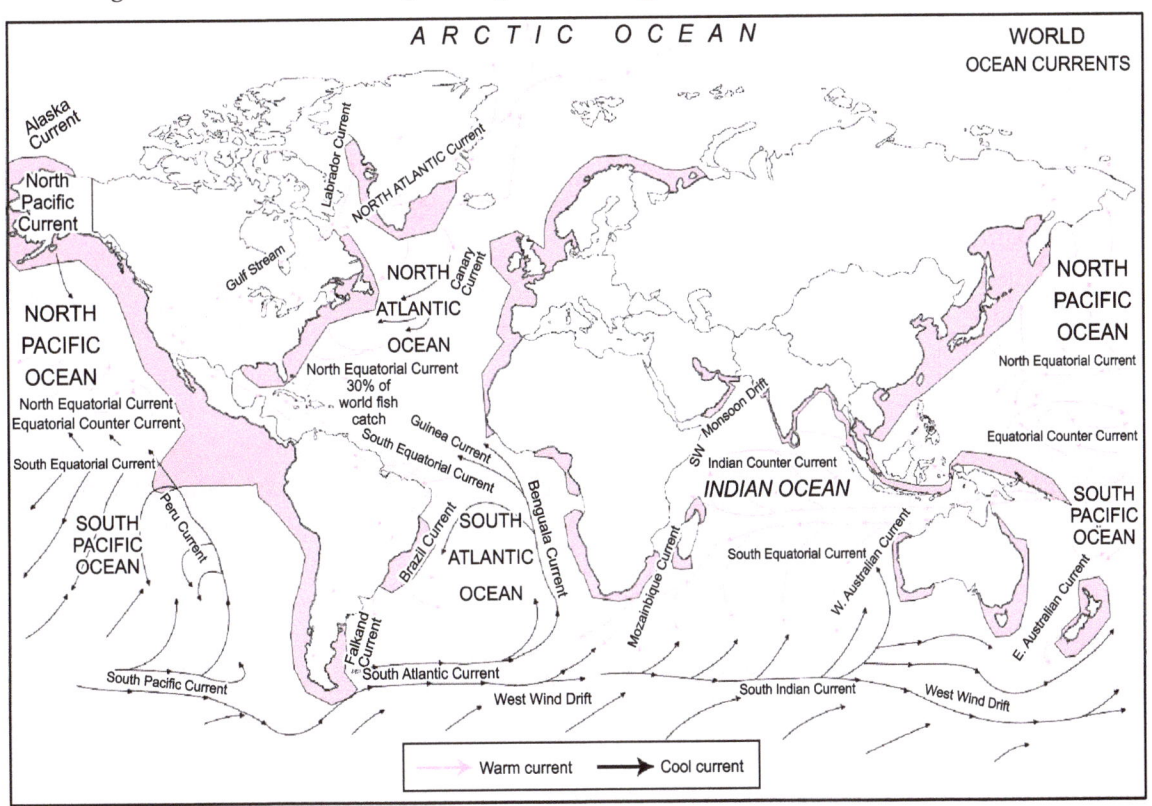

Fig. 10.3 : World Map Showing the Major Ocean Currents of the World.

The Currents of the Atlantic Ocean

South Equatorial Current

This current originates from the Western coast of Africa and flows along the Equator. On reaching Cape Sao Roque of the North East Brazil, it split into Northern Cayenne Current and the Southern Brazilian current. The Cayenne current flows along the Guiana coast and meet with the North Equatorial current.

North Equatorial Current

It splits into Antilles Current and Caribbean Current.

Counter Equatorial Current

It flows from west to east in between the North and South Equatorial Current.

The Cayenne Current

It is joined by the North Equatorial current which flows into the Caribbean Sea and then enters into the Gulf of Mexico. From the Gulf of Mexico, the warm water moves through Florida Strait in a north-easterly direction, up to the Cape Hatteras which is known as Florida current. Florida current comes under the influence of Westerlies and moves in a north-easterly direction towards the Newfoundland coast as Gulf Stream Drift.

Gulf Stream

This is a powerful, warm, swift and the largest of the western boundary currents of the North Atlantic Ocean. It originates in the Gulf of Mexico around 20°N and moves in the north-eastern direction along the east coast of North America. At about 30°W and 40°N, it splits into two with the northern stream crossing to northern Europe and the southern stream recirculating off West Africa. The Gulf Stream influences the climate of the east coast of North America from Florida to Newfoundland, and the west coast of Europe. Under the impact of the Westerlies, this warm water current reaches the western coasts of Europe, up to 70°N. The convergence of this warm current with Labrador Current near Newfoundland results in heavy fog. Water within the current is usually warm and blue, often lacking nutrients and incapable of supporting much marine life. Its presence has led to the development of different types of strong cyclones, both within the atmosphere and ocean. It is also a significant potential source of renewable power generation.

North Atlantic Drift

On reaching Newfoundland coast, the warm Gulf stream drift moves in the North-easterly direction and flows as North Atlantic drift which then divides into three directions eastwards to Britain, North-eastward to Scandinavia and the Arctic and southward as the cool Canary current past the Iberian coast.

It is a warm Atlantic Ocean Current that runs from the Grand Bank, near Newfoundland to Western Europe. In fact, the warm Gulf Stream Current is deflected towards the east under the influence of the Westerlies and Earth's rotation, and reaches Europe as the North Atlantic Drift. Due to it being a warm current, it keeps the ports of Europe free from ice even in winter. In fact, due to the North Atlantic drift, the climate of Western Europe and Northern Europe stays warmer than it would otherwise be.

Canary Current

It is the continuation of North Atlantic Drift along the western coast of Iberian Peninsula and North Africa in the southern direction. It completes the clockwise circuit in the North Atlantic Ocean by flowing southwards and merging with the North Equatorial current forming a Guro or Gyre, meaning cycle, as it flows along in the periphery of an ocean basin. Within the ring of current, a large amount of floating seaweeds collects and the area is referred to as the Sargossa Sea.

Labrador Current

The Labrador current, flowing from the south of Arctic Ocean, along the coast of Labrador and converging with the cold Irminger or East Greenland current, flows southward along east coast of Nova Scotia. It is a continuation of the West Greenland Current and the Baffin Island (Davis Strait) Current. It meets the warm Gulf Stream at the Grand Banks, southeast of Newfoundland and again north of the Outer Banks of North Carolina. The combination of these two currents produces heavy fogs, however it is also considered as most conducive for the fast growth of planktons, which is a feed for fish. It is because of these favourable conditions that the Grand Bank near Newfoundland has become an ideal fishing ground of the world. The average speed of the current is about 28 km per day. In spring and early summer, this current brings down huge icebergs from the Arctic Ocean to the eastern coast of Canada causing difficulties for navigation. The waters of the Labrador Current have a cooling effect on the Canadian Atlantic provinces and coastal New England, but rarely have a significant effect on waters south of Cape Cod.

In the South Atlantic, the circulation is anticlockwise. The Southequatorial current divides at Cape Sao Roque of Northeast of Brazil, and one branch, the warm Brazilian current moves along the Eastern coast of Brazil. Under the influence of the Westerlies at about 40°S latitude, Brazilian Current continues as the South Atlantic Current and merges with cold West Wind Drift. On reaching the western coast of Africa, it flows northward along the western coast of South Africa as cold Benguela current and merges with the South Equatorial current of the Atlantic.

Falkland Current

It flows towards north along the eastern coast of South America upto Argentina.

The Currents of the Pacific Ocean

Due to extensive and openness of the Pacific Ocean, there is a modification in the pattern of the circulation of currents in the Pacific Ocean. The warm waters of North Equatorial current flow westward under the impact of the rotation of the Earth from Central America across nearly 12,000 km to the island of Philippines. It comes under the influence of trade winds and the Equatorial current flow off the coast of eastern Philippines northwards into the East China Sea towards the southern cost of Japan as warm Kuroshio current.

Kuroshio Current

It is also sometimes known as the Black Stream, which is the English translation of *Kuroshio*. It is a strong, western boundary current in the western North Pacific Ocean. It develops partly due to the Coriolis force and partly due to the obstruction of the Philippines in the flow of the North Equatorial Current. It begins off the east coast of Taiwan and flows towards Northeast past Japan, where it merges with the easterly drift of the North Pacific Current. It is analogous to the Gulf Stream in the Atlantic Ocean, transporting warm, tropical water northward towards the Polar region. Its counterparts are the North Pacific Current to the north, the California Current to the east, and the North Equatorial Current to the south. The warm waters of the Kuroshio Current sustain the coral reefs of Japan. An off shoot of Kuroshio Current, also known as Tsushima current, enters into the Sea of Japan along the west coast of the islands. The relatively warm water of Tsushima current keeps the western coast of Japan warm even in the coldest month (January), when snowing is frequent in Honshu and Hokkaido. The average surface temperature of this current is around 18°C with a speed of about 30 km per day.

On reaching the coast of Japan, the warm Kuroshio current comes under the influence of westerlies and takes a North-easterly turn and reaches South of Gulf of Alaska. It splits into two branches – one branch moves into the Gulf of Alaska as warm British Columbian current and the other branch flows along the western coast of USA or California as cold Californian current. It then merges with the North Equatorial current.

Oyashio Current

The cold Bering current creeps southwards from the narrow Bering strait. It is known as the Kurile Current as it touches the island of Kurile while moving southwards along the coast of Kamchatka and is joined by Okhotsk current to meet the warm Kuroshio current as Oyashio current.

It is a cold subarctic Ocean current that flows south and circulates anticlockwise in the western North Pacific Ocean. It collides with the Kuroshio Current off the eastern shore of Japan to form the North Pacific Current. The current has an important impact on the climate of the Russian Far East, mainly in Kamchatka and Chukotka. The waters of the Oyashio Current form probably the richest fishing grounds in the world owing to the extremely high nutrient content of the cold water and the tides, which are about ten meters high in some areas further enhancing the availability of nutrients. It also causes Vladivostok to be the most equator-ward port to seasonally freeze and require icebreaking ships to remain open in winter. However, this has relatively little effect on the fish yield through the Sea of Okhotskas, the large tides do not encourage freezing to occur easily. It carries cold water and icebergs from the Arctic Ocean to the coast of Kurile (Russia) and Hokkaido (Japan).

South Equatorial Current

It flows westwards in the southern Pacific Ocean and splits into northern and southern branches near New Guinea. Due to the rotation of the Earth, it takes an anticlockwise turn and moves along the eastern coast of Australia as the warm East Australian current, bringing the warm equatorial water into the temperate water. It is propelled by the trade winds. The current turns eastward towards New Zealand under the force of westerlies in the Tasman Sea and merges with the part of the cold west wind drift as South pacific current. It is obstructed by the Southern tip of South America. It is then forced up towards the west coast of Chile as cold Humboldt or Peruvian current. The cold water chills any wind that blows on shore so that Peru and Chile coasts are practically rainless. The Peruvian current finally joins South Equatorial current, completing the South Pacific current cycle.

Counter Equatorial Current

It flows between north and south Equatorial Current in the opposite direction.

Major Ocean Currents of the Indian Ocean

Warm Currents

- **Indian Equatorial Current:** It flows westwards in the South Indian Ocean, splitting at Madagascar and flowing as Mozambique and Agulhas Current in the southern direction, both of which are also warm currents. *(Fig. 10.4)*

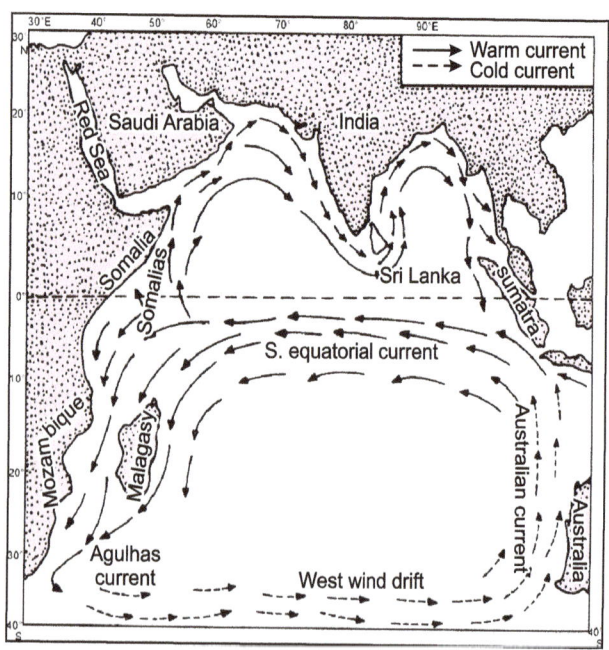

Fig. 10.4 : Currents of Indian Ocean during Summer

Cold Currents

- **Southwest Monsoon Current :** It flows along the coast of India in the easterly direction.
- **Northeast Monsoon Current :** It flows along the eastern coast of India during winter. *(Fig. 10.5)*

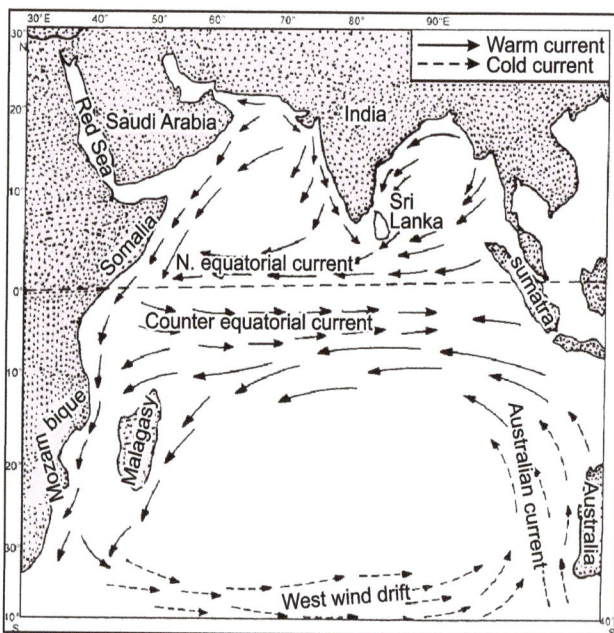

Fig. 10.5 : Currents of Indian Ocean during Winter

Effects of Ocean Currents

Ocean currents influence the distribution of temperature, pressure, winds, precipitation, and the climate of the coastal regions. This determines the agriculture and all the other economic activities of the region.

Temperature

When warm or cold ocean currents flow near a coast, they exert a significant climatic influence. The warm Equatorial currents usually raise the temperature of the places where they flow. On account of the influence of the cold Arctic Current, the Labrador Current remains frozen for almost nine months, while on account of the influence of the warm North Atlantic Drift, the British Isles enjoy a mild climate. The otherwise hot climate of Peru is greatly cooled by the Peru Current. On account of the influence of the North Atlantic Drift, the harbours of Norway, even beyond the North Cape are free from ice throughout the year, while Greenland in the same latitude is frozen all the year round. The warm Kuroshio keeps the ports of the Alaskan coast ice-free in winters. However, the cool Canaries current, flowing along the West Coast of North Africa has little cooling effect on the coast of Portugal and Spain in summer because at that time, the region comes under the influence of the off-shore Northeast Trade winds.

Rainfall

The winds passing over warm currents pick up moisture and bring rain. E.g. the North Atlantic Drift and the Kuroshio current brings in sufficient rainfall along the west coasts of Europe and east coasts of Japan respectively. Similarly, the east coast of Africa and the east coast of Australia have heavy rainfall owing to the winds passing over warm currents. On the other hand, cold currents do not pick up enough moisture, thus discouraging rainfall. E.g. The Kalahari Desert along the western coast of South Africa and Atacama Desert along the western coast of South America owe their existence to some extent to the Benguela and Peru Currents respectively.

Fog

The air above a warm current is warm and acquires a lot of water vapour. When it meets the cold air above cold ocean currents, the water vapours of the warm air are condensed into minute water particles, which form dense fog. E.g. Japanese coast has dense fog when the warm Kuroshio Current meets the cold Oyashio Current, and Newfoundland has dense fog when the warm Gulf Stream meets the cold Labrador Current. Ships face danger due to fog, as they are not able to locate icebergs that flow in cold currents. Many ships have sunk on account of accidents with these icebergs. However, in modern time, radar helps the ships to locate icebergs even in the darkness of dense fog.

Storms

Devastating storms follow the line of meeting of cold and warm currents. E.g. The hurricanes occurring off the coast of America follow the line where Gulf Stream joins with the cold Labrador Current.

Cyclones

The routes of cyclonic storms are influenced by ocean currents. They are caused by the low pressures brought about by the warming of large masses of ocean water. E.g. The Southeast of Iceland is one of the world's principle Cyclonic areas brought about by the warming of the North Atlantic Drift.

Transport

Due to the favourable influence of warm currents, harbours of cold countries are kept open in winter, facilitating trade and transport throughout the year. E.g. The coasts of UK, Norway, etc., should normally freeze in winter, but due to warm North Atlantic Drift currents, they remain unfrozen and transporting remains unaffected.

Navigation

Sailing vessels are aided or hindered by the direction of currents. Ships that sail in the direction of the current go faster than the ships going against the current and thus they save time and fuel. E.g. Vessels from England bound for Australia move towards Rio de Janeiro in order to have a favourable current across the South Atlantic and the Southern Ocean.

Fish Trade

The finest fishes are found in cold shallow waters. Places where cold and warm currents meet are ideal for the growth of plankton. These are very small organisms, which are food for fish. These regions have developed into major fishing grounds of the world. Newfoundland on the eastern coast of North America is the meeting point of the Gulf Stream and the Labrador Current.

TIDES

It is defined as the rise and fall of the surface water of the ocean due to gravitational forces of the sun and the moon. The waves produced by tides are called the tidal waves. The rise and movement of the ocean water towards the coast is called a tide and the resultant high water level is known as high tide water, whereas the fall and movement of the ocean water towards the sea is called the ebb and the resultant low water level is called the low tide water. The difference between high tide water and low tide water is called the tidal range. *(Fig. 10.6)*

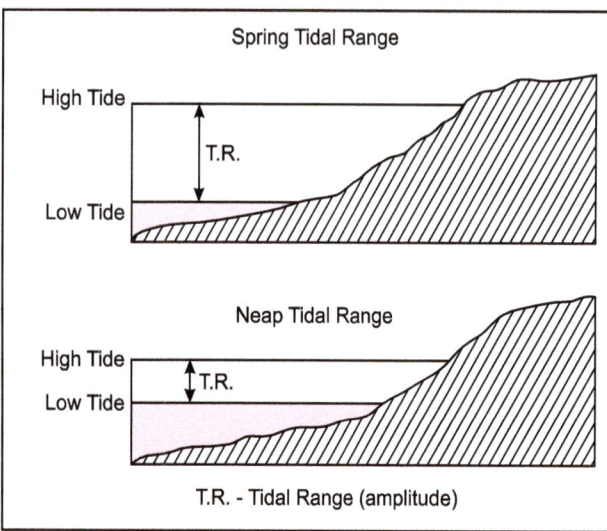

Fig. 10.6 : Tidal Range

Magnitude of Tides

The magnitude and height of the tide in an open ocean differs from that of a coastal area. The difference in height between the high and low tides in the open ocean may be only half a meter but in shallow marginal sea, it can increase to about 10 meters and in some estuaries, it can go up to 12 meters. The average height of a tide is about 4 meters.

Types of Tides

The different positions of the Sun and the Moon with the Earth result in a lot of temporal and spatial variation in the tide producing forces. Due to these variations in the intensity of tide producing forces, there occurs two important types of tides. *(Fig. 10.7)*

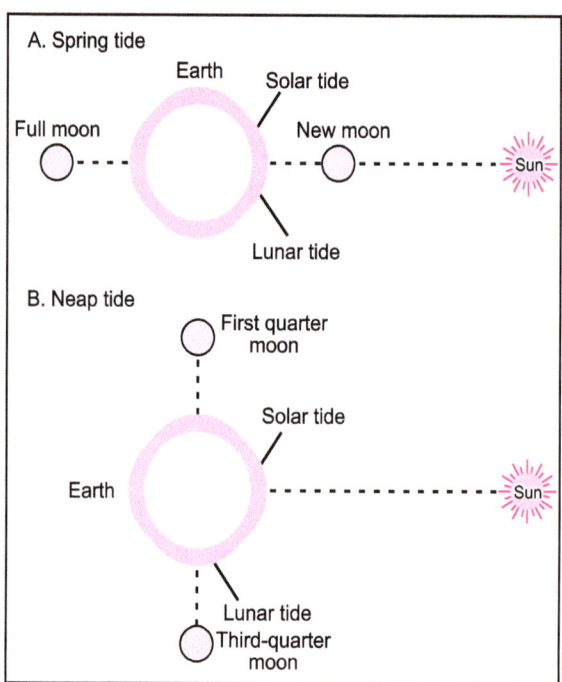

Fig. 10.7 : Spring and Neap Tides.

Causes of Tides

Gravitational Force

Tides have their origin in the gravitational forces of the sun and the moon. The surface of the Earth facing the moon experiences the maximum amount of gravitational force of the moon, while it experiences minimum amount of gravitational force at the opposite side of the Earth. Consequently, the ocean water facing the moon is attracted and pulled up causing high tides. At the same time, there is a simultaneous high tide on the opposite side of the Earth caused by the centrifugal force due to the gravitational force of the moon forming the outward bulge of the ocean water.

Rotation of the Earth

Tides are caused by the rotation of the Earth, which results in bringing every meridian into the position of two high tides and two low tides near each other in every 24 hours. Since the Moon and Earth rotate in the same direction. Consequently, it takes about 24 hours and 52 minutes or one lunar day to complete the sequence of two high tides and two low tides.

Influence of the Moon

Tides are caused by the influence of the moon on the Earth. The Sun too exerts some pull on the Earth but due to its far distance, the effect is much less as compared to the effect of the Moon on the Earth. The connection between the phases of the Moon and tides can be understood by observing the Moon rising about 50 minutes late everyday than the day before, and the high tide occurrs according to it.

Spring Tide

This type of tide is also known as high tide. It occurs when the Sun, the Moon and the Earth are almost in a same straight line. The gravitational forces of the sun and the moon working together with combined force results in a very high tide. The height of such spring tides is 20% more than that of the normal tides. Such tides occur twice during the lunar month, usually just after the New moon and Full moon and their timing remains fixed.

Neap Tide

This type of tide is also known as low tide. It occurs when the sun, the moon and the Earth are not in a straight line. The gravitational force of the sun opposes that of the moon and the difference between high and low tides is at its least. The height of such neap tides is 20% less than that of the normal tides. Such tides occur at the first and last quarters of the moon, when the sun and the moon are at right angles to each other.

Periodicity of Tides

According to the rotation of the Earth completing in roughly 24 hours, every place should experience tide after 12 hours, but this never happens. Each day, tide is delayed by 26 minutes as the moon rotates on its axis (west to east) while revolving around the Earth. Due to Earth's rotation from west to east, the tide centre shifts westward. When the tide centre completes one round, the Moon's position is ahead of the tide centre by that time. The revolution of the Moon around the Earth results in the tide centre taking another 52 minutes to come under the Moon. Thus, a particular tide centre takes about 24 hours 52 minutes to come under the Moon. During this time, there occurs another tide at the opposite side of the referred tide centre, which happens after 12 hours 26 minutes. Moon covers about 12° around the Earth in a day, so when the Earth has completed a 24 hours rotation, the Moon has gone about 12° ahead and hence the tide that occurred the previous day has to cover 12° more to come under the Moon, for which it takes about 52 minutes. Thus, the high tide on the next day comes after 24 hours and 52 minutes. This is the reason why tides do not take place at the same time every day.

Importance of Tides

- It washes away the coastline helping to form creeks and inlets.
- It helps in keeping the seashore and harbours clean by carrying away the dirt and debris from the coastline.
- It regulates the schedule of fishermen as they sail out and in with the tide.
- In certain harbours, tidal basins are constructed to store the tidal water.
- Tidal energy is utilized to produce electricity.
- Strong tidal currents help rivers in forming their lower flood plains, while preventing the formation of deltas.
- In cold countries, tides prevent the ports from freezing by bringing salt water and keeping the ocean water in constant motion.
- Low-lying areas around the sea coasts are flooded during high tides. Thus, the water is trapped in a place known as salt pans from which salt is produced.
- Marine animals like oysters and mussels that are attached to the rocks and have fixed positions depend on tides to bring them their food.

SUMMARY

- Hydrosphere refers to the total water realm of the Earth's surface zone including the oceans, surface waters of the lands, groundwater and water held in the atmosphere.
- Pattern of circulation of currents : (i) Atlantic Ocean Circulation, (ii) Pacific Ocean Circulation, and (iii) Indian Ocean Circulation.
- The temperature of ocean water is highest at the Equator (where it is warmed by the Sun) and coldest toward the poles.
- Ocean current refers to the persistent, dominant horizontally flowing ocean water.
- Gulf Stream is the strong northward moving warm water current off the east coast of North America that carries its water far into the North Atlantic Ocean.
- High tide is the high water corresponding to a tidal crest.
- Low tide is the low water position corresponding to a tidal trough.

EXERCISES

A. Answer the following questions

1. What is hydrosphere?
2. State in percentage the distribution of land and water surface on the Earth.
3. Why is the ocean water unfit for drinking?

4. What factors are responsible for the salinity of ocean water?
5. For what is the Gulf Stream famous?
6. What are ocean currents?
7. What do you mean by Coriolis effect?
8. Describe the circulation pattern of the following ocean currents:
    (i) The North Atlantic drift
    (ii) Gulf Stream of the Atlantic Ocean
    (iii) Oyashio Current of the Pacific Ocean
9. What happens when a cold current meets a warm current?
10. Why the Northern Hemisphere is called the Land Hemisphere?
11. Classify the following as cold or warm currents :
    (i) Kuroshio
    (ii) Canaries
    (iii) North Atlantic Drift
    (iv) Benguela
    (v) Gulf Stream
    (vi) Labrador
12. Name the three ways in which movement of ocean water takes place.
13. What are tides? How are they caused?
14. What is the time difference between two tides?
15. How many types of tides are there?
16. How are tides useful to man?
17. How do tides affect the coast line?
18. What is an island?
19. What is an archipelago?

B. Distinguish between the following

1. Spring tide and Neap tide.
2. Warm currents and Cold currents.
3. Surface currents and Deep water currents.

C. Give reasons

1. The Earth is known as the watery planet.
2. Newfoundland is considered to be dangerous for shipping.
3. In winter, the east coast of Canada is ice bound while the west coast is not.
4. The eastern coasts of USA are comparatively cold.
5. Northern Japan has severe winter as compared to southern Japan.
6. There is heavy rainfall in Queensland but the Atacama Desert is dry.
7. Winds are the main influence on the circulation of ocean currents.
8. The tidal range differs from sea to sea.
9. The tides help in navigational purposes.
10. Both sides of the Earth experience high tide at the same time.
11. The periodicity of high tide changes everyday.
12. The Sargasso Sea has a collection of seaweeds.
13. Rich fishing grounds are found on the Pacific Coast of North America and Northern Japan.

E. Map work

1. On an outline map of the world, show the direction of one current each of the Pacific, the Atlantic and the Indian Ocean.

F. Board Questions

1. Name a cold ocean current which affects fishing industry of Japan.
2. Give a reason for each of the following :
    (i) The waters of the Oyashio current form one of the richest fishing grounds in the world.
    (ii) The coast of Norway remains ice free during winter.
    (iii) Warm ocean currents create a milder climate.
3. Draw a well labelled diagram of a spring tide.
4. Draw a fully labelled diagram of a Neap tide.

CHAPTER 11
ATMOSPHERE

> **Composition and Structure :** Composition and Structure of the Atmosphere. Troposphere, Stratosphere, Ionosphere and Exosphere; Ozone in the Stratosphere, Its Depletion. Global Warming and its Impact.

The study of the Earth's atmosphere is termed as Meteorology. Present day evidences suggest that except Earth, no other planet has the exact mixture of gases or the heat and water conditions necessary to sustain life. Atmosphere is the gaseous cover surrounding a planet. The gases that make up the atmosphere are vital to our lives. Atmospheric changes occur all the time, but if we alter or change our atmosphere to a great extent, then it may drastically impact our environment and lives.

ATMOSPHERE

Atmosphere is defined as the gaseous envelope or blanket surrounding a planet. It is colourless, odourless and tasteless substance that is flexible and compressible. It is rich in oxygen that is essential for supporting all forms of life on the Earth. It protects the Earth from the harmful ultraviolet and infrared rays of the sun, acting like a shield for the planet. It helps to retain the necessary amount of warmth on the Earth and also helps to circulate water vapour resulting in rainfall. Owing to the presence of the atmosphere, the Earth does not experience extremes of temperature as found on other planets. The atmosphere is therefore, an important component of our environment.

Composition of the Atmosphere

The atmosphere is a thin layer of gases that surrounds the Earth. It is composed of 78% nitrogen, 21% oxygen, 0.9% argon, 0.03% carbon dioxide and tiny proportion of lighter Hydrogen and Helium. This thin gaseous layer insulates the Earth from extreme temperatures; it keeps heat inside the atmosphere and it also blocks the Earth from much of the Sun's incoming ultraviolet radiation. The Earth's atmosphere is about 300 miles (480 km) thick, but most of the atmosphere (about 80%) is within 10 miles (16 km) of the surface of the Earth. There is no exact place where the atmosphere ends; it just gets thinner and thinner, until it merges with the outer space. *(Fig. 11.1)*.

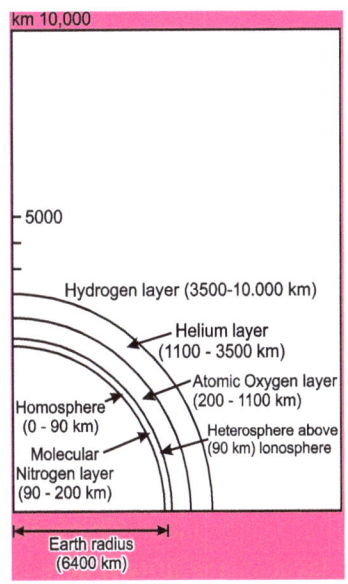

Fig. 11.1 : Composition of Atmosphere

Structure of Atmosphere

The atmosphere is held by the gravitational force of the Earth and is densest near the Earth's surface where the gravity is at its highest. It gradually thins out at higher levels. The outer limit of the atmosphere cannot be fixed as traces of the atmosphere have been found to extend upto a height of 10,000 km.

Layers of Atmosphere

The Earth's atmosphere is composed of layers, each of which is characterized by a particular kind of constituent. The proportion of the various gases and their temperatures vary across the different layers. Based on the characteristics of temperature and air pressure, there exist different types of layers of the atmosphere *(Fig. 11.2)*.

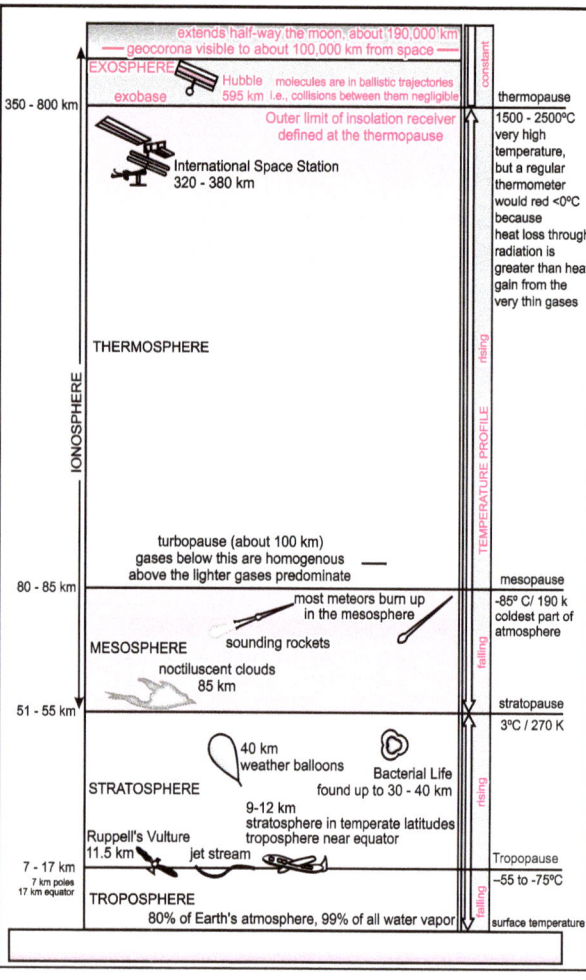

Fig. 11.2 : Structure of Atmosphere.

Troposphere

The Greek word 'tropos' meaning 'mixing' gave rise to the word 'troposphere'. This is the lowermost and densest layer of the atmosphere closest to the Earth's surface, extending up to about 10-15 km above the Earth's surface. The top of this layer is marked by the tropopause, where temperatures remain constant. This occurs at about 8 km at the poles and 18 km at the tropics and it can vary with seasons. The tropopause acts as a temperature inversion and forms a lid to the weather systems. Some scientists call the tropopause a "cold trap" because it is a point where rising water vapour cannot go higher because it changes into ice and gets trapped. If there were no cold trap, Earth would lose all its water. The troposphere is wider at the Equator than at the Poles. Temperatures decrease with height, which is known as the Normal lapse rate. The average decrease is 1°C for every 166 meter altitude gained. The heating caused by the solar energy reduces the density of air causing the air to rise. In the process of opposing the surrounding air, the air in this layer utilizes energy, resulting in a decrease in its temperature. The decreasing temperature causes the vapour content of the air to condense, resulting in an increase in the air mass. The tropopause acts like an invisible barrier and is the reason why most clouds form and weather phenomena occur within this layer. The air we breathe is from this very layer. Thus, this layer contains about 80% of the total mass of the atmosphere.

The most of the weather phenomena take place in this layer since it contains most of the water vapour. This layer is subjected to intense mixing due to both horizontal and vertical circulation

Stratosphere

The Latin word 'stratus' meaning 'spreading out' gave birth to the word 'stratosphere'. This layer lies directly above the troposphere and extends from about 15 to 50 km above the Earth's surface. The lower portion of the stratosphere has a nearly constant temperature with height, but in the upper portion, the temperature increases with altitude because of absorption of sunlight by ozone. The air is thin, cold and dry with a temperature of about 55°C. The layer is free of dust and cloud and ozone not only absorbs, but also filters out the UV rays. Warming is greater over the polar regions than in the tropical latitudes and these temperature differences cause strong horizontal air movements at great heights.

The Earth's ozone layer is located in this layer. The ozone layer is located in between 15-35 km above the surface of the Earth. The ozone layer contains high amounts of ozone gas. This layer absorbs the ultraviolet radiation of the sun, which would have otherwise proved harmful to the life on Earth. Only the highest clouds (cirrus, cirrostratus, and cirrocumulus) are in the lower stratosphere. Temperatures increase with height as ozone absorbs the ultraviolet rays. The temperature begins to fall again at about 50 km., this marks the end of the Stratosphere and is called Stratopause.

Mesosphere

This layer lies directly above the stratosphere, extending from 50 to 80 km above the Earth's surface. It is a cold layer where the temperature generally decreases with increasing altitude. As there is no water vapour or dust to absorb radiations, temperature declines rapidly to 110°C at an altitude of about 80 km near the mesopause (the upper limit of this layer). Very strong winds, about 3000 km/hr, characterize this layer. Most of the meteors and rock fragments burn up in this layer before they can enter and harm the Earth's atmosphere.

Thermosphere

This layer extends from 80 km above the Earth's surface to the outer space. The temperature is hot and may be as high as thousands of degrees as the few molecules that are present in this layer receive extraordinarily large amounts of energy from the Sun. However, the thermosphere would actually feel very cold to us because of the probability that, these few molecules will hit our skin and transfer enough energy to cause appreciable heat, is extremely low. The thermosphere is a thermal classification of the atmosphere, where the temperature increases with altitude. The thermosphere includes the exosphere and a part of the ionosphere.

- **Ionosphere :** This layer starts at about 43 to 50 miles (70-80 km) high and continues for about 400 miles (640 km). It constitutes about 0.1% of the atmospheric mass. This part of the atmosphere is ionized by the solar radiation and contains electrically charged particles like ions and free electrons. Ions are created when sunlight hits atoms and tears off some electrons. It contributes to the propagation of radio signals to distant places on Earth. It reflects radio waves back to the Earth, thus facilitating radio communication.

- **Exosphere :** It is the outermost layer of the Earth's atmosphere. It goes from about 400 miles (640 km) height to about 1000 miles (1600 km). The lower boundary of the exosphere is called the critical level of escape, where the temperature increases with altitude. The temperature are well above 1650 °C. The atmospheric pressure is very low as the gas atoms are very widely spaced. This layer is where the atoms and molecules escape into space. The atmosphere becomes very thin in this layer. The main gases present here are the lighter ones like hydrogen, helium and Argon.

Functions of Atmosphere

- Since air has some weight, it exerts pressure. Hence, it is pressed down and remains in contact with land and water, which enables the exchange of gases among them on a continuous basis.
- Due to this contact, soil is able to absorb oxygen and nitrogen.
- On account of evaporation, water vapour in air rise from oceans.
- Carbon dioxide present in the air absorbs the excess heat from the atmosphere and thus keeps the Earth warm at night.
- Energy radiated from the sun is responsible for maintaining the atmosphere in a dynamic state.
- Large masses of air are regularly moved up and down and across the Earth's surface.

Weather and Climate

The weather and climate have affected human lives as well as plants and animals in various ways. Their main elements are temperature, pressure, wind and moisture.

The physical condition of atmosphere at a given locality or an area is known as Weather. It generally refers to a short-term state of the day or week. It may change in a short period of time, i.e., the weather may be hot in day, windy and rainy in the evening and cool in the night. Several different types of weather can occur during the period of a year. Thus, the weather can be sunny, cloudy, rainy, sultry, cyclonic, etc. Weather conditions are recorded in meteorological observatories using various instruments and the weather forecasts are broadcasted on radio and television for public knowledge.

The average weather condition over a long period and over a large area is known as Climate. It generally refers to a long-term state of the week or month. Climate of a place often repeats itself year after year in a systematic and almost regular manner. Climate can be hot, cold, wet, humid or dry. The minor gases present in the air play a significant role in the climatic condition of a place. Carbon dioxide helps to absorb heat and provide necessary warmth to the Earth's surface. Ozone, another gas, helps in absorbing harmful ultraviolet rays and thus protects the Earth's surface.

OZONE

It is a pale, blue gas with a sharp irritating odour. It was first discovered by Christian Friedrick Schonbein in 1840. Ozone (O_3) is a special form of oxygen, made up of three oxygen atoms rather than the usual two oxygen atoms. It is present in rare amounts in the atmosphere. Approximately one molecule out of every two million present in the atmosphere is ozone. It is naturally produced by lightning or by electrical discharges and electric sparks from motors and machines.

Formation of Ozone Layer

- Ozone is formed when oxygen molecules absorb ultraviolet photons and undergo a chemical reaction known as photo dissociation or photolysis, where a single molecule of oxygen breaks down to two oxygen atoms.
- The free oxygen atom (O), then combines with an oxygen molecule (O_2) and forms a molecule of ozone (O_3). The ozone molecules in turn absorbs ultraviolet rays between 310 to 200 nm wavelengths and thereby prevent these harmful radiations from entering the Earth's atmosphere.

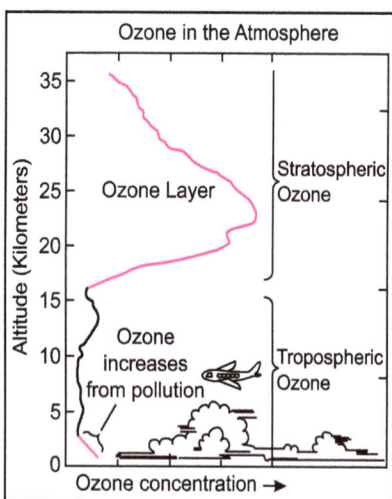

Fig. 11.3 : Ozone Layer

- In the process, ozone molecules split up into a molecule of oxygen and an oxygen atom.
- The oxygen atom (O) again combines with the oxygen molecule (O_2) to regenerate an ozone (O_3) molecule. Thus, the total amount of ozone is maintained by this continuous process of destruction and regeneration.
- The ozone layer is located between 10 and 50 km above the Earth's surface.
- In the troposphere, ozone is present only in small amounts generated by the action of ultra-violet rays on the molecules of nitrogen dioxide and accelerated by the sunlight acting on the pollutants in the air.
- In the stratosphere, it is present in significant amounts produced by the action of highenergy radiation from the sun striking some molecules of oxygen and converting them into ozone. *(Fig. 11.3)*

Importance of Ozone Layer

- It absorbs harmful Ultraviolet-B radiation from the sun, thereby preventing them from passing through the atmosphere of Earth.
- Ultraviolet rays of the Sun are associated with a number of health related and environmental issues.
- This layer absorbs the excessive heat from the atmosphere and thus helps to protect and evolve the terrestrial ecosystem.

Depletion of Ozone Layer

- In recent years, the thickness of this layer has been decreasing, leading in extreme cases of holes in the layer.
- The cause of ozone depletion is the increase in the level of free radicals such as hydroxyl radicals, nitric oxide radicals and atomic chlorine and bromine.
- The most important compounds, which account for almost 80% of the total depletion of ozone in the stratosphere, are chlorofluorocarbons (CFCs).
- CFCs are used as cleaning agents in refrigerators, fire extinguishers, car propellants, insulating foams, etc.
- These compounds are very stable in the lower atmosphere of the Earth, but in the stratosphere, they break down to release a free chlorine atom due to ultraviolet radiation.
- A free chlorine atom reacts with an ozone molecule (O_3) and forms chlorine monoxide and a molecule of oxygen.
- Chlorine monoxide reacts with an ozone molecule to form a chlorine atom and two molecules of oxygen.
- The free chlorine molecule again reacts with ozone to form chlorine monoxide. The process

continues and the result is the reduction or depletion of ozone in the stratosphere.

Effects of Ozone Layer Depletion

- Severe ozone layer depletion in a region, particularly over Antarctica and over the Arctic is known as the Ozone Hole. The depletion is caused by the destruction of ozone by CFCs and other compounds, such as carbon tetra-chloride and carbon tetra-fluoride. The amount of ozone in ozone holes is about 55% to 60% of the normal concentration in the ozone layer.
- Increase in the surface level of ozone can enhance the ability of sunlight to synthesize vitamin D, which can be regarded as an important beneficial effect of ozone layer depletion.
- A 1% loss of ozone leads to a 2% increase in UV radiation. Continuous exposure to UV radiation affects humans, animals and plants, and can lead to skin problems, depression of the immune system and fatal eye diseases like corneal cataracts that often leads to blindness.
- Disturbance of the thermal structure of the atmosphere probably results in causing changes in atmospheric circulation.
- Ozone is considered to be a greenhouse gas. A depleted ozone layer may partially dampen the greenhouse effect. Therefore, efforts to tackle ozone depletion may result in increased global warming.
- Phytoplankton, an important component of the marine food chain, can also be affected by ozone depletion. Studies in this regard have shown that ultraviolet rays can influence the survival rates of these microscopic organisms by affecting their orientation and mobility.
- The effects of ozone depletion are not limited to humans only, as it can affect animals and plants as well. It can affect important food crops like rice by adversely affecting cyanobacteria, which helps them to absorb and utilize nitrogen properly.
- The increasing concern for the causes and effects of ozone depletion led to the adoption of the Montreal Protocol, in the year 1987, to reduce and control the industrial emission of CFCs.
- International agreements have succeeded to a great extent in reducing the emission of these CFC compounds. However, more cooperation and understanding among all the countries of the world is required to completely solve this problem.

GLOBAL WARMING

Global Warming is an average increase in the temperature of the atmosphere near the Earth's surface and in the troposphere, which can contribute to changes in global climate patterns. It can occur from a variety of causes, both natural and human induced. In common usage, global warming often refers to the warming that can occur as a result of increased emissions of greenhouse gases from human activities. Therefore, it is closely linked to the enhanced greenhouse effect, which is an increase in the concentration of greenhouse gases in the atmosphere leading to an increase in the amount of infrared or thermal radiation near the surface. Most scientists agree that enhanced greenhouse effect leads to rising temperatures, referred to as global warming. The results of global warming do not limit themselves to a mere warmer weather, but also to an erratic climate that, if left unchecked, could cause pervasive natural disasters and species extinction.

Causes of Global Warming

The causes for the existence of global warming are not limited to natural causes only, but comprise man-made or anthropogenic causes too.

Greenhouse Effect

The major natural greenhouse gases are water vapour, which causes about 36-70% of the greenhouse effect on Earth, carbon dioxide (CO_2), causes 9-26%, methane, greenhouse effect causes 4-9% and ozone of the causes 3-7%. Other greenhouse gases include nitrous oxide, sulfur hexafluoride, hydrofluoro-carbons (HFCs), perfluorocarbons (PFCs) and chlorofluorocarbons (CFCs). Greenhouse gases in the atmosphere act like a mirror and reflect back to the Earth a part of the heat radiation, which would otherwise be lost to space. The higher the concentration of greenhouse gases like carbon dioxide in the atmosphere, the more heat energy is being reflected back to the Earth. The emission of carbon dioxide into the environment mainly from burning of fossil fuels (oil, gas, petrol, kerosene, etc.) has increased dramatically over the past five decades. The increase of greenhouse gas concentration (mainly carbon dioxide) led to a substantial warming of the

Earth and the sea, called global warming. In other words, it can be said that the increase in the man-made emission of greenhouse gases is the cause for global warming. *(Fig. 11.4)*

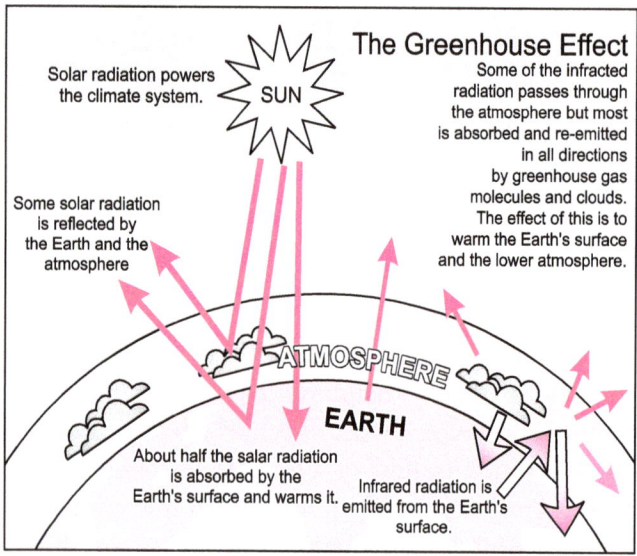

Fig. 11.4 : Greenhouse Effect.

Pollution

This is one of the biggest man-made problems. Pollution comes in many shapes and sizes. Burning fossil fuels is one thing that causes pollution. Fossil fuels are fuels made of organic matter such as coal, or oil. When fossil fuels are burned, they give off carbon dioxide (CO_2).

Population

Since CO_2 contributes to global warming, the increase in population makes the problem worse because we breathe out CO_2. Also, the trees that convert CO_2 to O_2 are being demolished because we cut the trees to use the land as property for our homes and buildings.

Deforestation

Clearing away of forests and forest ecosystems on a large-scale has posed several dangers to life on Earth. Trees are essential for absorbing excess carbon dioxide in air. However, deforestation is also a natural cause of global warming because forest fires can occur naturally and these are responsible for tearing through huge areas of forest and woodland. The fires produce carbon-filled smoke and also remove trees that can photosynthesize. The smaller plants that will replace them will take time to grow before they can efficiently photosynthesize. This leads to more carbon dioxide in the air and is thus one of the natural global warming causes.

Agriculture

A huge 30% of methane emissions that are released into the Earth's atmosphere come from agriculture. The majority of this comes from the result of the digestive system of animals such as cows. The number of animals, such as cows, that are bred for purposes such as killing for meat is high and thus, larger amount of methane is emitted than through natural breeding. The decomposition of manure also produces methane in environment that are low in oxygen.

Ocean Pollution

The waste dumped by humans into water bodies is not the only source of pollution that is found in oceans. Every ocean supports vast range of ecosystems, these ecosystems produced wastes that contributes to natural global warming causes.

Effects of Global Warming

Global warming is already affecting the humankind, plants and animals in a number of ways such as increased ocean levels, droughts and changed weather patterns. It is well recognized by scientists around the world as a serious public health and environmental concern. Below is the list of effects that global warming has on the environment, climate and humankind.

Melting of Glaciers

The melting of glaciers will create an excess of problems for humankind and the animals living on the Earth. Due to increased global warming, the level of the sea will rise, leading to flooding and this will in turn create havoc in human life. Apart from raising the sea levels, it will also endanger several species of animals and thus will hamper the balance of the ecosystem. Moreover, these large glaciers reflect light back into the space, and with the meltdown of these glaciers, the Earth will be further warmed.

Rise in Sea level

The sea levels have risen and the mass of the polar icecaps has significantly reduced over the last century. It can have disastrous effects on human habitations on sea coasts, as one-third of human population lives within 60 km of a coastline. Many towns and cities could even be submerged under water. With coastal areas taking a battering, this means flooding occurs, people are left homeless, there are huge costs due to damages and ultimately there is less land across the globe for a growing human race to live on.

Climate Change

Increased precipitation in the form of rain has already been noticed in Polar and Sub-Polar Regions. Warming of atmosphere will considerably increase its moisturecarrying capacity. While the troposphere warms up, the stratosphere will cool down. This would cause widespread changes in rainfall patterns due to changed pattern of airmass movements. More global warming will lead to more evaporation, which will cause more rains. Animals and plants cannot easily adapt to increased rainfall. Plants may die due to it and animals may migrate to other areas, which can cause entire ecosystem to become off-balance.

Diseases

As the temperature becomes warmer, it will have an effect on the health of humans and the diseases they are exposed to. With the increase in the rainfall, waterborne diseases like malaria are likely to spread. With global temperatures rising, disease carrying insects will migrate to populous regions. The Earth will become warmer and, as a result, heat waves are likely to increase that will cause a major blow to the people.

Hurricanes Frequency

As the temperature of the oceans rises, hurricanes and other storms are likely to become stronger. With the increase in the global warming, the water in the ocean warms up and it heats up the surrounding air, creating hurricanes. More evaporation means more hurricanes.

Health Problems

One of the serious effects of global warming is the health issues that are caused by many of the contributing factors. Those who live and work in builtup areas are subjected to air pollution or 'smog' that is created primarily by vehicle emissions and industrial pollution. It is not healthy to breathe this dirty air everyday as it can lead to a decline in the immune system and the onset of health problems such as asthma and bronchitis. This could be common in many big cities across the world as the population tries to fight against global warming effects.

- Atmosphere is defined as the gaseous envelope or blanket surrounding the Earth, protecting it from the harmful ultraviolet and infrared rays of the sun.
- The atmosphere of the Earth is composed of 78% nitrogen, 21% oxygen, 0.9% argon, 0.03% carbon dioxide, and trace amounts of other gases.
- Layers of the Earth : (i) Troposphere, (ii) Stratosphere, (iii) Mesosphere, and (iv) Thermosphere.
- Weather is the short-term physical condition of atmosphere at a given locality or an area.
- Climate is the average weather condition over a long period and over a large area.
- Ozone is a special form of oxygen, made up of three oxygen atoms. It is present in rare amounts in the atmosphere.
- Global Warming is an average increase in the temperature of the atmosphere near the Earth's surface and in the troposphere contributing to changes in global climate patterns.

A. Answer the following questions

1. What is meant by atmosphere?
2. What is the importance of atmosphere?
3. What types of solid particles are present in the atmosphere?
4. What is the significance of the solid particles?
5. Name and define the different types of layers of the atmosphere.
6. What are the properties of troposphere?
7. Why is stratosphere found ideal for flying aircrafts?
8. State the properties of ionosphere.
9. What is Ozone Layer?

10. What is the importance of ozone layer in the atmosphere?
11. What are the causes responsible for the depletion of the ozone layer?
12. What are the effects of the Ozone Depletion?
13. Explain the Greenhouse Effect.
14. What is meant by Ozone Hole?
15. In which layer of the atmosphere do all weather conditions occur?

B. Define the following terms
1. Global Warming
2. Greenhouse Effect
3. CFCs

C. Distinguish between the following
1. Troposphere and Stratosphere.
2. Ionosphere and Exosphere.
3. Weather and Climate.

D. Give reasons
1. The Earth does not experience extreme temperatures like other planets.
2. The amount of water vapour in the atmosphere varies from place to place.
3. The layers of the atmosphere become thinner with altitude.

E. Board Questions
1. What is global warming ?
2. (i) Name the two most important gases present in the atmosphere.
   (ii) Mention the percentage of both these gases named by you.
3. Why is the Ozone layer very significant in the atmosphere ?
4. Why is the height of tropopause over the Equator more than over the poles ?

CHAPTER 12: INSOLATION

Meaning of Insolation : Meaning of Insolation and Terrestrial Radiation. Factors affecting Temperature : Latitude, Altitude, Distance from the Sea, Slope of Land, Winds and Ocean Currents.

The Sun, by the process of Solar Radiation, continuously radiates heat and light energy in all directions. The complex process of the flow of energy from the Sun to the Earth, and then into the space, involves energy transmission, in the form of heat in the atmosphere. Sun is the only primary source of light and heat on the Earth through which the Earth receives its heat, which is a tiny fraction of the huge amount of energy radiated by the Sun.

INSOLATION

The total amount of solar energy received by the Earth in the form of short wave rays is known as Insolation. The Sun radiates nearly half of its energy at wavelengths of visible light. As the insolation enters the atmosphere, a part of it reaches the Earth, some part gets absorbed, and some gets reflected, i.e., out of the total 100% solar energy, only 51% reaches the Earth, 14% is absorbed by the atmospheric layers including ozone during insolation, and about 35% gets reflected back into the space.

Terrestrial Radiation

About 51% of the insolation reaches the Earth, which on getting heated, is radiated back into the atmosphere by the Earth's surface in the form of long waves. This heat radiated by the Earth's surface is known as Terrestrial Radiation.

Heat Balance

It is defined as the state of equilibrium that exists on Earth between incoming insolation from the sun and the outgoing terrestrial radiation from the Earth. The Earth therefore maintains a heat balance between the heat and cold variations in different regions. Thus, it can be said that the Earth controls the delicate balance between the heat received and the heat given out. Overall, there is neither a heat gain nor loss.

The heat balance is a worldwide average balance as low latitude areas receive more radiation than they lose, while the opposite occurs near the poles. The heat required to preserve the balance is transferred by the movement of air masses and ocean currents. *(Fig. 12.1)*

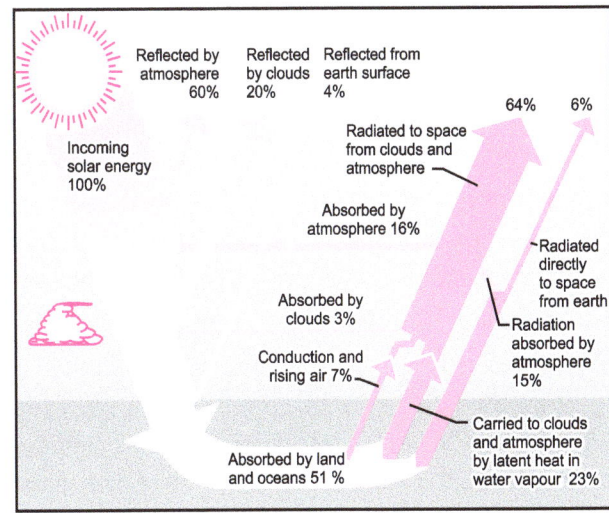

Fig. 12.1 : Heat Budget.

The heat balance is maintained by the following factors :

- The spherical shape of the Earth changes the horizontal distribution of insolation between latitudinal zones.

- In the latitudes between 37°N and 37°S, the incoming radiation is much higher than the outgoing radiation.
- In the middle and high latitudes, the outgoing radiation is in excess of the incoming radiation, while the outgoing radiations are in excess only when the surplus energy from the low latitudes is transported to the idle and high latitudes by the circulation of winds and ocean currents.
- The sunrays fall vertically overhead at the Equator and slanting at the Poles. This difference in the direction of the sunrays causes difference in the heating effect on the Earth's surface.
- The difference in the heating of the Earth and its atmosphere helps in the circulation of air and water in the atmosphere and the oceans. This helps to maintain the heat balance in the Earth's atmospheric system.

Heat Budget

The balance of incoming and outgoing radiation is known as the Heat Budget. *(Fig. 12.1)*

At any particular point on the Earth, a total of 100 units of heat are received at the top of the atmosphere. This heat is dispersed by the atmosphere in the following manner :

- Heat received by the Earth (insolation) = 51 units
- Heat reflected back into the space by the layers of atmosphere or lost by scattering = 35 units
- Heat absorbed by the atmosphere = 14 units
  ∴ Total = 100 units

Out of 35 units of heat that are reflected back into the space or lost by scattering, as described above, 27 units are reflected back from the top of the clouds, 6 units are scattered into the space and 2 units are reflected back from the snow covered areas of the Earth.

Since the Earth's surface receives about 51 units of heat from the Sun as insolation, which is radiated back to the atmosphere and space by the Earth, it can be said that the total energy received from the Sun is radiated by the Earth in the following manner :

- Heat radiation absorbed and radiated back to the atmosphere by the Earth = 34 units
- Heat radiated directly by the Earth into space = 17 units
  ∴ Total = 51 units

Thus, in these ways the heat budget is balanced in the atmosphere. It can be seen that a total of 48 units (14 units from insolation and 34 units from terrestrial radiations), are radiated back to space gradually.

Heat Zones

The fact that the Earth is spherical in shape and revolves on its axis around the Sun in an inclined position is the reason for the unequal distribution of heat on the Earth's surface. The intensity of insolation is greatest where the Sunrays strike vertically. This occurs at noon at the latitude equal to the Sun's declination ranging between the Tropic of Cancer in the north to the Tropic of Capricorn in the south during the Equinoxes. As we go towards the Poles, the angle diminishes and the same amount of solar energy spreads over a larger area on the Earth's surface. Hence, the Poles receive the least heat per unit area. In this way, the amount of insolation varies from lower to higher latitudes depending on the position of the Earth in its orbit with respect to the Sun. This unequal distribution of insolation on the Earth's surface results in the existence of different heat zones on the planet. *(Fig. 12.2)*

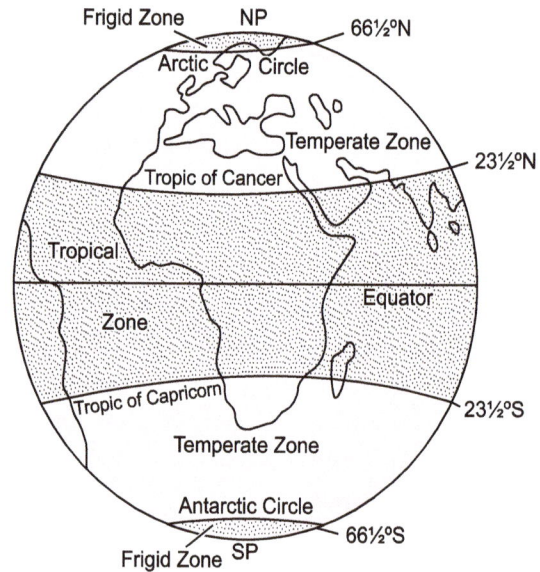

Fig. 12.2 : Heat Zones

Torrid Zone

The region between the Tropic of Cancer and Tropic of Capricorn marks the limit of the overhead Sun. So, all places between 23½°N and 23½°S receive the maximum amount of insolation as the sunrays are more or less vertical throughout the year. Hence, the heat is concentrated over a smaller area. In this region, the amount of insolation received during the day is more than the terrestrial radiation lost at night. Due to this fact, this region could become hotter and hotter with every passing day, but this does not happen. This is because a balance is maintained as the surplus heat from this region is transported to the higher latitudes by the circulation of wind and ocean currents.

Temperate Zone

In this zone, due to the spherical shape of the Earth, the amount of insolation received decreases with an increase in latitude. Beyond the Torrid Zone, the sunrays fall in a slanting position. This zone comprises the regions between 23½° and 66½°, i.e., between the Tropic of Cancer and the Arctic Circle in the north and the Tropic of Capricorn and the Antarctic Circle in the south. In each of the two Temperate Zones, the angle of incidence and duration of sunshine is greater in summers than in winters. The contrast between summers and winters is greater in this zone than in the Tropical Zone.

Frigid Zone

This zone comprises the zones beyond the Arctic and Antarctic Circles surrounding the poles. In these zones, the amount of insolation received is very less due to the extremely low angle of incidence of sunrays. The rays are always in a slanting position covering a very large distance. Thus, the summer temperatures are quite low in these regions. In this region, the amount of the insolation received is much less than the amount of terrestrial radiation given out in space. The circulation of winds and ocean currents transfer surplus energy from the lower latitudes to the middle and higher latitudes, thus balancing the energy shortage in this zone.

Factors Affecting the Distribution of Temperature

The horizontal distribution of temperature is affected by different types of physical factors.

Latitude

In the low latitudes, the sunrays are direct and have to travel a lesser extent through the atmosphere. Hence, the heat of these rays is more intense. But, in high altitudes, the sunrays are slanting and have to pass through a greater extent of atmosphere. Hence, these rays lose heat and so the areas in the high latitude are not very hot as compared to the equatorial regions. The temperature zones are formed on the Earth's surface in this way. Therefore, places close to the Equator have higher temperature and are warmer than the places away from the Equator as the Sunrays reach the Earth directly after passing through the layers of the atmosphere.

Altitude

The height of a place above the mean sea level is known as the altitude of that place. Temperature of the atmosphere and altitude are interrelated. With an increase in height, temperature decreases. The lower layers of atmosphere contain more water vapour and dust than the upper layers. Therefore, the lower layers of the atmosphere does not easily let heat escape back into space. So, the places on lower altitudes remain comparatively warmer. On the other hand, places at higher altitudes will hardly manage to remain warm because at high altitudes, the air is refined on account of less content of dust particles and water vapour. The result is that the heat rapidly escapes from the ground at higher altitudes. The rate at which the temperature falls as we go upwards is known as the Normal Lapse Rate.

Direction of Winds

Onshore winds are the winds that blow from sea to land and offshore winds are the winds that blow from land to sea. E.g., a cold wind blowing from the interior of the continent during winter further reduces the temperature of the places along their path. Generally, winds blowing from the lower latitudes (Equator) are warmer than those winds coming from higher latitudes. Some of the local winds are hot and dry like the Loo, whereas the Bora and Mistral are the cold winds. Winds affect the temperatures of the regions over which they blow. During winters, the offshore winds lower the temperature while they raise it in summers. On the other hand, the onshore winds coming from the sea raise the winter temperatures and lower the temperatures in summer. Moreover, warm winds that blow from the sea into land are moisture-laden and cause rainfall on land, especially when they strike against a barrier.

Ocean Currents

Warm currents blow from Equatorial to Polar Regions, while cold currents blow from Polar Regions to lower Equatorial latitudes. Warm currents can be noticed on the eastern margins of the continents in the middle latitudes, while the cold currents flow at the western margins of the continents. Ocean currents influence the temperature of the coastal lands by increasing or decreasing the temperature of the Earth's surface

Distance from the Sea

Since water is fluid and transparent, sunrays pass through it to a great depth. Water is mobile and warm water mixes easily with the cold water. Because of this, water is neither gets heated nor cooled quickly. However, the land surface is opaque and rigid, so, the sunrays influence a limited portion of it. Thus, the sunrays heat a piece of land more rapidly because the heat obtained by the area does not mix with other areas of land. Hence, the land gets heated or cooled more quickly than water. Thus, during the day, the land is hotter than the sea. The hot air over the land becomes lighter and goes upwards. This creates a low pressure area over the land. The air above the sea is cooler during this time. When this air blows towards the low pressure area over the land, it lowers the temperature of the air on land. Such cool breeze that blows over the Earth is known as Sea Breeze that cools the coastal regions. At night, the sea is warmer than the land and the cooler land breeze blows towards the sea, these making the air above sea cooler. The main contrast is between the landmasses and the ocean as there is differential heating of land and water. Thus, the interchange of breeze maintains the heat balance.

Humidity

Water vapour in the air absorbs heat during the day time and retains it at night, preventing loss of heat, especially near the Earth's surface where humidity is highest. Thus, humid tropics have high temperatures even at night, though there is little cloud cover. E.g., the high temperature in the deserts is due to absence of clouds, thus increasing the diurnal range of temperature, whereas the reverse can be noticed in the equatorial regions where there are clouds for the greater part of the afternoon.

Slope of the Land

An area with a steep slope experiences a more rapid change in temperature than a gentle one. That is why, mountain ranges with an east-west alignment like the Alps have a higher temperature on the south-facing sunny slope, than the north-facing sheltered slope. Similarly, temperature may be lower in the valley than higher up the slopes. It happens on calm, cold winter nights when there is a clear sky and the air is very dry. Due to these conditions, the heat from the Earth's surface escapes rapidly back into space, making the upper slopes warmer. The cold is further increased by the sinking of the cool air from the mountain sides. In this way, there is a reversal in the vertical distribution of temperature. In this case, temperature decreases down in the valleys. This process is known as the Inversion of Temperature.

Natural Vegetation

Every surface has different properties. Vegetation checks radiation from upper layers of soil. A crop covered field absorbs between 60-80% of the solar energy while a snow covered field absorbs only about 20%. A forest area absorbs about 90% of the solar energy. Thus, vegetative cover absorbs more sunshine than snow fields. Most of this absorbed energy is used by plants in the process of transpiration. This explains why these areas do not become very hot.

Nature of the Soil

If the soil can retain more water, then it heats or cools less rapidly. Dark coloured soil absorbs more heat than the light coloured soil, hence giving rise to differences in temperature. The loamy and clayey soils retain water while, the sandy soils absorb and release heat more quickly.

MEASUREMENT OF TEMPERATURE

Many devices have been invented to accurately measure temperature. Temperature is measured basically by using two scales, namely the Centigrade Scale and the Fahrenheit Scale. These scales transformed the measurement of temperature into meaningful numbers.

The Centigrade Scale has 100 divisions while the Fahrenheit Scale has 180 divisions. Each scale can be converted into the other by using a specific formula.

$°F = (°C \times 9/5) + 32$

$°C = (°F - 32) \times 5/9$

Range of Temperature

From the beginning of dawn, the temperature gradually increases until midday and then remains constant for a couple of hours before starting to decrease. Though the angle of incidence is at its highest around noon, the maximum temperature is recorded at about 3 o'clock in the afternoon, the reason being the heating of the atmosphere taking place from below and consequently creating a time lag.

The difference between the maximum and minimum temperature on any single day is called as the diurnal range of temperature. There are two types of ranges of temperature :

Mean Monthly Range Temperature

It is the average of mean temperatures of all the days in a month. In the Climate Data, it is calculated on the basis of average values of mean temperatures of the days for each month.

Mean Annual Range Temperature

It is the difference between the mean temperature of the hottest month and the mean temperature of the coldest month. It is also understood as the seasonal difference in temperature.

SUMMARY

- Insolation is the total amount of solar energy received by the Earth in the form of short wave rays.
- Terrestrial Radiation is the heat radiated by the Earth's surface back to the atmosphere.
- Heat Balance is defined as the state of equilibrium that exists on Earth between incoming insolation from the sun and the outgoing terrestrial radiation from the Earth.
- Heat Budget is the balance of incoming and outgoing radiation.
- Heat Zones of the world : (i) Torrid Zone, (ii) Temperate Zone, and (iii) Frigid Zone.
- Diurnal Range of temperature is the difference between the maximum and minimum temperature on any one day.

EXERCISES

A. Answer the following questions

1. What is Insolation? State its importance.
2. Name the factors that affect the insolation over the Earth's surface.
3. What are the factors affecting the distribution of temperature?
4. State two characteristics of the temperate zone.
5. What are the different Heat Zones?
6. What is inversion of temperature?
7. Define the different types of ranges of temperature.
8. What is meant by the range of temperature?

B. Define the following terms

1. Insolation
2. Heat Balance
3. Heat Budget
4. Normal Lapse Rate

C. Distinguish between the following

1. Insolation and Terrestrial Radiation.
2. Torrid Zone and Temperate Zone.

D. Give reasons

1. The atmosphere is heated more by terrestrial radiation than by insolation from the sun.
2. The vertical sunrays give more insolation than the slanting rays.
3. South facing slopes are much warmer than north facing slopes in the Northern Hemisphere.
4. Distance from sea affects the temperature of a place.
5. Land gets heated up faster than the sea.
6. The temperature of a place depends largely upon its latitude.
7. Desert areas experience a high temperature at day while a much lower temperature at night.
8. The Earth's surface receives only about 51% of the solar energy.

E. Board Questions

1. What do you understand by terrestrial radiation ?
2. Give a reason for each of the following :
   (i) New Delhi is warmer than Mumbai in summer.
   (ii) Areas near the Equator remain warm nearly throughout the year.

CHAPTER 13
ATMOSPHERIC PRESSURE AND WINDS

Meaning of Factors : Meaning and Factors that affect Atmospheric Pressure. Major Pressure Belts of the World. Factors affecting Direction and Velocity of Wind–Pressure Gradient, Coriolis Effect. Permanent Winds–Trades, Westerlies and Polar Easterlies. Periodic Winds–Land and Sea Breezes, Monsoons. Local Winds–Loo, Chinook, Foehn and Mistral. Variable Winds–Cyclones and Anticyclones. Jet Streams–Meaning and Importance.

Air is a tangible medium exerting pressure on any solid or liquid surface exposed to it. This pressure is tremendous, but we do not notice it because the pressure within our body is able to counterbalance the outside pressure. The pressure of air is not uniform everywhere due to the differential heating of the atmosphere. It differs from place to place and from time to time. The variations in the pressure of our atmosphere at different elevations have important effects on the climate. These variations cause horizontal movements of air called winds that transport heat and moisture from one place to another. Air pressure is crucial to all forms of life on Earth as it plays a vital role in controlling temperature variation and precipitation.

ATMOSPHERIC PRESSURE

Atmospheric or air pressure is the force per unit area exerted on the Earth's surface by the weight of the air above the surface. The force exerted by an air mass is created by the molecules that make it up and their size, motion, and number present in the air. These factors are important because they determine the temperature and density, and thus pressure of the air.

Molecules are significant for measuring air pressure because if the number of air molecules above a surface increases, there are more molecules to exert pressure on a surface and thus, the total atmospheric pressure increases. By contrast, if the number of molecules decreases, so does the air pressure.

Measurement

Air pressure is measured with the instrument known as *mercury or aneroid barometer*. A mercury barometer measures the height of a mercury column in a vertical glass tube (Fig. 13.1). As air pressure changes, the height of the mercury column changes. It drops when pressure falls and rises when it increases. An aneroid barometer uses a coil of tubing with most of the air removed. (Fig. 13.2) The coil then bends inward when pressure rises and bows out when pressure drops. Using such instruments, scientists have set the standard of normal sea level pressure at about 1013.2 millibars (force per square meter of surface area).

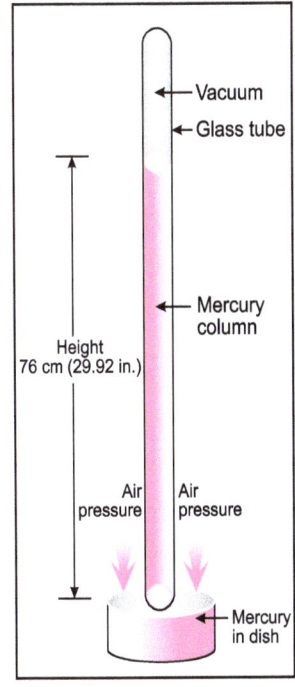

Fig. 13.1 : Mercury Barometer

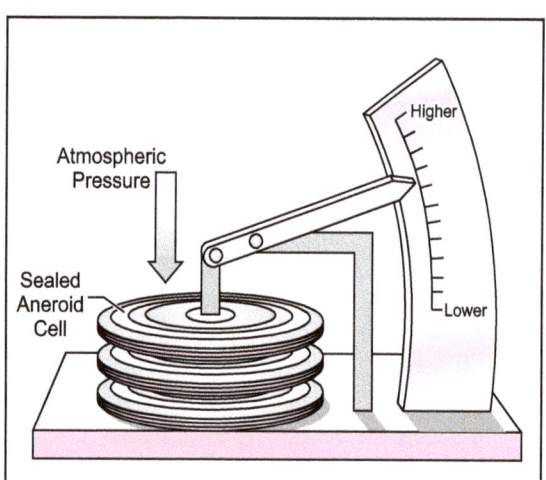

Fig. 13.2 : Aneroid Barometer.

Factors Affecting Atmospheric Pressure

Atmospheric pressure depends mainly on the following factors :

Altitude

Atmospheric pressure decreases with an increase in altitude. It is highest at sea level. As one goes up, the density of air decreases, and so does the pressure exerted by it. This is due to the air that is composed of gases and is thus, highly compressible. Earth's gravity pulls the molecules of air and other gases downwards towards the ground. Thus, the lowest layer is the densest as it is the most compressed. The mercury falls about 1 cm for every 110 m of ascent. Due to insufficient oxygen supply or air at high altitudes, mountaineers experience weakness, nausea or breathlessness. Therefore, they carry oxygen cylinders on their expeditions.

Temperature

Atmospheric pressure decreases with increase in temperature. When air is compressed, without any heat being added to it, its temperature is raised. On the contrary, when the air is allowed to expand, without any addition or subtraction of heat, its temperature falls. At the surface of the Earth, the pressure is greater than above. If the air is forced to rise, it moves into a region of lower pressure and therefore, it expands and becomes cooler. Similarly, any mass of air moving down will face a higher pressure leading to compression and increased temperature.

There are three ways through which the temperature of air is forced to rise :

- Heating by contact with earth's surface.
- By blowing against a mountain side.
- Descent of a heavier mass of air through cooling.

These vertical movements do not extend indefinitely upwards. Above a certain altitude, their effect is imperceptible, and beyond that, the temperature does not decrease.

Water Vapour

Moist air exerts less pressure than dry air. Warmer air has more capacity to hold moisture. Therefore, air with higher quantity of water vapour (moist air) exerts lower pressure, while air with low quantity of water vapour (dry air) shows higher pressure.

Rotation of the Earth

Air at the Poles are pushed towards the Equator by the rotation of the Earth. There is high pressure at the Poles due to low temperatures. Because of rotation, the air coming down from Poles occupies more space as it expands and its pressure falls. These low pressure belts are along parallels of 60° N and 60° S. As air always moves from high pressure to low pressure, the air moves away from the Poles from the higher level to take its place.

Isobars

The pressure of air is shown on weather maps by the means of lines known as isobars, which means of equal weight. An isobar is an imaginary line drawn on a map joining all places of equal atmospheric pressure, at sea-level. When the isobars are far apart, there is little difference of atmospheric pressure and the weather is calm. When the isobars are close together, there is a great difference in atmospheric pressure and the weather is stormy.

PRESSURE BELTS OF EARTH

The horizontal distribution of atmospheric pressure is not uniform all over the globe. It is largely affected by a variation in temperature and the rotation of the Earth. There is a pattern of alternate high and low pressure belts over the Earth, which are created due to the unequal heating of land and water that can be attributed to the spherical shape of the Earth. The Equatorial region receives a great amount of heat throughout the year. Warm air being light, the air at the Equator rises creating a low pressure. At the Polar region, the cold air sinks and high pressure is created.

There are four major types of pressure belts on the Earth *(Fig. 13.3)*. These belts are not continuous because the surface of the Earth is made of both land and water.

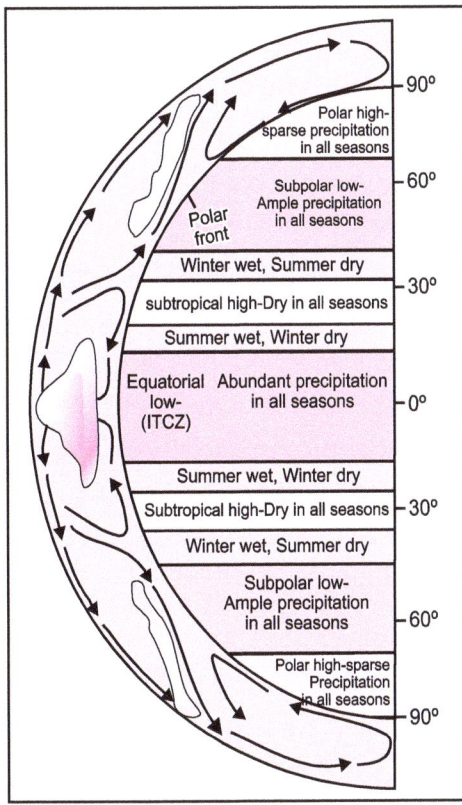

Fig. 13.3 : Four major types of pressure belts on the Earth.

Equatorial Low Pressure Belt

This belt extends up to 5° North and South of the Equator. This region receives the direct rays of the Sun throughout the year. The hot air expands and rises as convection current, thus creating a low pressure. This is a calm region with little wind movement and hence, is also known as 'Doldrums' (meaning dull). Despite the calm and light winds, the doldrums are characterized by turbulent and stormy weather, with heavy rains, thunderstorms and squalls. The doldrums are variable, both in position and extent, usually moving northwards and southwards with the Sun due to shifting of the pressure belts.

Sub-Tropical High Pressure Belt

This belt extends up to 30–35° North and South of the Equator. The hot air rising at the Equator reaches the upper layers of the atmosphere and cools down. This cool air spreads on either side of the Equator in the upper layers of the atmosphere. When it reaches near 30°N and 30°S of the Equator, it starts sinking, creating a high pressure there. The air from the sub-polar regions also descends here due to the rotation of the Earth. This adds to the already existing high pressure in the area. In these belts, calm conditions prevail with light, dry winds. This belt is also known as Horse Latitudes. The dominant winds in the Subtropical high are called the Westerlies.

In ancient times, due to the absence of surface winds and the weight of the high pressure air, the sailing ships would get stuck in the same place for many days. In order to conserve food and water, the sailors used to throw the horses on the ship into the sea. Hence, this belt got the name Horse Latitudes.

Sub-Polar Low Pressure Belt

This region lies between the latitudes 60–65° North and South of the Equator. Here, low pressure is created because of the Earth's rotation, which moves the bulk of air towards the sub-tropical and Polar Regions, thereby making the air less dense. Moreover, the rising currents of air in these low pressure belts tend to lower the pressure still further. This region is marked by violent storms in winter. The sub-polar low pressure belt is more developed in the Southern Hemisphere than that in the Northern Hemisphere.

Polar High Pressure Belt

At the North and South Poles, the temperatures always remain extremely low due to low insolation. As a result, the air remains cold, heavy and dense, creating a high pressure. These areas are known as Polar Highs and are characterized by permanent Ice Caps. Of the two Polar Regions, the Antarctic High is significant in terms of both strength and persistence. In the Arctic, a polar high pressure belt is less pronounced, and when it does form, it tends to locate over the colder northern areas in winter rather than directly over the relatively warmer Arctic Ocean.

Shifting of Pressure Belts

The main cause for the formation of the pressure belts is the uneven distribution of temperature on the Earth's surface, which can be attributed to the Earth's revolution around the Sun and the inclination of the Earth's axis. Consequently, the pressure belts follow the apparent annual migration of the Sun. They swing either to the north (between December and June) or to the south (between June and December) of the Equator. When the Sun is overhead the Tropic of Cancer (21st June), the pressure belts shift 5°N and when it shines vertically overhead on Tropic of Capricorn (22nd December), they shift 5°S from their original position. The shifting of the pressure belts cause seasonal changes in the climate, especially between the latitudes 30° and 40° in both hemispheres. In this region, the Mediterranean type of climate is experienced because of the shifting of pressure belts southwards and northwards with the overhead position of the Sun. During winters, Westerlies prevail and bring rainfall. During summers, dry trade winds blow offshore and are unable to bring rainfall to these regions. When the Sun shines vertically over the Equator on 21st March and 23rd September (the Equinoxes), the pressure belts remain balanced in both the hemispheres. *(Fig. 13.4)*

Effects of Shifting of Pressure Belts

- Pressure belts affect the direction in which winds blow. Thus, the shifting of pressure belts causes some places to be in different wind belts during the year.

- Due to the swing of the pressure belts according to the seasons, the precipitation (snow and rainfall) associated with them also changes.

Eg : The Mediterranean regions of the world sometimes come under the influence of Trade Winds and sometimes under the influence of Westerlies due to the shifting of pressure belts. As such, the Mediterranean regions experience winter rain due to the influence of the Westerlies.

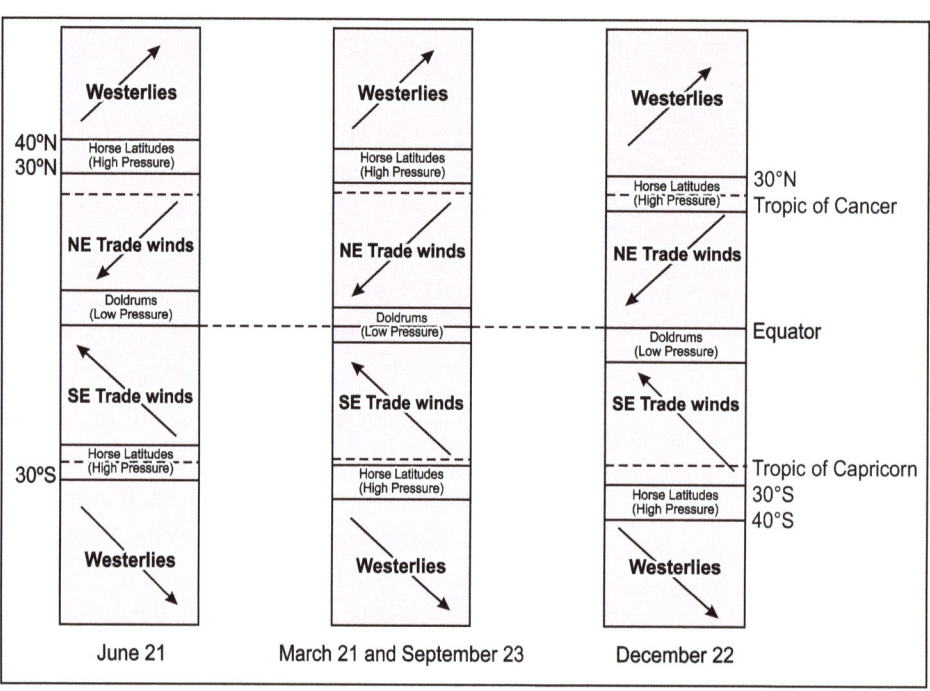

Fig. 13.4 : Shifting of Pressure Belts

WINDS

Air moving in a horizontal direction is called wind. It is caused due to the uneven heating of the Earth by the Sun. Wind always blows from high pressure to low pressure areas. Greater the difference in pressure, higher the wind speed.

In the atmosphere, there is a vertical movement (ascent and descent) of air. This vertical movement is known as Air Current. The air currents together with the winds, comprise a system of atmospheric circulation. *(Fig. 13.5)*

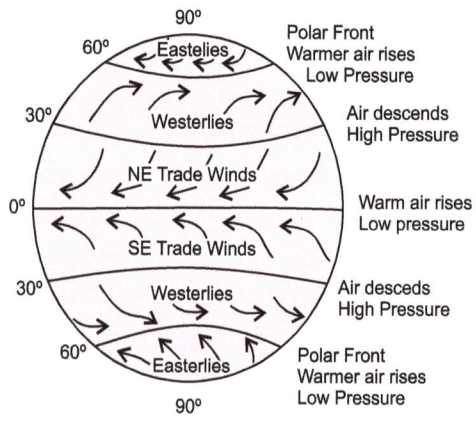

Fig. 13.5 : Atmospheric Circulation

Factors Affecting the Direction and Velocity of Wind

The direction and speed of wind are controlled by a number of factors :

Pressure Gradient

It is the rate of change of pressure between two points on two isobars. The direction and amount of pressure gradient determines the direction and velocity of winds. The greater the difference in two points, the steeper is the pressure gradient, and the higher is the wind speed.

Coriolis Force

Due to the rotation of the Earth, a force called Coriolis force is produced, which tends to deflect the winds to their right in the Northern Hemisphere, and to their left in the Southern Hemisphere *(Fig. 13.6)*. This is known as the Ferrel's Law and this effect is called the Coriolis Effect.

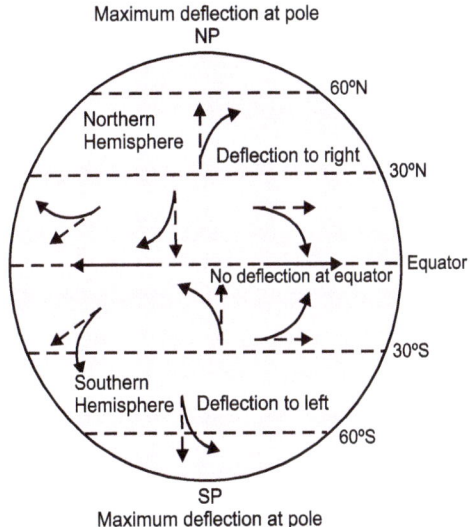

Fig. 13.6. : Coriolis Effect.

TYPES OF WINDS

Permanent/Prevailing/Planetary Winds

These winds blow from highpressure belts to lowpressure belts constantly throughout the year in the same direction. There are mainly three types of planetary winds on the Earth *(Fig.13.7)* :

Trade Winds

These steady winds blowing from the subtropical high-pressure belt to the equatorial lowpressure belt in both the hemispheres. The name 'Trade' is derived from a nautical expression 'to blow tread', which means to blow along a regular path.

Characteristics

- Constantly blow from subtropical highpressure areas between 30° latitudes in both the hemispheres towards the equatorial lowpressure belt.
- Trade Winds are noted for their steadiness and persistent direction.

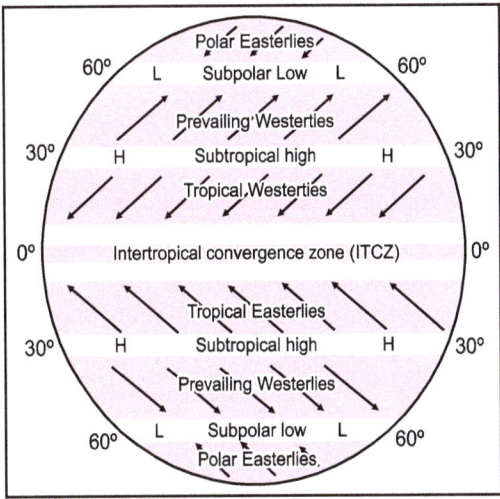

Fig. 13.7 : Types of winds.

- When they cross the open oceans, they pick up a lot of moisture. They bring heavy rainfall to the eastern coasts of continents lying within the tropics because they blow onshore.
- On the western coasts of continents, these Trade Winds do not bring any rainfall. It is because here there are 'offshore' winds or winds blowing just parallel to the shores, as they blow offshore.
- These winds blow from north-east to south-west in the Northern Hemisphere and from south-east to north-west in the Southern Hemisphere.
- Following the apparent movement of the Sun, the Trade Wind belts swing northward and southward.
- The North-east and the South-west Trade winds converge with each other near the Equator.

Westerlies

These are the winds blowing from the subtropical high pressure belt to the sub-polar low pressure in both the hemispheres. They are named Westerlies as they generally blow from the west.

Characteristics

- They are found in the latitudinal belt between 35° and 60°, North and South.

- Their direction is south-west in the Northern Hemisphere and north-west in the Southern Hemisphere.
- These winds are not as constant in strength and direction as the Trade Winds.
- The region of the Westerlies is characterized by frequent cyclones and anticyclones.
- They are also known as 'Anti-Trade Winds', because their movement is in the opposite direction from that of the Trade Winds.
- In the Northern Hemisphere, landmasses cause considerable disruption in the westerly winds.
- In the Southern Hemisphere, the Westerlies gain great strength and persistence because of the vast expanse of oceans in their belt. This made the ancient mariners to name them the 'Roaring Forties' (40°South), the 'Furious Fifties' (50° South) and the 'Screaming Sixties'(60° South).
- They become highly fluctuating towards poles.
- Since they blow from sea to land, they are moisture-laden and bring rainfall to the eastern parts of the continents in the Temperate Zone.

Polar Easterlies

The winds that originate in the North and South Polar Regions and blow towards circumpolar low pressure zone are known as the Polar Winds. These winds are called Polar Easterlies because they generally blow from the east.

Characteristics

- They are found in both the hemispheres in the latitude belt between 60° and 90°, North and South.
- They are deflected as much as 90° from their normal path due to the Coriolis Force.
- Their direction is north-east in the Northern Hemisphere and south-east in the Southern Hemisphere.
- In the Northern Hemisphere, due to local seasonal changes, these winds blow in several directions.
- In the Southern Hemisphere, these winds blow almost regularly.
- Colliding with the Westerlies, they give rise to temperate cyclones.
- Polar winds are extremely cold and dry as they come from the ice cap regions.

Periodic Winds

The winds that change their direction periodically due to changes in pressure and temperature are called as periodic winds. They blow in a particular direction during a particular period of the day or year. Land and sea breezes and monsoon winds are typical examples of periodic winds.

Land and Sea Breezes

These occur in the coastal areas due to the differential heating of land and sea.

- **Sea breeze :** During daytime, land gets heated faster than the sea. The warm air over the land rises, creating a low pressure. The hot air that rises over the land, is replaced by horizontal movement of a cool breeze from the sea, since sea is relatively cooler, and so a high pressure is created. The winds blow from sea (high pressure) to land (low pressure). These are called Sea Breezes. *(Fig. 13.8)*

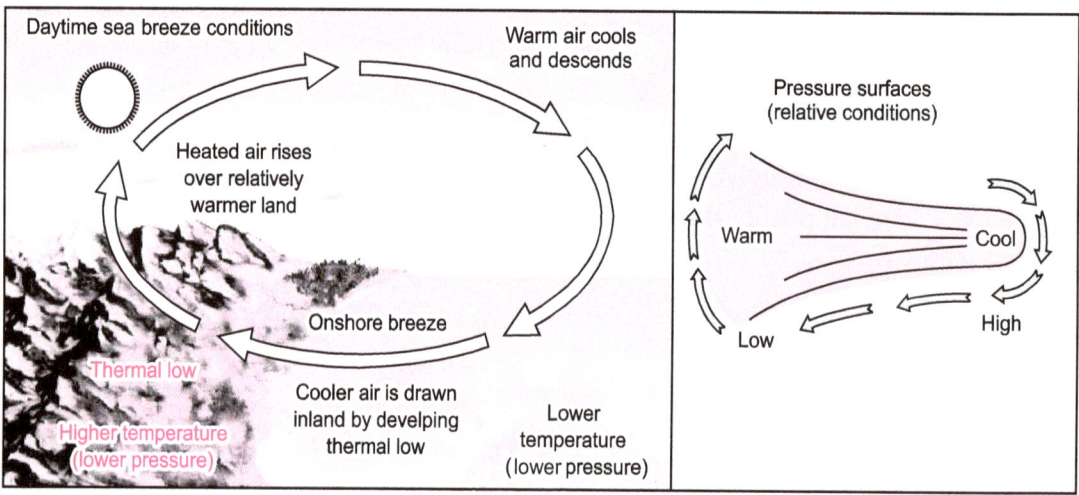

Fig. 13.8 : Sea Breeze.

- **Land Breeze :** During the night, land gets cooled faster than the sea. High pressure over the land causes the winds to blow from land to sea. These are called Land Breezes. *(Fig. 13.9)*

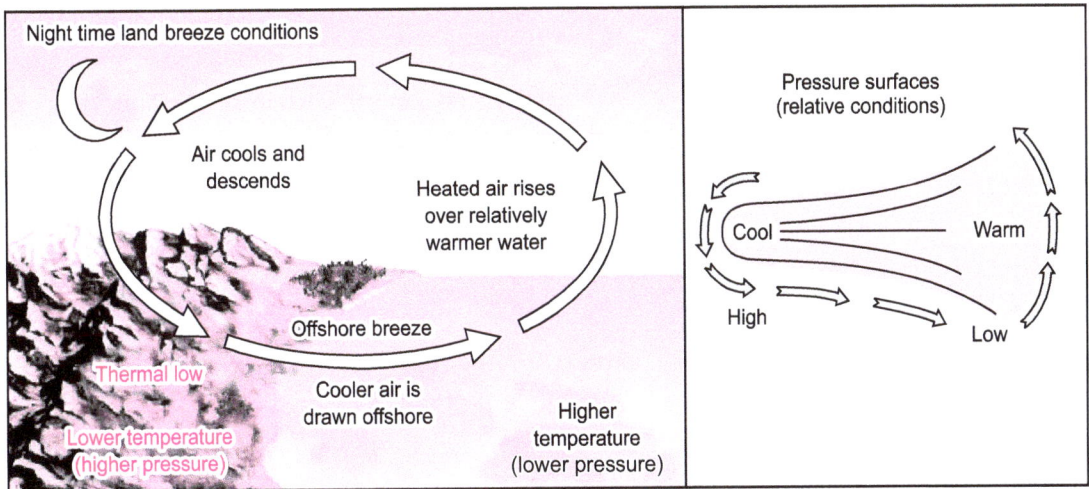

Fig. 13.9 : Land Breeze.

Monsoon Winds

Monsoons are seasonal winds, which blow from land to sea during winter, and sea to land during summer. They occur in the tropical regions and are particularly well-developed over South-west Asia and Northern Australia. They are divided into summer and winter Monsoons.

Summer Monsoon : In summer, the vast land-mass of Asia gets intensely heated creating a low pressure over the land. Over the adjoining Indian Ocean, land is comparatively cool, and a high pressure is developed there. The low pressure area attracts the south-easterly Trade winds of the Southern Hemisphere, which cross the Equator and enter the Northern Hemisphere *(Fig. 13.10)*.

they overshadow the Northeast Trade winds in this region.

- **Winter Monsoon :** In winter, the conditions are just the reverse. A high pressure develops over Central Asia upto the north-west Indian plain. *(Fig. 13.11)* At the same time, a low pressure develops over the Indian Ocean. As these winds blow from land to sea, they bring cold, dry weather. In some areas, while crossing the oceans, they gather moisture. Thus, they bring sporadic rainfall to the Tamil Nadu coast of India, the Vietnamese Coast and the west coast of Japan. The winter monsoons blow in a north-east direction. Hence, they are also called as North-East monsoons.

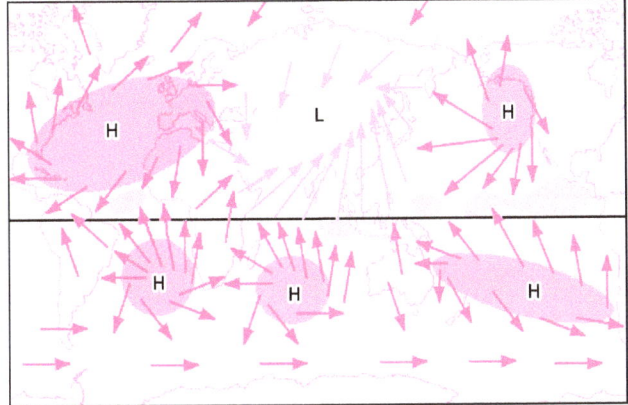

Fig. 13.10. : Summer Monsoon in Asia.

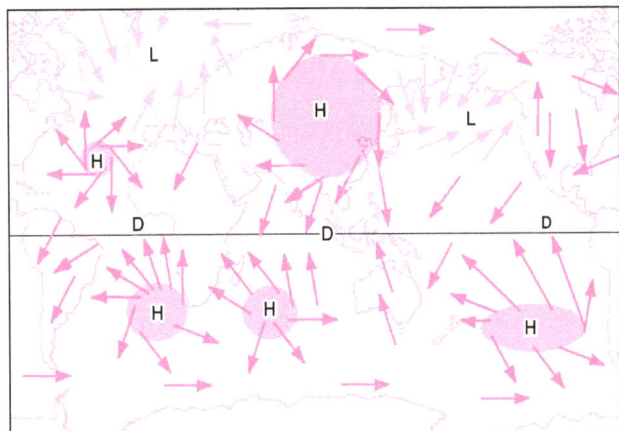

Fig. 13.11. : Winter Monsoon in Asia.

Local Winds

These winds blow over small areas for a short period. They are developed due to temperate depressions (systems with low pressure centers).

They are then deflected to the right due to the rotation of the Earth, and blow over the Asian sub-continent from the south-west. As these winds blow from sea to land, they bring heavy rainfall to Southeast Asia. These winds are so powerful that

They may be warm or cold depending upon the area from which they blow. *(Fig. 13.12)*

- **Depression Winds**

Hot Winds : Air is drawn in from the tropical regions in front of the depressions, giving rise to hot winds. These winds are usually hot and dusty, and become humid when they cross a sea surface. Eg. : Sirocco, Leveche, Khamsin, Zonda.

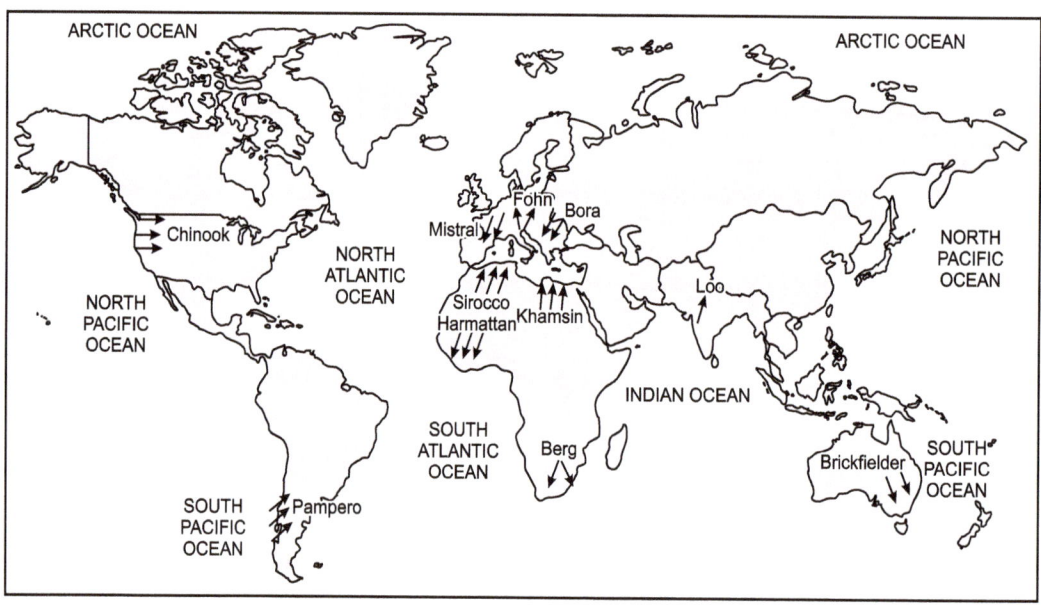

Fig. 13.12 : Some Local Winds of the World.

- **Cold Winds :** Air is drawn from the polar regions in the rear of the depression, giving rise to cold winds. These winds are very strong and gusty and bitterly cold. Eg. Mistral, Bora, Pampero, Boran.
- **Descending Winds :** These are warm winds, which descend from the mountain slopes onto the lowlands. *Ex.* Chinook, Fohn, Berg, and Nor'wester.

Some Local Winds Around the World

- **Loo :** A hot wind that blows usually in the afternoon in the plains of Northern India during May and June.
- **Foehn :** A warm, dry wind that blows down the leeward side of mountain ranges in Switzerland and Austria in central Europe.
- **Chinook :** A warm, dry wind that blows down the eastern slopes of the Rocky Mountains of North America.
- **Mistral :** A violent, dry, cold wind that blows from Central France and the Alps to the Mediterranean.

- **Pampero :** A dry, bitterly cold wind that sweeps through the Pampas of South America.
- **Brickfielder :** A hot and dry wind in the desert of Southern Australia that occurs in the summer season.
- **Sirocco :** A hot, spring time wind blowing from the Sahara in Africa to the Mediterranean Coasts.
- **Harmattan :** A dry and dusty wind that blows south from the Sahara into the Gulf of Guinea.
- **Khamsin :** A hot, dry and dusty wind that blows in Egypt, moving eastward along the Mediterranean Sea.
- **Bora :** A strong, cold and very dry north-easterly wind blowing along the eastern coast of the Adriatic Sea.
- **Berg :** A hot, dry wind in South Africa blowing from the plateau down to the coast.

Variable Winds

These winds blow for a short duration and change their speed and direction frequently, depending upon the change of atmospheric pressure. Cyclones and anticyclones are examples of variable winds *(Fig. 13.13)*.

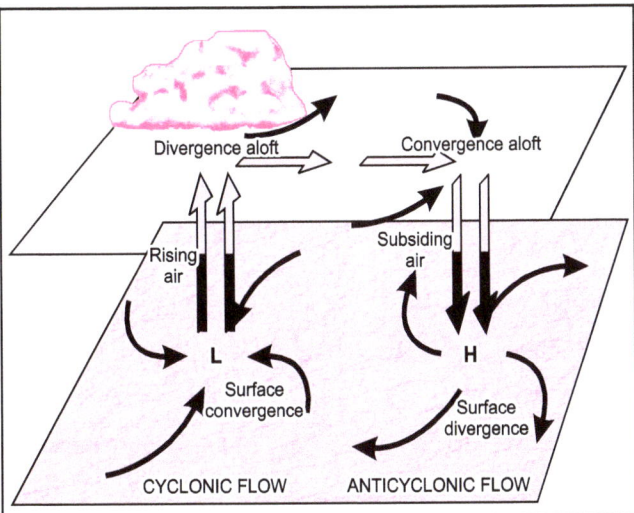

Fig. 13.13 : Cyclones and Anticyclones

Cyclones

It is a low pressure system with winds blowing anticlockwise in the Northern Hemisphere and clockwise in the Southern Hemisphere. Strong winds blow from all directions towards the center in a spiral motion. The eye of the cyclone is a region of calm weather formed at the center of a strong cyclone. These winds bring heavy rain and cause extreme damage to life and property. There are two types of cyclones :

- **Tropical Cyclones :** They originates between 8°N to 20° North and South of the Ocean in the Tropical region. High temperature and high humidity of the air is responsible for its origin. Tropical cyclones are common in the Bay of Bengal and Arabian Sea. In the South China Sea, they are known as Typhoons, in the Caribbean Sea, they are known as Hurricanes. They are known as Willy-Willies in the Northern Australia and Tornadoes in the Mississippi basin of USA.

Depressions : These are the cyclones of the temperate latitudes, especially in Europe.

Hurricanes : These are the tropical cyclones in the Gulf of Mexico, the Caribbean Sea and the western Pacific Ocean.

Cyclones : The tropical storms of the Indian Ocean are known as cyclones..

Typhoons : These are the tropical cyclones that originate in China.

Tornadoes : These storms are form on land very suddenly, looking like a twisting funnel of air. They are most common in the USA.

- **Temperate Cyclones :** They are of frontal origin where the convergence of warm Westerlies from the South and the polar Easterlies from the North take place. They are much larger than the Tropical cyclones and are more frequent in winters than in summer. They bring rainfall but are not destructive as Tropical storms, as the wind moves at a speed of only 30 to 50 km/hr.

Anticyclones

It is a high pressure system with winds blowing clockwise in the Northern Hemisphere and anti-clockwise in the Southern Hemisphere. Gentle winds blow out from the central high pressure area in all directions in a spiral motion. They bring fine weather and clear skies.

JET STREAMS

Jet streams are the high velocity winds, which can influence the weather and climatic conditions of the region. Two types of Jet streams that move at the Tropical belt of 30°North latitude are :

- **Westerly Jet Stream :** The Westerly jet stream which blow over the subtropical belt are intersected by the Himalayas, are able to bring the temperate cyclone from the Mediterranean region. It is responsible for the snowfall in the Himalayan region and rainfall in the North West of the Subcontinent.

- **Easterly Jet Stream :** The easterly jet stream helps to bring tropical monsoon causing rainfall in most parts of India.

Importance of Jet streams

Jet streams are important because :

(i) They contribute to worldwide weather patterns and as such, they help in forecast weather based on their position.

(ii) Jet streams don't generally follow a straight path — the patterns are called peaks and troughs — so they can shift, causing some to point at the poor forecasting skills of meteorologists.

(iii) It is also used for possible future power generation.

(iv) Jet streams act as an invisible director of the atmosphere. Jet streams are useful to form a border between hot and cold air.

(v) In addition, they are important to air travel because flying in or out of them can reduce flight time and fuel consumption.

- Atmospheric or air pressure is the force per unit of area exerted on the Earth's surface by the weight of the air above the surface.
- Air pressure is measured with a mercury or aneroid barometer.
- Factors affecting atmospheric pressure : (i) Altitude, (ii) Temperature, (iii) Water vapour, and (iv) Rotation.
- An isobar is an imaginary line drawn on a map joining all places of equal atmospheric pressure, at sea-level.
- Four major pressure belts on the Earth : (i) Equatorial low pressure belt, (ii) Sub-Tropical high pressure belt, (iii) Sub-Polar low pressure belt, and (iv) Polar High Pressure Belt.
- The main cause for the formation of the pressure belts is the uneven distribution of temperature on the Earth's surface, which can be attributed to the Earth's revolution around the Sun and the inclination of the Earth's axis.
- Wind is the air moving in a horizontal direction.
- Types of winds : (i) Permanent winds (Trade winds, Westerlies and Polar Easterlies), (ii) Periodic winds (Land and Sea Breeze, Summer and Winter Monsoon), (iii) Local winds, and (iv) Variable winds (Cyclones and Anticyclones).

A. Answer the following questions

1. What is atmospheric pressure?
2. What is the effect of rotation on pressure distribution over the globe?
3. How does humidity affect pressure distribution?
4. Name the major Wind Belts.
5. What are periodic winds?
6. Why are the summer monsoons known as South-West Monsoons in the Indian subcontinent ?
7. What do you understand by Local Winds? Give examples.
8. Name two types of variable winds.
9. What is a Cyclone?
10. What are Anticyclones? Why are they associated with dry weather?
11. How are cyclones named differently in different parts of the world?
12. What are the Jet Streams? What is the significance of Jet Streams?

B. Define the following terms

1. Isobars
2. Doldrums
3. Horse Latitudes

C. Distinguish between the following

1. Summer and Winter Monsoons.

D. Give reasons for the following

1. There is a seasonal shifting in pressure belts.
2. Temperature and pressure are inversely related to one another.

E. Diagram / Map work

1. Draw two labelled diagrams showing the pressure and wind belts of the Earth.

F. Board Questions

1. Which pressure belt is known as 'horse latitude'? Why?
2. (a) (i) Mention two factors that affect atmospheric pressure.
      (ii) Give one way in which Monsoon is similar to and one way in which it is different from Land and Sea breezes?
   (b) Give a reason for each of the following:
      (i) Trade winds move from South-east in Southern hemisphere.
      (ii) Chinook is popularly called snow eater.
   (c) (i) Name the four main pressure belts of the world.
      (ii) What is a front?
   (d) (i) Name two types of variable winds.
      (ii) Why are they known as variable winds?
      (iii) What is the importance of Jet streams in the climate of India?
3. (a) (i) What is the meaning of the term pressure gradient?
      (ii) How does it affect the velocity of wind?
   (b) How does the Coriolis Force vary from lower to higher latitude?
   (c) Distinguish between each of the following:
      (i) Permanent and Periodic Winds.
      (ii) Cyclones and Anticyclones.
      (iii) Land Breeze and Sea Breeze.
   (d) Give a reason for each of the following:
      (i) The Westerlies in the Southern Hemisphere blow with a greater force than those in the Northern Hemisphere.
      (ii) As we go higher atmospheric pressure decreases.
      (iii) Cyclones are frequent in summer in the tropical region.

CHAPTER 14

HUMIDITY PRECIPITATION

Humidity : Meaning and Difference between Relative and Absolute Humidity, Condensation–forms (Clouds, Dew, Frost, Fog and Mist). Precipitation–form (Rain, Snow, and Hail). Types of Rainfall–Relief / Orographic, Convectional, Cyclonic / frontal with examples from the different parts of the World.

Humidity is a measure of the dampness of the atmosphere, which varies greatly from place to place at different times of the day. There is a definite limit to the quantity of moisture (dampness) that can be held by the air at a specified temperature. On the other hand, Precipitation means 'condensation of atmospheric water vapour'. When the air is cooled below the dew point, the condensed water droplets forming clouds grows larger and cannot remain suspended in the air. This causes precipitation.

HUMIDITY

Moisture (dampness) is added to the atmosphere by the process of evaporation. Humidity refers to the amount of water vapour present in the air. It is inversely proportional to heat. Hotter the air, the more is the water vapour present in it. When the atmospheric pressure is low, water vapour is less. Humidity is responsible for most of the weather phenomena. In the absence of humidity, there would be no rainfall or any other form of precipitation.

Absolute Humidity

Absolute humidity refers to the total amount of water vapour present in a given volume of air. It is expressed in gram per cubic meter. Eg., If the absolute humidity is $10g/m^3$, it means that in one cubic meter of air, the amount of water vapour present is 10 g.

Relative Humidity

It refers to the ratio between the absolute humidity of a given mass of air and the maximum amount of water vapour that it could hold at the same temperature. It is expressed in percentage.

$$\text{Relative Humidity (R.H.)} = \frac{\text{Actual amount of water vapour}}{\text{Maximum water holding capacity}} \times 100$$

If the temperature of an air mass is 25°C, and if its relative humidity is 60%, then it can still add 40% more water vapour at the same temperature before it becomes saturated or Relative Humidity reaches 100%.

If a sample of air holds $20g/m^3$, at 25°C but has the capacity to hold $20g/m^3$ at this temperature; the Relative Humidity would be :

$$R.H. = \frac{20}{25} \times 100 = 80$$

Thus, the R.H. of air is 80% at 25°C temperature.

Relative humidity changes with an increase or decrease of air temperature, and addition or reduction of water vapour. When the air is fully saturated, relative humidity is 100%. Dew point is the temperature at which air gets fully saturated.

EVAPORATION

Vapour is the gaseous state of water. Evaporation is the process by which water is converted into water vapour by the heat of the Sun. Evaporation occurs at all temperatures, but it is more rapid at higher temperatures. Boiling is an example of evaporation at a particular temperature. It takes 600 calories of energy to convert 1 g of water into water vapour. Evaporation is a cooling process and it has a cooling effect on evaporating bodies. When rain falls through the dry layers, the surrounding air is cooled due to evaporation.

Factors Affecting Evapouration
Amount of Water Available

Rate of evaporation is greater over the oceans than over the continents.

Temperature

As the temperature of air increases, its capacity to hold moisture also increases. Hence, evaporation is directly proportional to the temperature of evaporating surface. Warmer the evaporating surface, higher the rate of evaporation. E.g., Clothes dry faster in summer than in winter.

Relative Humidity

The rate of evaporation is closely related to the relative humidity of air. Since the moisture holding capacity of air at a given temperature is limited, drier air evaporates more water than moist air.

Wind Speed

Evaporation depends on the wind speed as well. When the winds are light, a thin layer of air just above the surface gets saturated because of which the difference between the vapour pressure between ground and air is very small. This results in very low evaporation. On the other hand, when the wind velocity is high, turbulence is set up in the air. Moisture evaporated from the ground is mixed upward and the vapourpressure difference between the atmosphere and the surface remains large. Thus, the rate of evaporation is accelerated. Eg., Clothes dry faster under a fan.

Area of the Evaporating Surface

The area that is exposed to evaporation directly influences the rate of evaporation. Larger the surface area, greater is the rate of evaporation of the liquid. E.g., A spread out wet cloth dries faster than a folded one.

Air-pressure

Evaporation is also affected by the atmospheric pressure exerted on the evaporating surface. Lower pressure on open surface of the liquid results in the higher rate of evaporation. E.g., Pressure cooker.

CONDENSATION

Condensation is the process by which water vapour (gas) is converted into water (liquid) or ice. For condensation to take place, the atmosphere must be fully saturated *(Fig. 14.1)*. In other words, the maximum vapour pressure must have been reached. Also, the nature of water requires that

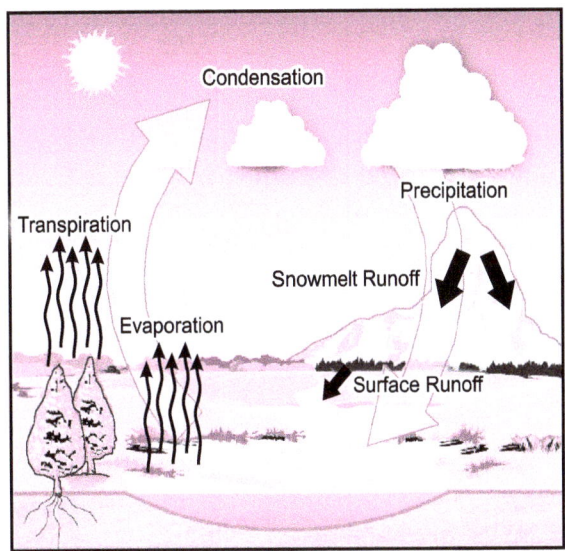

Fig. 14.1 : Water Cycle

there should be a surface upon which water can condense. This surface might be blades of grass, windows, etc. In the atmosphere, condensation often takes place around dust particles, or other particulates such as smoke, and even microscopic bacteria.

Condensation takes place under the following conditions:

- There is a high amount of water vapour in the atmosphere.
- Minuscule particles of dust, salt, and even smoke act as condensation nuclei.
- The temperature of air is below dew point.

Forms of Condensation

There are many different forms of condensation. Some are listed below:

Clouds

A cloud is a mass of small water droplets or tiny ice crystals that float in the air. It is composed of millions of little droplets of water or ice crystals when temperature is very low (below dew point). Clouds can form when water vapour becomes liquid, i.e., when humid air is cooled, water vapour condenses into tiny particles. It condenses around small particles such as dust or smoke. These impurities are known as condensation nuclei. The products of condensation are so tiny that they remain suspended in the air. As more and more droplets are added, the cloud grows in size. When the air becomes fully saturated (relative humidity 100%), the moisture comes down as rain.

Types of Clouds

Clouds are classified based on their shape (Cirrus, Cumulus, Stratus) and height (low, middle, high) at which they are formed. *(Fig. 14.2)*

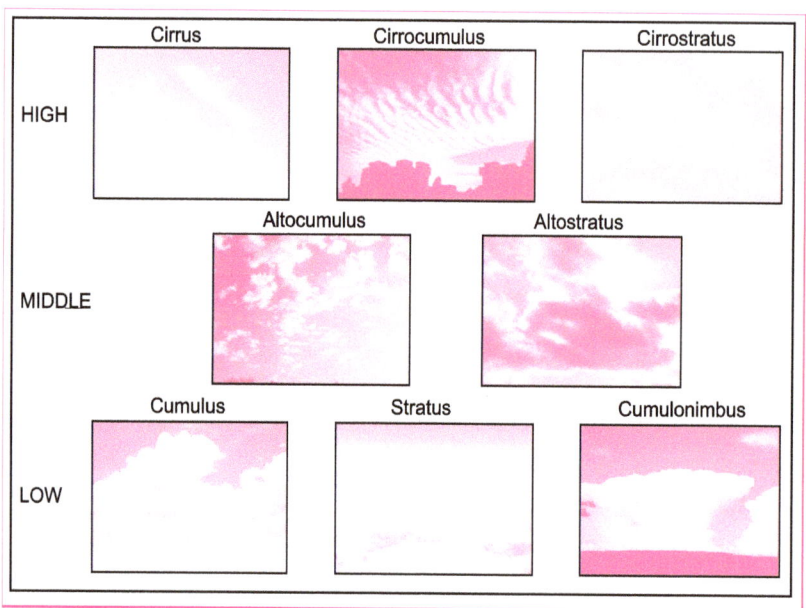

Fig. 14.2 : Types of Clouds

- **Based on Shape**

Cirrus : These clouds are wispy, feathery and composed entirely of ice crystals. They often are the first sign of an approaching warm front or upper-level jet streak.

Cumulus : These clouds are puffy, piled up with a flat base.

Stratus : These clouds are uniform and flat, producing a gray layer of cloud cover which may be precipitation-free or may cause periods of light precipitation or drizzle.

- **Based on Height**

Low Clouds : These clouds are not given a prefix, although their names are derived from 'strato' or 'cumulo', depending on their characteristics. Low clouds occur below 6500 feet, and normally consist of liquid water droplets or even super cooled droplets, except during cold winter storms when ice crystals (and snow) comprise much of the clouds. Eg., Stratus, Cumulus.

Middle Clouds : The bases of clouds in the middle level of the troposphere, given the prefix 'alto', appear between 6,000 and 20,000 feet. Eg., Altocumulus, Altostratus.

High Clouds : These clouds occur above about 20,000 feet and are given the prefix 'cirro'. They are mostly made up of ice crystals. Eg., Cirrus, Cirrostratus, and Cirrocumulus.

Fog

It is a collection of liquid water droplets or ice crystals suspended in the air at or near the Earth's surface. It is considered a low cloud. Unlike a cloud, the water vapour in fog comes from sources close to the fog like a large water body or a moist ground. Fog forms when water evaporates from a surface or is added to the air. This evaporation can be from the ocean or another body of water or moist ground like a marsh or a farm field, depending on the type and location of the fog. As water begins to evaporate from these sources and turns into water vapour, it rises into the air to form water droplets. These droplets then condense to form fog when the process occurs close to the ground.

Mist

This is formed in the same way as fog, but is less dense. If the visibility is more than 1–2 km, the fog is called as Mist.

Dew

Small drops of water can be seen on grass, plants and trees shining like pearls in the early hours of morning. These water-drops are called dew. Dewdrops are formed due to condensation of water vapours. During the night when the hot air comes in contact with some cold surface, water vapour present in it condenses on the cold surface in the form of droplets. Dew formation is more when the sky is clear and less when it is cloudy.

Frost

It occurs when a thin layer of moist air near the ground cools to below freezing point and immediately forms ice crystals, without first condensing as liquid (Dew). These crystals coat any cold surface including stone, grass, leaves, berries, and even cobwebs. Sometimes, frost is so thick and white that it is mistaken for snow.

PRECIPITATION

This is a very common phenomenon in the atmosphere of our Earth. This is the process by which water from the atmosphere falls on the Earth. It occurs when tiny particles of water join to form large-sized particles that become too heavy to remain suspended in the air. Moisture may be precipitated either in solid or liquid states. Rain, drizzle, snow, sleet and hail are the common forms of precipitation.

Forms of Precipitation

Rain

Precipitation that reaches the ground in liquid form is called Rain. It is the most common form of precipitation. Water droplets in a cloud collide and conjoin to form larger droplets. When the droplets become too large to be sustained on the air currents, they begin to fall down as rain. Rain drops are 0.5 mm to 6.35 mm in diameter.

Drizzle

Drizzle is a light rain precipitation consisting of liquid water drops smaller than those of rain, and generally smaller than 0.5 mm in diameter.

Snow

These are the crystals or grains of ice, which form directly from water vapour. It is formed in the extremely cold upper clouds. If the air temperature near the ground is below freezing point, snow falls, otherwise, it melts and comes down as rain.

Sleet

It refers to a mixture of snow and rain, as well as raindrops that freeze on their way down. Unlike snow, the raindrops pass through a liquid form before freezing. The result is that they are not light and fluffy.

Hail

Hailstones are frozen lumps of ice produced by thunderstorms. Deep within the cumulonimbus clouds, ice crystals form and begin to fall towards the Earth's surface. As this happens, wind gusts pick up the ice crystals pushing them back up high into the clouds. As they begin to fall, they continue growing in size. Again, a wind gust might catch the growing hailstone, pushing it back up high into the cloud. This process is repeated several times until the hailstone becomes so large that it is too heavy for the wind to carry, causing it to fall towards the Earth. They are very destructive and dreaded form of solid precipitation as they destroy agricultural crops and claim human and animal life.

Measurement of Precipitation

Rainfall is measured using an instrument called Rain Gauge. It has a large metal cylinder. A funnel is fitted on the top of a glass bottle kept in the cylinder *(Fig. 14.3)*. The cylinder is kept above the level of the funnel to ensure that rain is not splashed out of the funnel. A measuring tape is used to measure the amount of rainfall. The measurements are taken twice or thrice a day.

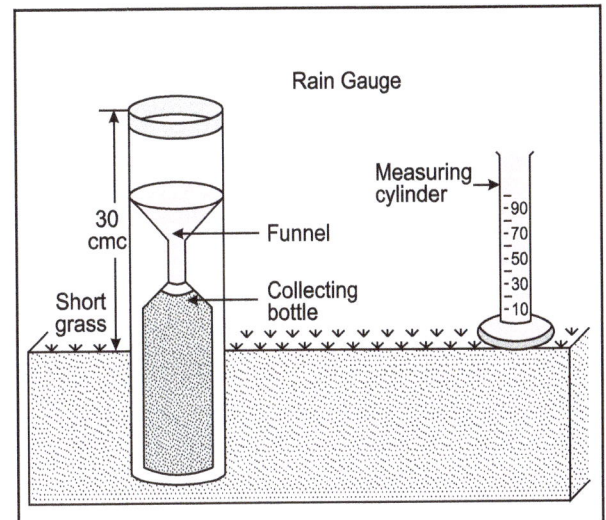

Fig. 14.3 : Rain Gauge.

Types of Rainfall

According to the way the cooling of the warm moist air mass takes place, rainfall can be of the following types :

Convectional Rainfall

This type of rainfall is caused by convection where the surface layer of the atmosphere is heated causing the moisture-laden air to rise. *(Fig. 14.4)* As it rises, it cools to form clouds. The unequal heating of the Earth's surface causes convection. The resulting condition is that, more widespread areas of colder air separate rising currents of warm air. The colder air slowly sinks to take the place of rising warm air. The condition of rising currents of warm air separated by widespread areas of slowly sinking air is referred to as convection. This is typical of thunderstorms during a hot summer. Convectional rain can also be found all the year round in regions near the Equator.

Examples : Areas such as South East England during warm sunny spells, the Amazon Rainforest, the United Kingdom does experience some convectional rainfall during the summer, particularly in the South East of the country, Coromandel coast in India receives rainfall in summer.

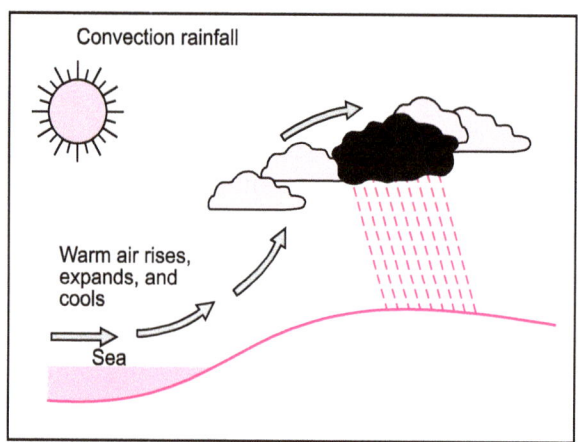

Fig. 14.4 : Convectional Rainfall

Orographic or Relief Rainfall

This type of rainfall occurs when an air mass is forced to rise over a mountain range *(Fig. 14.5)*. The air cools as it rises. The amount of moisture that air can hold decreases with decreasing temperature. So, the water vapour in the rising airstream condenses, and rain falls on the windward side of the mountain. The air descending on the leeward side contains less moisture, resulting in a rain shadow area where there is little or no rain.

Examples of Orographic Rainfall

Examples : Areas such as Eastern Brazil, East China, South Eastern United States, in the North-East of India the Himalayan barrier causes orographic rainfall.

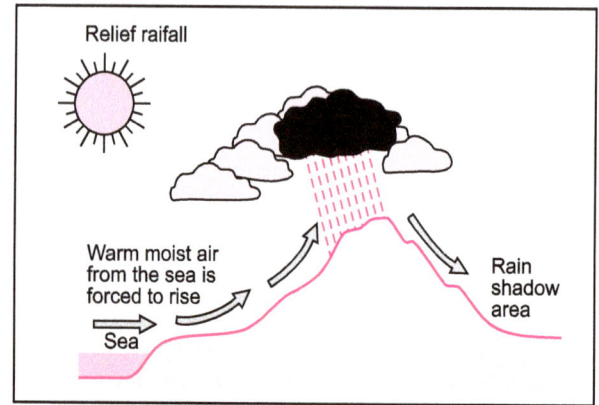

Fig. 14.5 : Relief Rainfall

Cyclonic or Frontal Rainfall

This type of rainfall is caused by depressions. Cyclonic rain originates where warm tropical air meets cold polar air. The warm air overrides the cold air. *(Fig. 14.6)* When contrasting air masses make contact, an abrupt zone or boundary is formed. This boundary is called a front and is accompanied by rather abrupt changes in temperature, pressure and humidity. When a mass of warm air moves into a region of cold air, the warm air overrides the cold air mass, forcing the cold air to retreat. This situation is called a warm front, which is characterized by several days of rain. A cold air mass moving into a warm air mass produces a frontal surface, which is more vertical than that of a warm front. This situation produces a cold front. Cold air masses advance rapidly and force the warm air mass upward where it becomes cooled. The movement of the air mass is rapid enough to produce cumulonimbus clouds. Rainfall is heavy but occurs for a brief duration.

Examples : Winter rainfall in Northwest India, in northwest Europe.

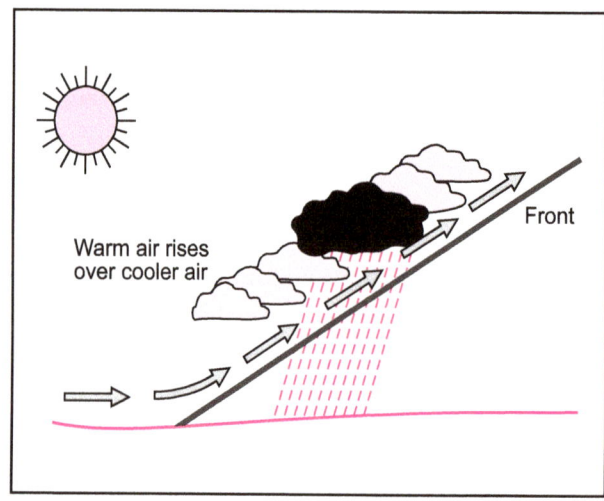

Fig. 14.6 : Frontal Rainfall

Isohyets

An *isohyet* is a line, which is used to connect the areas on the map receiving the same amount of rainfall. Hence, the distribution of rainfall on a map is shown with the help of isohyets.

World Distribution of Rainfall

Based on the total amount of annual precipitation, we can classify the world into the following four rainfall regions. *(Fig. 14.7)*

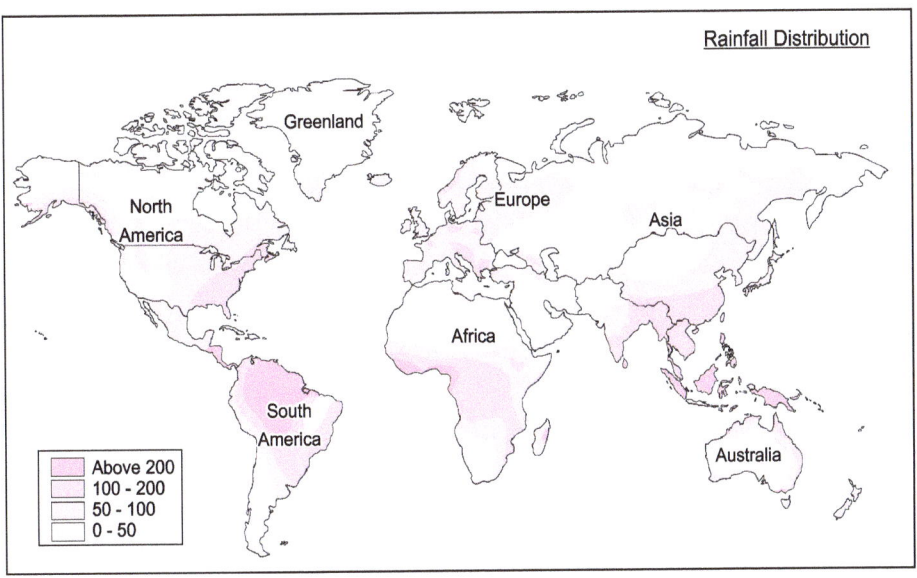

Fig. 14.7 : World Rainfall Distribution.

Areas of Heavy Rainfall

This belt includes regions receiving more than 200 cm of annual rainfall. The main areas are the Equatorial belt, the mountain slopes along the western coasts in the cool temperate zone, and the coastal areas of the monsoon lands. E.g., Amazon Basin, Congo Basin, Indonesia, Malaysia, Bangladesh, Western Coast of India, Northeast India, Southeast Asia, South China, Philippines, Sri Lanka, Northwest Europe, West Coast of Canada, Southern part of Chile, South Island of New Zealand and Tasmania.

Areas of Moderate Rainfall

This belt includes regions receiving 100–200 cm of annual rainfall. These areas lie adjacent to the areas of heavy rainfall. E.g., East Brazil and East China.

Areas of Low Rainfall

This belt includes regions receiving 50–100 cm of annual rainfall. The main areas lie in the central part of the tropical lands and in the eastern and interior parts of the temperate lands. E.g., Eastern parts of Canada, Central Europe, Argentina and south-eastern parts of Africa.

Areas of Scanty Rainfall

This belt includes regions receiving less than 50 cm of annual rainfall. The main areas are the rainshadow areas of mountain ranges, interior of continents, areas of high latitudes, western margins of the continents in the tropical areas and the arid deserts. E.g., Central region of North America and Central Asia, the Sahara Desert, Arabian Desert, Kalahari Desert, Atacama Desert, Californian Desert, Great Australian Desert, Greenland, Northern USSR and Northern Canada.

 SUMMARY

- Humidity refers to the amount of water vapour present in the air. It is inversely proportional to heat, the hotter the air, the more is the water vapour present in it.
- Absolute humidity refers to the total amount of water vapour present in a given volume of air.
- Relative humidity refers to the ratio between the absolute humidity of a given mass of air and the maximum amount of water vapour that it could hold at the same temperature.

- Evaporation is the process by which water is converted into water vapour by the heat of the Sun.
- Condensation is the process by which water vapour (gas) is converted into water (liquid) or ice.
- Forms of Condensation : Clouds, Fog, Mist, dew and Frost.
- The process through which water from the atmosphere falls on the Earth is called precipitation.
- Forms of precipitation: Rain, drizzle, snow, sleet and hail.
- Precipitation that reaches the ground in liquid form is called rain.
- Drizzle is a light rain precipitation consisting of liquid water drops smaller than those of rain, and generally smaller than 0.5 mm in diameter.
- Snow consists of crystals or grains of ice, which form directly from water vapour.
- Sleet refers to a mixture of snow and rain, as well as raindrops that freeze on their way down.
- Hailstones are frozen lumps of ice produced by thunderstorms.
- Rainfall is measured using an instrument called rain gauge.
- Types of rainfall : (i) Convectional, (ii) Orographic, and (iii) Cyclonic.
- An Isohyet is a line, which is used to connect the areas on the map receiving the same amount of rainfall.

EXERCISES

A. Answer the following questions

1. What are the factors affecting evaporation?
2. What determines the amount of water vapour in the air?
3. How is relative humidity determined?
4. Name four chief forms of condensation.
5. Describe the process of cloud formation. Name the types of clouds.
6. Mention the different forms of precipitation.
7. What is cyclonic rainfall?
8. Name two regions of heavy rainfall.
9. How is precipitation measured? Explain the working of this instrument.
10. Describe the world distribution of rainfall.

B. Define the following terms

1. Precipitation
2. Drizzle
3. Condensation nuclei
4. Evaporation

D. Give reasons for the following

1. Humid air is lighter than dry air.
2. Coasts receive more rainfall than the interior of the continents.
3. The windward sides of mountains receive more rainfall than the leeward sides.

E. Diagram / Map work

1. Draw labelled diagrams showing convectional, orographic and cyclonic rainfall.
2. On an outline map of the world, show the areas of heavy and low rainfall.

F. Board Questions

1. (a) Differentiate between Fog and Mist.
   (b) What is condensation ? Name two form of condensation.
   (c) (i) Name three different types of rainfall.
       Which is most common in the Equatorial region ?
       (ii) Why do polar regions receive very low rainfall ?
   (d) Draw a fully labelled diagram showing the occurrence of rainfall caused by a mountain barrier.

2. (a) Explain the following terms :
   (i) Humidity
   (ii) Condensation
(b) Distinguish between the following :
   (i) Snow and Hail
   (ii) Cloud and Fog
(c) Give a reason for each of the following :
   (i) The rain shadow areas are generally dry.
   (ii) Convectional rainfall occurs almost daily in the Equatorial region.
   (iii) Humidity in the air decreases with height from the Earth's surface.
(d) Study the diagram given below and answer the questions that follow :

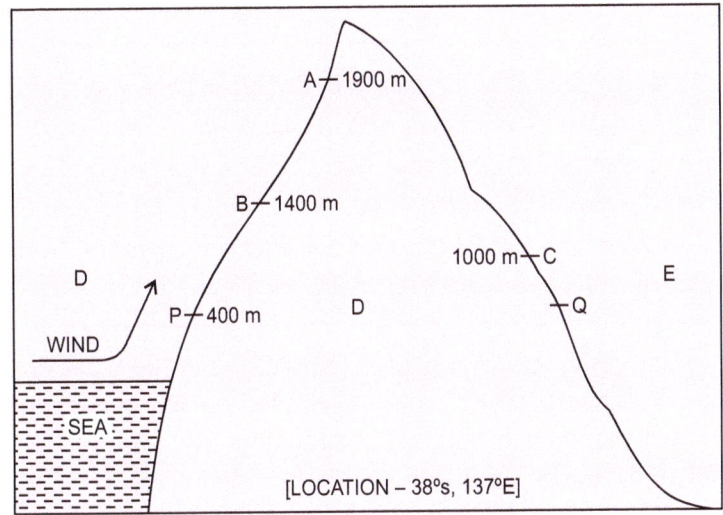

   (i) Write whether place P or place Q will have less rainfall?
       Give a reason for your answer.
   (ii) Write whether place B or place C will have lower temperature?
       Give a reason for your answer.
   (iii) Between position D and E in the given diagram :
       1. Which will be called windward side?
       2. Which will be called rain shadow area?

CHAPTER 15
POLLUTION AND ENVIRONMENT

Humidity : (a) *Types–Air, Water (Fresh and Marine), Soil, Radiation and Noise.*
(b) *Sources–Noise : Traffic, Factories, Construction Sites, Loudspeakers, Airports. Air : Vehicular, Industrial, Burning of Garbage. Water : Domestic and Industrial Waste. Soil : Chemical Fertilizers, Biomedical Waste and Pesticides. Radiation : X-rays; Radioactive Fallout from Nuclear Plants.* (c) *Effects–On the Environment and Human Health.* (d) *Preventive Measures–Car Pools, Promotion of Public Transport, No Smoking Zone, Restricted use of Fossil Fuels, Saving Energy and Encouragement of Organic Farming.*

The living organisms and their environment together constitute an ecosystem. Both the components of the ecosystem maintain a balance. Smaller, or to some extent, larger changes, occurring in the ecosystem gets adjusted by reciprocal changes in one or the other component. However, very large changes destroy the balance of the ecosystem and thus, the control of one component of ecosystem over the other gets lost. Environmental resistance to these changes fails to work, thus producing a state of disturbance. This disturbed state of the environment is called pollution.

POLLUTION

Pollution is defined as an undesirable change in the physical, chemical, or biological characteristics of air, water, and soil that may harmfully affect the life or create a potential health hazard to any living organism. In a broader sense, pollution means to destroy the purity of the ecosystem and cause instability, disorder, harm or discomfort to the environment and living organisms. In simple terms, pollution is the contamination of the environment as a result of human activities. Nearly everyone causes pollution. The sources of contamination that pollute the environment are known as pollutants. Pollutants are the components of pollution, which can be either foreign substances or naturally occurring environmental contaminants. The sources of pollution or the types of pollutants can be further classified as air, water, soil, radiation, and noise pollutants. The introduction of massive quantities of waste matter at any point in the biosystem overloads it, thus, disrupting the natural recycling mechanisms. In recent years, pollution signifies a wider range of disruptions to the environmental quality. Large numbers of people are continually taking initiatives to reduce pollution and clean up the environment.

Sources of Pollution and Major Pollutants

Pollutants are substances or chemicals, which change the natural balance of the environment, thus, causing pollution. In simple terms, a pollutant is a waste material that pollutes air, water or soil. Pollutants stimulate, initiate or terminate the vital metabolic reactions of the organisms. Pollutants are generally out of place resources that get accumulated in large quantities in the environment due to human activities. Three factors that determine the severity of a pollutant are: its chemical nature, its concentration, and its persistence.

Types of Pollutants

Pollutants are mostly divided into two categories :

Biodegradable Pollutants
- Domestic sewage, cloth, paper, wood, vegetable wastes, etc., comes under this category.
- They can be decomposed by micro-organisms.

- However, the decomposition becomes practically difficult when such materials accumulate in large quantities.

Non-degradable Pollutants

- Substances like aluminium cans, plastic, compounds of mercury, DDT, glass, etc., are non-degradable waste materials.
- These are neither decomposed by micro organisms nor do these materials break down by physical and chemical agents present in the environment.

Major Pollutants

There are many different kinds of pollutants, but some of the bigger problems result from :

- **Gases :** Carbon Monoxide (CO), Sulphur dioxide (SO_2), Hydrogen Sulphide (H_2S), Oxides of Nitrogen (NO, NO_2), Halogens (Chlorine, Bromine, Iodine, etc.), and to lesser extent Carbon dioxide (CO_2).
- **Particulate Matter :** Dust, Soot, Grit, etc.
- **Acid droplets :** Sulphuric and Nitric acid.
- **Metals :** Chromium, Lead, Zinc, Mercury, Nickel, Cadmium, etc.
- **Agrochemicals :** Insecticides, Pesticides, Herbicides, Weedicides, etc.
- **Organic Substances :** Benzene, Benzpyrene, Alkyl benzene sulphonates (ABS)
- **Fluorides**
- **Photochemical-Oxidants :** Ozone, Peroxyacetyl nitrate (PAN), Ethylene, etc.
- **Radioactive Substances :** Uranium, Plutonium, Strontium, Iodine, etc.
- **Noise**

Causes of Pollution

In the last 200 years several fundamental trends have been observed that became the major forces behind the different forms of pollution. However, three main causes are considered fundamental to pollution. *(Fig. 15.1)*

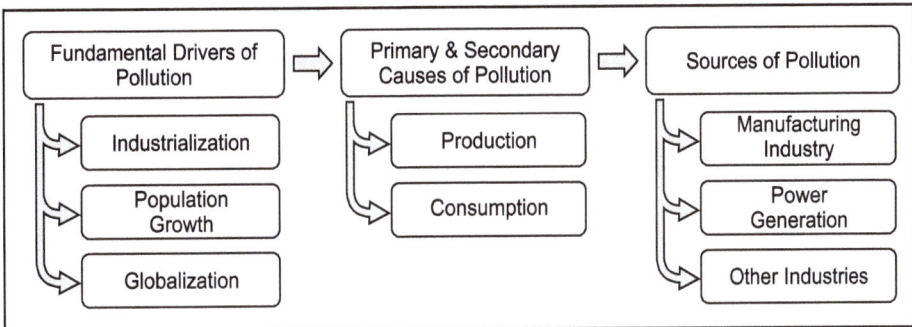

Fig 15.1 : Fundamental Causes of Pollution

Industrialization is the first fundamental cause of pollution. Among other things, industrialization led for the widespread use of fossil fuels (oil, gas & coal), which are now the main sources of pollution.

Population growth is the second fundamental cause of pollution. With population, numbers literally exploding around the world, the demand for food and other goods goes up. This demand is met by expanded production and use of natural resources, which in turn leads to higher levels of pollution.

Globalization is another major cause of pollution. Globalization has become an effective facilitator of environmental degradation. Developing countries usually have much looser laws on environmental protection, thus resulting in increased pollution rates.

TYPES OF POLLUTION

The increase in pollution over the years by man has caused severe damage to the earth's ecosystem. It is responsible for global warming, adversely affecting all the lives on earth. Over the years, there is an extreme increase in the rate of human diseases and death rate of various animals and plants on earth. This is all because of the pollution caused by human activities. There are many types of pollution that have the most hazardous affect on our lives. Pollution can be broadly classified into the five major types: air, water, soil, radiation, and noise pollution.

Air Pollution

Air pollution can be defined as the presence of one or more contaminants in the atmosphere, which may be harmful to the environment. It is perhaps the most common and the most dangerous type of pollution. It is one of the major problems that we are facing today. It involves the direct release of chemicals into the environment. *(Fig. 15.2)* The chemicals then become the part of the air around us that all the living things take in. Atmospheric pollution originates from all the parts of the world and travels around knowing no borders.

Fig. 15.2 : Waste Gases Produced by Factories

Sources

The sources of air pollution may be natural and man-made (anthropogenic). *(Fig. 15.3)*

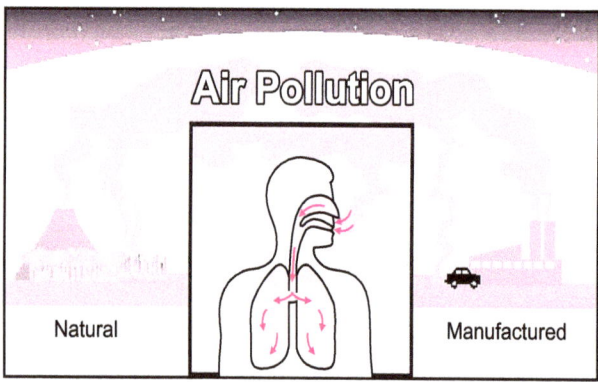

Fig. 15.3 : Causes of Air Pollution

Natural Sources

- These are volcanic eruptions, forest fires, sea-salt sprays, biological decay, photochemical oxidation of terpenes, marshes, extraterrestrial bodies, pollen grains of flowers, spores, etc.
- Radioactive minerals present in the earth's crust may be the sources of radioactivity in the air.

Man-made Sources

- These may include thermal power plants, industrial units, vehicular emissions, burning of fossil fuels, agricultural activities, etc.

- Thermal power plants are the major source of generating electricity and emitting pollutants like fly ash and SO_2.
- Fertilizer plants, smelters, textile mills, tanneries, refineries, chemical industries, paper and pulp mills are also the sources of air pollution.

Automobile Exhausts

- The toxic vehicular exhausts are a source of considerable air pollution.
- In big cities, around 60% of atmospheric pollution is caused by internal combustion engines like scooters, cars, buses, trucks, etc.

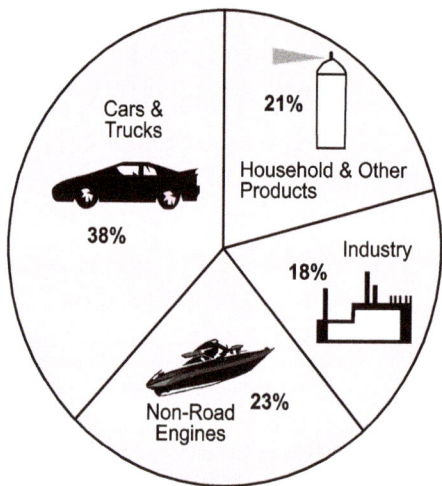

Fig. 15.4 : Sources of Air Pollution

- The two wheelers and three wheelers contribute about 60% of total Carbon Monoxide (CO) and 80% of total hydrocarbons.
- Jet aeroplanes, air conditioners, cleaning solvents and refrigerators release aerosols. These are chlorofluorocarbons (CFCs) and are known to cause serious damage.

Indoor Air Pollution

- In the underdeveloped and developing countries like India, most people use fuels like coal, dung-cakes, wood and kerosene in their kitchens.
- Complete combustion of fuels produces CO_2 which may not be toxic but incomplete combustion produces toxic Carbon Monoxide gas.
- Burning of coal produces sulphur dioxide.

Smog

- The combination of smoke particles and fog in the air is referred to as smog. Industries and vehicle pollution are usually the ones responsible for the formation of the smoke particles, while fogs are a result of air being cooled to the point where it can no longer hold all of the water vapour it contains.

Common Pollutants

Most air pollutants cannot be seen or smelled, but they still exist in dangerous proportions resulting in health hazards. The main types of pollution causing gases in the air include :

- Sulfur dioxide
- Nitrogen oxides
- Ammonia
- Carbon dioxide
- Carbon monoxide
- Volatile Organic Compounds (VOCs)
- Ozone
- Persistent Organic Pollutants (POPs)
- Airborne particles
- Toxic metals
- Radioactive pollutants

Effects

Air pollution has negative impacts on human health, crops, forests, fisheries, semi-natural ecosystems, and materials (e.g. corrosion), etc. It also causes a change in the worldwide climate. According to the WHO, air pollution is a major environmental risk to health and is estimated to cause approximately 2 million premature deaths worldwide per year. Air pollution is responsible for major health effects, can kill plants and trees by destroying their leaves, and can kill animals, especially fish in highly polluted rivers. Some major impacts of air pollution on environment are listed below :

Effects on Human Health

- High amount of CO in the air causes difficulty in breathing, suffocation, dizziness, unconsciousness and even death.
- Air pollutants, like cigarette smoke cause lung cancer, asthma, chronic bronchitis and emphysema.
- SO_2 causes constriction of respiratory passage.
- Ozone causes eye sore, and burning sensation in the chest of humans. It also breaks molecules of DNA causing skin cancer and cataract.
- Many other air pollutants like benzene (from unleaded petrol), formaldehyde, toxic metals and dioxins (from burning of polythene) may cause mutations, reproductive failure and even cancer.

Effects on Plants

- Hydrocarbons cause premature leaf fall, flower bud shedding, curling of petals and discolouration of sepals.
- Sensitive plants like alfalfa, barley, cotton, wheat, apple, etc., are affected by SO_2.
- Ozone is harmful to tobacco, tomato, bean, and pine plants.
- Peroxyacetyl Nitrate (PAN), a secondary pollutant can cause Hill reaction in plants by blocking photolysis of water and inhibiting photosystem-II.
- Arsenic poisons the plants useful for fodder.
- High concentration of fluoride causes chlorosis and necrosis of leaf tips and leaf margins.
- Air pollutants enter through stomata of leaves and destroy chlorophyll thereby affecting photosynthesis.
- Nitrogen oxides reduce the yield of crop plants.

Effects on Aquatic Life

Air pollutants combine with rainwater causing high acidity in fresh water lakes. This condition affects aquatic life especially fish communities.

Control

Efforts to prevent Air Pollution generally focus on both sources of air pollution and waste reduction, and on reuse and recycling of materials. Thus, cleaning and processing, using non-polluting technologies and materials, reduced generation of waste water, converting hazardous by-products to non-threatening forms, etc. are some of the ways to control Air pollution. The following measures can help to prevent air pollution :

- Reuse things like paper and plastic bags. This will contribute a lot towards reducing the effects of air pollution and global warming.
- Barium compounds should be added to the fuel to reduce the amount of exhaust gases.
- The amount and quality of exhaust gases should be controlled.
- Industries should be set up in specific areas.

- Techniques of filtration and purification of different gases by electrostatic precipitators should be adopted.
- Low sulphur emitting coal should be used in industries.
- Nitrogen oxides should be removed from the combustion process.
- Vehicular pollution may be checked by regular tune-up of engines, replacement of old vehicles, use of fuel efficient engines (to reduce CO and hydrocarbon emission).
- Non-conventional sources of energy may be taken up.
- Fumes from aerosols and chemicals like paint should be avoided to control air pollution.
- Maximum number of trees should be planted (plants absorb particulate pollutants).

Water Pollution

Around 75% of the earth's surface is covered with water and more than half of the total population of earth's species resides in water. Moreover, life without water is impossible. Water pollution is contamination of water by addition of foreign matter that deteriorates the quality of the water. Water pollution covers pollutions in liquid forms like ocean pollution and river pollution. As the term implies, water pollution occurs in the oceans, lakes, streams, rivers, underground water and bays, in small water bodies. It involves the release of toxic substances, pathogenic germs, substances that require much oxygen to decompose, easy-soluble substances, radioactivity, etc., that gets deposited in the bottom and their accumulations interfere with the condition of aquatic ecosystems. For example, the eutrophication, depletes oxygen in water bodies due to excessive algae growth resulting from enrichment of pollutants. Water pollution not only affects the aquatic life but also affects the whole food chain by also transferring the contaminants to the people feeding on these animals. The pollution of water has far reaching effects. It not only affects the availability of safe drinking water, but also harms the environment. Polluted water is not only unfit for drinking and for other domestic uses, but it is also not suitable for most industrial and agricultural use.

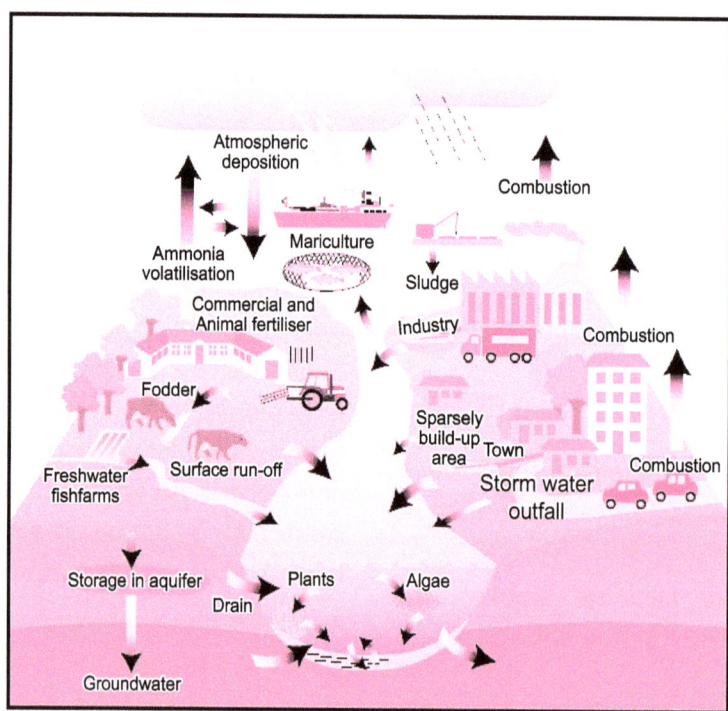

Fig. 15.5 : Sources of Water Pollution

Sources

Just like air and soil pollution, water pollution is caused by the direct interference of hazardous pollutants. The sources of these pollutants are the large industries and factories that dispose off their waste in lakes and ponds. Some common sources are listed below :

- **Sewage and Other Wastes :** Sewage is the water borne waste generated from home (domestic waste), animals and food processing plants. It includes human excreta, paper, cloth, soap, detergents etc. There is uncontrolled dumping of wastes of rural areas, towns, cities into ponds, lakes and rivers. The major constituents of sewage include organic matter and biological pollutants. The other pollutants include suspended solids, heavy metals, cyanide, oil, etc.
- **Household Detergents :** Household detergents are released into drains and ultimately are carried into lakes, rivers, etc. The major constituents of detergents include mostly compounds of phosphate, nitrate, ammonium and alkyl benzene sulphonate (ABS).
- **Industrial Wastes :** Industries release their wastes into lakes and rivers. A wide variety of both organic and inorganic pollutants are also present in effluents from breweries, tanneries, dying textiles, paper and pulp mills, steel industries, mining operations, etc.
- **Agricultural Wastes :** These include chiefly the chemicals used as fertilizers and pesticides (biocides). Their discharges reach into the water bodies and disturb the natural ecosystem.

Common Pollutants

Below is the list of most common water pollutants :

Organic Water Pollutants

- Insecticides and herbicides, a range of organohalides.
- Bacteria from livestock operations.
- Food processing waste including pathogens.
- Tree debris from logging operations.
- VOCs including solvents and hydrocarbons.
- Dense non-aqueous phase liquids (DNAPLs) such as chlorinated solvents.
- Detergents and chemical compounds found in cosmetics products.

Inorganic Water Pollutants

- Heavy metals
- Acidity caused by industrial discharges such as sulfur dioxide by power plants.
- Chemical waste
- Fertilizers from agricultural use
- Silt from construction sites, logging, slash and burn operation.

Effects

Polluted water breeds viruses, bacteria, intestinal parasites and other harmful micro-organisms, which can cause waterborne diseases like diarrhea, dysentery, and typhoid. Few other hazardous effects are :

- Water pollution affects both terrestrial animals like humans and marine animals.
- Water pollution has been related to events such as ocean acidification and coral reef bleaching. Polluted water is likely to cause waterborne diseases like typhoid, dysentery, gastroentritis, hepatitis, etc.
- Pollutants like heavy metals, pesticides, cyanides and many other organic and inorganic compounds reaching the water bodies are harmful to aquatic life.
- Mercury released by chlorine and caustic soda factory reaches man through food chain. It affects nervous system leading to death. In 1953, Japan suffered Minamata disease (Minamata Bay of Japan) due to Mercury poisoning.
- Lead is highly toxic to plants and animals.
- Liver and kidney damage, mental disorder, gastrointestinal trouble, residual paralysis are some important problems occuring because of the presence of lead in the water bodies.
- Excess Nitrate in drinking water causes blue baby syndrome or Methemoglobinemia by which it interferes with the oxygen-carrying capacity of the blood.
- Excess of fluoride (Fluorine) in drinking water causes dental fluorosis. Fluorides also destroy leaf tissues.
- Artificial fertilizers destroy the microbes of the top soil, so the soil easily becomes poor.

Control

There are several methods by which water pollution can be prevented or checked :

- The waste water should be treated before its discharge into lake or river.
- Primary treatment of sewage should be done, which includes physical processes like sedimentation, floatation, etc.

- Secondary treatment using micro-organisms in oxidation pond or activated sludge (soft mud) process is also very helpful.
- Algal blooms should be removed from time to time.
- In place of non-biodegradable ABS (for household detergent), degradable Linear Alkyl Sulphonate (LAS) may be used.
- Advanced treatment for nitrates and phosphate may prevent eutrophication.
- Judicious use of agrochemicals like pesticides and fertilizers may reduce their surface run-off and leaching.
- Use of nitrogen fixing plants may be practised to supplement the use of fertilizers.
- Integrated pest management process may be adopted in order to reduce reliance on pesticides.
- The nutrient-rich water may be used as fertilizer in the field.
- Separated drainage of sewage and rainwater should be provided to prevent overflow of sewage with rainwater.
- Treatment of factory effluents should be done in such a way that only harmless substances are released.
- Planting trees would reduce pollution by sediments and will also prevent soil erosion.
- Above all, enforcement of strict and appropriate laws should be made.

Types of Water Pollution

Thermal Pollution

Thermal pollution is the degradation of water quality by any process that changes ambient water temperature. A common cause of thermal pollution is the use of water as a coolant by power plants and industrial manufacturers.

Sources

A common cause of thermal pollution is the use of water as a coolant by power plants and industrial manufacturers. When water used as a coolant is returned to the natural environment at a higher temperature, the change in temperature decreases oxygen supply, and affects the ecosystem composition. Rainwater discharged from urban areas percolates to surface waters from roads and parking lots can also be a source of elevated water temperatures.

Effects

- The dissolved oxygen content of water is decreased as the solubility of oxygen in water is decreased in high temperature.
- High temperature becomes a barrier for oxygen penetration into deep cold waters.
- Toxicity of pesticides, detergents and chemicals in the effluents increases with increase in temperature.
- The composition of flora and fauna changes because the species sensitive to increased temperature due to thermal shock will be replaced by temperature tolerant species.
- Metabolic activities of aquatic organisms increase at high temperature and require more oxygen level falls under thermal pollution.
- Discharge of heated water near the shores can disturb spawning and can even kill young fishes.
- Fish migrations are affected due to formation of various thermal zones.
- When a power plant first opens or shuts down for repair or other causes, fish and other organisms adapted to particular temperature range can be killed by the abrupt rise in water temperature. This is also known as 'thermal shock.'
- Many aquatic species will fail to reproduce at elevated temperatures.
- A large increase in temperature can lead to the denaturing of life-supporting enzymes by breaking down hydrogen and disulphide bonds within the quaternary structure of the enzymes. Decreased enzyme activity in aquatic organisms can cause problems such as the inability to break down lipids, which leads to malnutrition.

Control

The following methods can be employed for control of thermal pollution :
- Cooling ponds
- Spray Ponds
- Cooling towers

Marine Pollution

Many toxic pollutants enter into the sea as a result of industrialization. In sea, the pollutants get diluted and the organic matter is further broken down in river water. Still many pollutants, specially the unmanageable ones, remain unchanged or are partially degraded causing marine pollution. Tankers and other shipping industries like petroleum, refinery, lubricating oil using industry, metal industry, paint industry, etc., automotive wastes refineries, ship-accidents, and offshore production adds to marine pollution. Oil in sea water can spread over a large area of the sea remain dispersed or gets adsorbed on the sediments. It can have adverse effects on marine life.

Sources

The main sources of marine pollution are :

- Rivers, which bring pollutants from their drainage basins.
- Catchment area i.e. coastline where human settlements in the form of hotels, industry, agricultural practices have been established. Oil drilling and shipment.
- Oil spills are another dangerous kind of marine pollutant. Oil spills adversely affect the environment and are responsible for almost all forms of pollution, such as air, water, wind, and land pollution. An oil spill is the release of a liquid petroleum hydrocarbon into the environment, especially marine areas, due to human activity. Oil spills mostly describe marine oil spills, where oil is released into the ocean or coastal waters. Oil spills may be due to releases of crude oil from tankers, offshore platforms, drilling rigs and wells, spills of refined petroleum products

Fig. 15.6 : Oil Spills Polluting the Marine Environment

(such as gasoline, diesel) and their by-products, heavier fuels used by large ships such as bunker fuel, or the spill of any oily refuse or waste oil. One obvious physical effect of pollution is the result of oil spills that are caused by ship collisions or other accidents. Another significant route by which oil enters the marine environment is through natural oil seeps. Oil spilled into the seas coats everything it touches. It fouls boat hulls, pier pilings, and shore structures. It spoils the beauty of the nature by killing fishes and birds, and makes beaches unusable. In addition to the physical effects, oil spills require costly cleanup operations.

Common Pollutants

- Sewage sludge
- Industrial effluents
- Synthetic detergents
- Agrochemicals
- Solid wastes
- Plastics
- Metals
- Waste heat released by industries

Control

Marine pollution can be controlled by undertaking the following measures :

- Toxic pollutants from industries and sewage treatment plants should not be discharged in coastal waters.
- Runoff from non-point sources should be prevented to reach coastal areas.
- Sewer overflows should be prevented by having separate sewer and rainwater pipes.
- Dumping of toxic, hazardous wastes and sewage sludge should be banned.
- Developmental activities on coastal areas should be minimized.
- Oil and grease from service stations should be processed for reuse.
- Oil ballast should not be dumped into sea.
- Ecologically sensitive coastal areas should be protected by not allowing drilling.

Soil Pollution

Soil is the upper layer of the earth curst which is formed by weathering of rocks. Organic matter in the soil makes it suitable for living organisms. Dumping of various types of materials especially domestic and industrial wastes causes soil pollution. Soil pollution involves the contamination of soil by the release of harmful substances into the soil. Unlike air pollution, which has a direct affect on human lives, soil pollution causes an indirect damage to humans and other animals. Soil remediation techniques are being developed and redeveloped by scientists in order to restore contaminated soil.

Sources

- Domestic wastes include garbage, rubbish material like glass, plastics, metallic cans, paper, fibres, cloth rags, containers, paints, varnishes, etc.
- Sewage tanks are harmful and toxic, which pollute the soil. The sewage sludge contains many pathogenic organisms, bacteria, viruses and intestinal worms, which cause pollution in the soil.
- Thermal power plants generate a large quantity of 'fly ash'. Huge quantities of these wastes are dumped into the soil, thus contaminating it.
- Industrial wastes also contain some organic and inorganic compounds that are refractory and non-biodegradable.
- Soil also receives excreta from animals and humans.

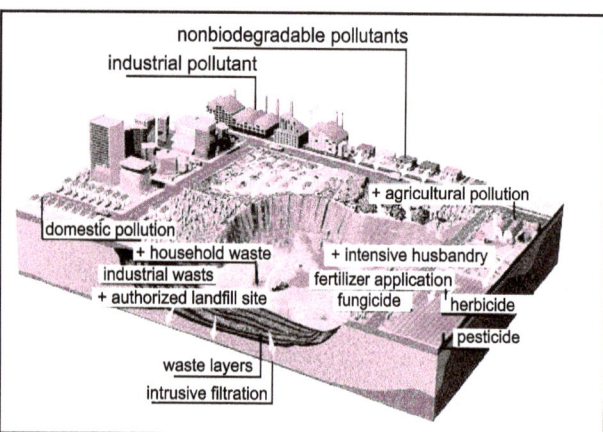

Fig. 15.7 : Sources of Soil Pollution

- **Urban and industrial wastes :** These wastes consists of medical waste from hospitals, municipal solid waste from homes, offices, markets (commercial waste), small cottage units, and horticulture waste from parks, gardens and orchards, etc. The urban solid waste materials that can be degraded by micro-organisms are called biodegradable wastes. For example, vegetable wastes, stale food, tea leaves, egg shells, peanut shells, dry leaves, etc. Urban and industrial development has also been associated with both physical degradation and chemical contamination of soils. Problems of physical degradation includes erosion, compaction and structural damage.

Common Pollutants

- By-products produced during the production of nuclear fuel.
- Nuclear power reactors.
- Use of Radionuclides in industries for various applications.
- Nuclear tests carried out by Defense Personnel.
- Disposal of nuclear waste.
- Uranium mining.

Effects

- Sewage and industrial effluents which pollute the soil ultimately affect human health.
- Various types of chemicals like acids, alkalis, pesticides, insecticides, etc., in the industrial discharges affect soil fertility by causing changes in physical, chemical, and biological properties.
- Some of the persistent toxic chemicals accumulate in food chain and ultimately affect human health.
- Pesticide persistence is toxic and causes bioaccumulation in food chain.
- Heavy metals used in pesticide survive for a number of years before they are degraded and hence, are responsible for much environmental problem, both for animals including humans and plants.

Control

- Effluents should be properly treated before discharging them in the soil.
- Solid wastes should be properly collected and disposed off by appropriate methods. Biodegradable organic waste should be used for generation of biogas.
- Recovery of useful products from the waste should be done.
- Effective persistence and toxicity of chemicals should be minimised.
- Alternative non-chemical strategies of pest disease and weed control should be adopted by which environmental problems may be alleviated.
- Biological methods of control should be implemented involving the use of predatory species to control the specific target organism.

- Cultural methods like use of tillage, crop rotation, etc., should be practised.
- Microbial degradation of biodegradable substances is also one of the scientific approaches for reducing soil pollution.

Radiation / Nuclear Pollution

Radioactive substances are present in nature. They undergo natural radioactive decay in which unstable isotopes spontaneously give out fast moving particles, high energy radiations or both, at a fixed rate until a new stable isotope is formed. These particles and its rays pass through paper and wood but can be stopped by concrete wall, lead slabs or water. Damage caused by different types of radiations depends on the penetration power and presence of the source inside or outside body. There are basically two kinds of radiation : Non-ionising – Ultraviolet radiation and Ionising – X-rays, V-rays, alpha and beta particles.

Sources

Damage caused by different types of radiations depends on the penetration power and the presence of the sources inside or outside the body.

Natural Sources
- Cosmic rays from outer space
- Radionucleotides in the earth such as Radium-224, Uranium-235, 238, Thorium-232, Carbon-14, and Potassium-40.

Anthropogenic or Man-made Sources
- Nuclear Power Plants
- Nuclear weapons
- Disposal of nuclear waste
- Uranium mining

Radioactive / Nuclear Fallout : It is the residual radioactive material propelled into the upper atmosphere following a nuclear blast, so called because it 'falls out' of the sky after the explosion and shock wave have passed. It commonly refers to the radioactive dust and ash created when a nuclear weapon explodes. This radioactive dust, consisting of material either directly vapourized by a nuclear blast or charged by exposure, is a highly dangerous kind of radioactive contamination. It can lead to the contamination of aquifers and devastate the affected ecosystem even years after the initial exposure.

Effects
- Both ionising and non-ionising radiations break the backbone of the chain(s) of DNA molecule.
- Chromosome is also affected by radiation. Single break, or two or more breaks in chromosome may take place. Stickiness or dumping of the chromosomes is another effect of radiation.
- Due to the effects of radiation, the cell may die before it divides, or there may be delay in cell division.
- Miscarriages, eye cataract, congenital abnormalities in birth, cancer of bone, thyroid, and breast cancer are some of the effects of radiation.
- Alpha particles have less penetration power but have more energy than beta particles. So, they become dangerous when they enter the body by inhalation or through blood. Alpha particles cannot penetrate the skin easily to reach the internal organs, whereas the beta particles can damage the internal organs easily.

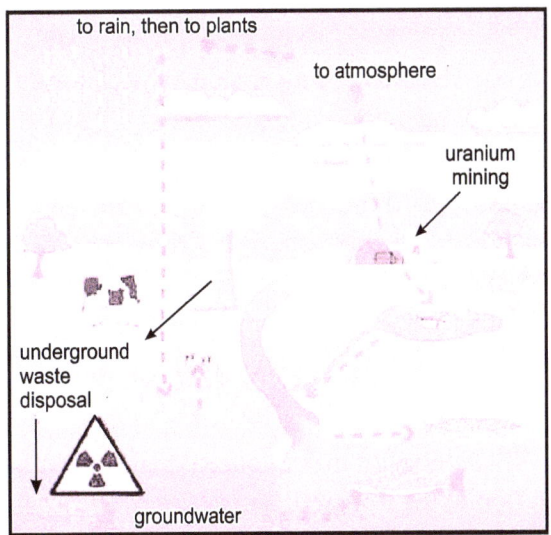

Fig. 15.8 : Nuclear Radiation Moving Through Air, Water, Plants, and Animals

- Non-ionising radiations i.e., Ultraviolet rays are also harmful to the organisms. UV-rays break DNA, RNA and Proteins.
- Longer exposure of skin to UV radiations causes a skin disease called Xeroderma Pigmentosum.
- Nuclear explosions are likely to cause heavy atmospheric pollution by dust and soot. This may result lowering of temperature to the extent that rivers, lakes, etc., would freeze.

Control

- Setting of Nuclear power plants should be carefully done after considering the long and short term effects.
- Proper and careful disposal of wastes from laboratory involving the use of radio isotopes should be done.
- Competition for acquiring nuclear weapons should be prohibited.
- Radioactive materials may be used for peaceful purposes.
- Appropriate safety measures should be taken for any leakage from nuclear reactors.

Noise Pollution

Noise is defined as an unpleasant sound that has an adverse affect on the human ear. Noise pollution is the increase in the rate of noise in the environment. Noise can be extremely dangerous. It penetrates into human mind and controls it. Too much noise leads to severe psychological illness and badly affects the behavior. It leads to hypertension, stress, aggression and annoyance. Moreover, it causes depression and forgetfulness. Noise pollution is caused by moving vehicles, man-made machines and loud music.

Noise levels can be measured by decibel method (decibel is the unit of sound):

Decibel, one tenth of a Bel, where one bel represents a difference in level between two intensities I_1, I_0 where one is ten times greater than the other. Thus, the intensity level is the comparison of one intensity to another and may be expressed:

$$\text{Intensity level} = 10 \log_{10} (I_1/I_0) \text{ (dB)}$$

Sources

We can classify major sources that lead to noise pollution to the following categories :

- Road traffic noise
- Air traffic
- Rail traffic
- Neighbourhood and domestic noise
- Incompatible land use
- Industrial noise

Common Pollutants

- Moving vehicles
- Man-made machines
- Loud music

Effects

Noise pollution has the following hazardous effects :

- Interferes with human communication as in a noisy area, communication is severely affected.
- Hearing damage: Noise can cause temporary or permanent hearing loss. It depends on the intensity and duration of sound level.
- Continuous exposure to noise affects the functioning of various systems of the body. It may result in hypertension, insomnia (sleeplessness), gastrointestinal and digestive disorders, etc.

Control

Following measures can be adopted to reduce the sources of noise:

- Noise making machines should be kept in containers with sound absorbing media. The noise path will be interrupted and will not reach the workers.
- Proper oiling will reduce the noise from the machinery.
- Use of sound absorbing silencers in transportation vehicles: Silencers can reduce noise by absorbing sound. For this purpose various types of fibrous material could be used.
- Planting more trees having broad leaves.
- Through Law : Legislation can ensure that sound production is minimized at various social functions. Unnecessary horn blowing should be restricted, especially in vehiclecongested areas.

EFFECTS OF POLLUTION ON ENVIRONMENT, HUMAN HEALTH, AND OTHER ORGANISMS

Pollution effects are indeed many and wide-ranging. There is no doubt that excessive levels of pollution cause a lot of damage to human and animal health, tropical rainforests, as well as the wider environment. The effects in living organisms may range from mild discomfort to serious diseases such as cancer to physical deformities, e.g., extra or missing limbs in frogs. Pollution not only causes physical disabilities but also results in psychological and behavioural disorders in people.

Effects of pollution are broadly classified into physical and biological effects that vary from mildly irritating to lethal. The more serious of the two are the biological effects.

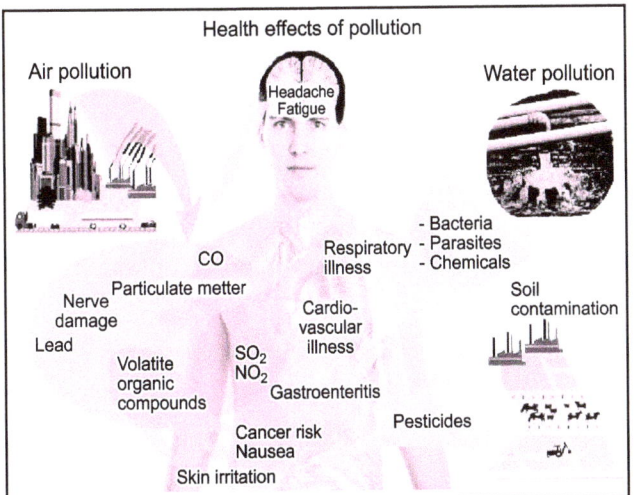

Fig. 15.9 : Health Effects that Arise from Different Types of Pollution

Physical Effects

The physical effects of pollution are those that we can see, but they also include effects other than the actual physical damage. Air pollutants damage a wide variety of materials. Burning oil and coal produce sulfur oxides, which cause steel to erode two to four times faster than normal. When combined with other pollutants (soot, smoke, lead, asbestos, and so on), sulfur oxide particulates cause corrosion to occur at an even faster rate. Air pollutants speeds the erosion of statues and buildings, which in some instances, destroys works of art.

Biological Effects

The most serious result of pollution is its harmful biological effects on human health and on the food chain of animals, birds, and marine organism. Pollution can destroy vegetation that provides food and shelter. It can seriously disrupt the balance of nature, and, in extreme cases, can cause the death of humans. Pesticides, which include herbicides and insecticides, can damage crops, kill vegetation, and poison birds, animals, and fishes. Most pesticides are non-selective, they kill or damage life forms other than those intended. For example, pesticides used in an effort to control or destroy undesirable vegetation and insects often destroy birds and small animals. Some life forms develop immunity to pesticides used to destroy them. When that happens, we develop more potent chemicals and the cycle repeats itself. The widespread use of pollutants, such as soil, chemicals, and fertilizers, pollutes our waterways. The biological effect of water pollution is its danger to our water supplies. Water pollutants are also dangerous to all forms of marine life. Oil is a specially harmful pollutant. It kills surface swimming animals and sea birds, and once it settles on the bottom, it harms the shell fish and other types of marine life.

The following are some of the major harmful effects of pollution :

- Loss of raw materials.
- Unnecessary expenditure on pollution control.
- Health hazards due to pollution related diseases like asthma, cancer, etc.
- Increase in death rate.
- Decrease in the working efficiency of man.
- Damage to crops.
- Damage to buildings, metals, cloth, paints, varnishes, etc.
- Environment of earth becoming unfit for living.

PREVENTIVE MEASURES

The aim of preventive measures is to reduce the pollution. The following measures that can be adopted to reduce the pollution :

- Carpool
- Promotion of public tranport
- No smoking zone
- Restricted use of fossil fuels
- Saving energy
- Encouragement of organic farming

Carpooling

Carpooling or car sharing means a number of people using a single car for their journey or travel in stead of using individual cars. This approach reduces fuel consumption thereby reducing the pollution as well as reduces individual cost of travel. It is an eco-friendly approach of the urban life.

Carpooling reduces emission of carbon dioxide, eliminates stress of driving for some people, reduces traffic congestion on the roads, helps Municipality Corporation for better car parking management. Carpooling is often being used by school children and office goers. Use of Odd and Even number vehicle in alternate day as tried out in the city of Delhi, is another way to reduce pollution and traffic congestion.

Promotion of Public Transport

Public transport is one of the best measures to reduce pollution arising out of vehicles as well to reduce vehicles on road, thus reducing traffic congestion. This is an alternative means of transport to private vehicles and the authority must improve the same in all cities and metros. People should also be encouraged to use the same as a means of primary mode of travel.

No Smoking Zone

Smoking is another means of increasing pollution affecting public health. This not only affects the smokers but also the people around them who are not smoking. The smoking causes heart disease, lung cancer, chronic bronchitis, asthma, etc.

The ill-effects can be eliminated or minimized if No Smoking Zones are created or marked. The closed spaces like offices, hospitals, restaurants, public malls, public transport, busy crossings, etc. must include these zones and proper and adequate sign should be put up. The law on prohibiting smoking in public places should be strictly followed.

Restricted Use of Fossil Fuels

Fossil fuels comprising of coal, natural gas and mineral oil are the main sources of energy. When fossil fuel is burnt to derive energy, it emits carbon dioxide in large quantities. Carbon dioxide absorbs heat from the atmosphere preventing terrestrial radiation to go back to space and this causes global warming. When carbon dioxide concentration exceed beyond set standards, it can lead to kidney damage, asphyxiation, coma and deduces development of RBC and causes pulmonary malfunction.

Acid deposition is caused mainly by sulphur oxide and nitrogen oxide from the thermal power plants, factories and automobiles that use coal or mineral oil. Such deposition is responsible for acid rain which damages vegetation, monuments, water bodies and the soil.

Restricted use of energy or saving of energy will reduce consumption of fossil fuel. This can be achieved by :

- Carpooling, fuel efficient cars and vehicles in automobiles.
- Use of electro-static precipitator in factories and power plants which use coal as fuel.
- Use of natural gas and nuclear power to reduce emmisions
- Use of low pollutant fuel like CNG gas which reduces in sulphur, dust and ash content of coal

Saving Energy

Saving energy will help to reduce consumption of fossil fuel. Alternatively, use of renewable energy will help to save energy thereby to save natural resources. Alternative energy can be obtained from the following:

- **Solar Energy** : This is a great source of energy which can be generated and converted into electricity without causing any pollution. Tropical countries like India, Pakistan, Bangladesh, USA, European countries, African countries, Australia etc. can generate such energy in abundance.

  Solar energy can be used for lighting, water heating, cooking etc. as well as can be put through in the power grid.

- **Wind Energy** : This is also another source to generate electricity which can be used for various purposes. Wind is used to drive a wind mill and run electrical generators. Asia's largest wind firm of 10 megawatt is located in Gujarat and is being used to pump drinking water.

- **Biogas** : It is the most important energy in rural areas. Biogas plants produce enriched fertilizer as a by-product. The use of biogas improves sanitation and provide smokeless and efficient cooking fuel. It can also be used for power generation and lighting.

Encouragement of Organic Farming

Organic farming is a technique which involves production of food, feed and fiber in natural ways without the use of synthetic substances. It aims at increasing productivity while reducing the production cost and minimizing the environmental impact of farming.

Organic farming is a system of cultivation with the help of integrated pest management, integrated nutrient supply and integrated natural resources management systems.

Organic farming aims at mutually keeping relationships between agricultural productivity and conservation of nature. The local people have developed such knowledge from thousands years of living in harmony with the nature. It aims to bring together agricultural development and conservation of biodiversity in the same landscapes. It relies on ecologically balanced agricultural principles like usage of organic waste, biological pest control, green manure, crop rotation, mineral and rock additives etc.

LOCAL AND GLOBAL ISSUES RELATED TO POLLUTION (CASE STUDIES)

Bhopal Gas Tragedy

Hundreds of people have died from the effects of toxic gases which leaked from a chemical factory near the central Indian city of Bhopal. The accident happened in the early hours of December 3rd, at the American-owned Union Carbide Pesticide Plant three miles (4.8 km) from Bhopal. In the early morning hours of December 3rd, 1984, a poisonous grey cloud (forty tons of toxic gases) from Union Carbide India Limited (UCIL's) pesticide plant at Bhopal spread throughout the city. Water carrying catalytic material had entered Methyl Isocyanate (MIC) storage tank No. 610. What followed was a nightmare. The killer gas spread through the city, sending residents scurrying through the dark streets. No alarm ever sounded a warning and no evacuation plan was prepared. When victims arrived at hospitals breathless and blind, doctors did not know how to treat them, as UCIL had not provided emergency information. It was only when the sun rose the next morning that the magnitude of the devastation was clear. Dead bodies of humans and animals blocked the streets, leaves turned black, and the smell of burning chilli peppers lingered in the air. Estimates suggested that as many as 10,000 may have died immediately and 30,000 to 50,000 were too ill to ever return to their jobs. The leakage caused many short term health effects in the surrounding areas. Apart from MIC, the gas cloud may have contained phosgene, hydrogen cyanide, carbon monoxide, hydrogen chloride, oxides of nitrogen, monomethyl amine (MMA) and carbon dioxide, either produced in the storage tank or in the atmosphere. The gas cloud was composed mainly of materials denser than the surrounding air, stayed close to the ground and spread outwards through the surrounding community. The initial effects of exposure were coughing, vomiting, severe eye irritation and a feeling of suffocation.

Chernobyl Russian Nuclear Power Plant Explosion

The Chernobyl Power Plant in Chernobyl, Ukraine was nuclear fission powered and was capable of producing four times the power output of the Huntly power station. However at 1:23 am on the 26th of April, 1986, a failed reactor test resulted in the world's worst nuclear disaster, subsequently displacing over 200,000 people, and instantly killing a further 54 residents and emergency workers. The Chernobyl Nuclear Power Station included four nuclear reactors, each capable of producing one gigawatt of electric power. At the time of the accident, the four reactors produced about 10 percent of the electricity used in Ukraine. On April 26th, 1986, the operating crew planned to test whether the Reactor No. 4 turbines could produce enough energy to keep the coolant pumps running until the emergency diesel generator was activated in case of an external power loss. During the test, power surged unexpectedly, causing an explosion and driving temperatures in the reactor to more than 2,000 degree Celsius melting the fuel rods, igniting the reactor's graphite covering, and releasing a cloud of radiation into the atmosphere. The precise causes of the accident are still uncertain, but it is generally believed that the series of incidents that led to the explosion, fire and nuclear melt down at Chernobyl was caused by a combination of reactor design flaws and operator error. The number of people that will ultimately be affected by this disaster is estimated to be around 11 times that of the cancer deaths expected from the combined bombings of the Hiroshima and Nagasaki in 1945. The biggest challenge facing communities still coping with the fallout of Chernobyl is the psychological damage to 5 million people in Belarus, Ukraine and Russia.

SUMMARY

- Pollution is an undesirable change in the physical, chemical, or biological characteristics of air, water, and soil that adversely affects the ecosystem.
- A pollutant is any substance that negatively impacts the environment or organisms that live within the affected environment.
- The ultimate cause of pollution is human activity itself. However, industrialization, population growth, and globalization are the major causes of environmental pollution.
- Air pollution is the contamination of air by the discharge of harmful substances that causes health problems.
- Water pollution is contamination of water by foreign matter that deteriorates the quality of the water.
- Marine pollution may cause oxygen depletion and severely affect the health of whole ecosystems.
- The earth has suffered massive environmental degradation with the advent of industrialization resulting in soil pollution.
- The radioactive pollution is defined as the physical pollution of air, water, and soil by radioactive materials.
- Noise pollution typically refers to human-made noises that are either very loud or disruptive in manner.
- Maximum noise pollution occurs due to one of modern science's best discoveries the motor vehicle, which is responsible for about 90% of all unwanted noise worldwide.
- The effects of all kinds of pollution in living organisms may range from mild discomfort to serious diseases.
- Excessive levels of pollution are causing a lot of damage to human and animal health, tropical rainforests, as well as the wider environment.
- Pollution not only causes physical disabilities but also results in psychological and behavioural disorders in people.
- Preventive measures towards pollution include : carpool, public transport, no smoking zone, restricted use of fossil fuels, saving energy and encouragement of organic farming.

A. Answer the following questions

1. Define pollution? Name the different kinds of pollution?
2. Describe the main types of pollution.
3. What are the causative agents of pollution?
4. What do you mean by pollutant? Name some common environmental pollutants.
5. Describe air pollution and its causative agents.
6. What is Smog? How is it harmful?
7. What is water pollution? Describe its various types.
8. What is thermal pollution? How does it cause pollution?
9. Define marine pollution.
10. What is soil pollution? Describe its control measures.
11. Describe noise pollution? What are the main sources of noise pollution?
12. What preventive measures would you adopt to control noise pollution?
13. What is radioactive pollution? Describe its effects on environment.
14. Describe nuclear fallout.
15. Write a note on oil spills.
16. Describe the health effects of pollution.
17. Mention the preventive measures that can be used to lessen pollution levels.
18. How can consumption of fossil fuel be reduced? List out the alternative sources of energy.
19. Write a note on Bhopal Gas Tragedy.
20. How was the Chernobyl Tragedy caused?
21. What safety measures should be undertaken to control pollution?

22. What is organic farming? State the characteristic features of organic farming.
23. How are the effects of pollution devastating?

B. Define the following terms
1. Sewage
2. Eutrophication
3. Urban and Industrial wastes
4. Nuclear fallout
5. Decibel
6. Oil spill
7. Pollutant
8. Ecosystem
9. Organic farming

C. Distinguish between the following
1. Pollution and Pollutant.
2. Biodegradable and Non-degradable pollutants.
3. Natural and Man-made sources.
4. Indoor pollution and Outdoor pollution.
5. Physical effects of Pollution and Biological effects of pollution.
6. Water pollution and Soil pollution.
7. Solar energy and Wind energy.

D. Give reasons
1. Pollution destroys the purity of the ecosystem.
2. Pollutants affect the vital metabolic reactions of the organisms.
3. Population growth is a fundamental pollution cause.
4. Water pollution affects the fish communities.
5. Soil pollution decreases the yield of crops.
6. Oil ballast should not be dumped into the sea.
7. More and more trees should be planted.
8. Carpooling is an eco-friendly approach.

E. Board Questions
1. (a) What do you understand by 'SMOG'? Why is it dangerous?
   (b) Give a reason for each of the following:
      (i) Vehicles are the main source of air pollution.
      (ii) The use of CFCs is the main cause of the depletion of the ozone layer.
   (c) (i) What are the sources of radioactive pollution?
      (ii) How does radioactive pollution harm the environment?
   (d) (i) Mention any two processes utilise by organic farming.
      (ii) Give two points why organic farming is important.
2. (a) (i) How does excessive use of chemical fertilizers harm the environment?
      (ii) What may be done to reduce such pollution?
   (b) (i) How are automobiles responsible for creating air pollution?
      (ii) What may be done to reduce the pollution caused by vehicles?
   (c) How are industries responsible for creating water pollution?

CHAPTER 16
NATURAL REGIONS OF THE WORLD

Humidity : *Location, Area, Climate, Natural Vegetation and Human Adaptation. Equatorial region, Tropical Grasslands, Tropical Deserts, Tropical Monsoon, Mediterranean, Temperate Grasslands, Taiga and Tundra.*

Have you ever wondered why one area of the world is a desert, another a grassland, and another a rainforest? Why there are different forests and deserts with different types of life in each area? The answer is *climate*.

Climate is the characteristic condition of the atmosphere near the Earth's surface at a certain place on earth. It is the long-term weather of that area, which includes the region's general pattern of weather conditions, seasons and weather extremes like hurricanes, droughts, or rainy periods. Two of the most important factors determining an area's climate are air temperature and precipitation.

A *natural region* is a group of areas where the conditions of relief, temperature, rainfall, natural vegetation and consequently the cultural environment are more or less similar. The particular set of climatic conditions is called a *climatic type*.

We may divide the world into a number of major natural regions whose physical features, rock structure, soils, climate and resultant products and human activities are similar over large areas. Plant and animal life are adapted to their surroundings. Man too, has adjusted himself to his environment, though in many cases the appearance and habits of people living in similar natural regions differ greatly. Natural regions would, of course, exist whether man existed or not, but no study of them can be considered complete without some knowledge of the activities of their human inhabitants.

The basic factor for dividing the world into major natural regions is climate. The climate influences soil, flora, fauna, and the vegetation of the region.

The climatic regions are named after the vegetation type prevalent there. The relation between climate and human activities is especially striking in regions where the primary activities like agriculture, animal husbandry and forestry are dominant. Each climatic type is suitable for the cultivation of certain crops, which can tolerate a certain range of temperature and need a certain minimum water supply. Thus, the major natural regions are named after the climatic or vegetation type.

It should be noted that there are no fixed or well-defined boundaries between the major types of climate. All climatic boundaries are transitional in nature. They exist in the form of broad transition zones, across which the characteristics of one climatic type gradually merge into its neighbouring type. However, a careful study of each climatic type gives a generalized idea of associated aspects like vegetation, animal life, soils or landforms of a region.

Every natural region has a combination of different climatic elements. Such classification of the combinations of these elements is known as *climatic classification*, with each type having some common characteristics. The climate zones are based on the following factors:

- The temperature, pressure, winds and humid conditions are equally responsible for the difference in human response under different climatic types.
- Landforms differ in different climatic regions.

- Soils too vary considerably as climatic conditions influence the weathering of rocks.
- Wildlife and vegetation greatly vary from one climate type to another.
- Water run-off in rivers and streams differ considerably.
- Varying climatic conditions support different cropping seasons and methods.

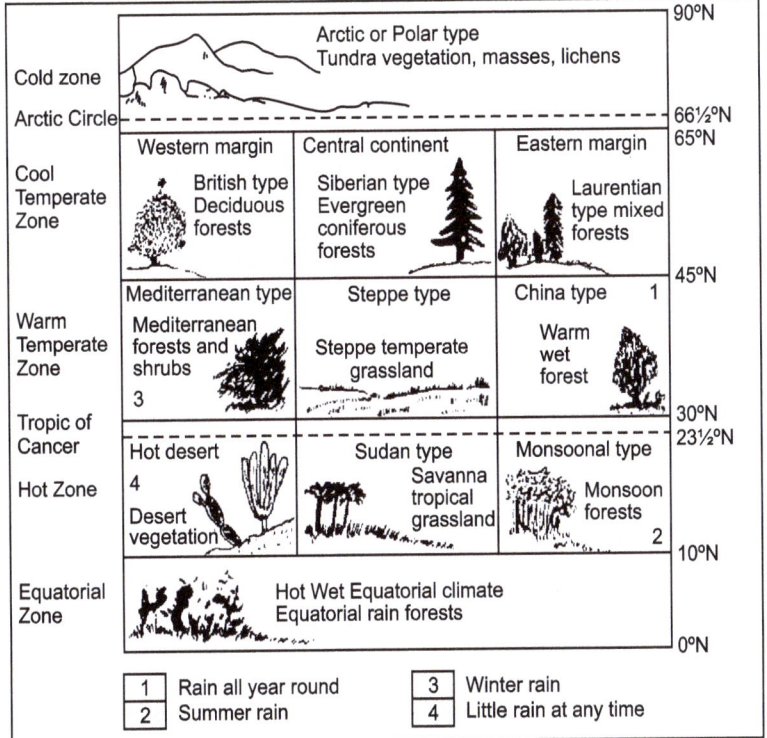

Based on climatic classification, the world is divided into different natural regions as follows :

Tropical Region: It includes the Equatorial Region, Tropical Grasslands, Tropical Monsoon Region, and Tropical Deserts.

Sub-tropical Region: It includes the Mediterranean region and China-type Region.

Temperate Region: It includes the Cool Temperate West Coast Region, Temperate Grasslands, and Temperate Deserts.

Polar Region: It includes the Taiga Region and Tundra Region.

MAJOR NATURAL REGIONS OF THE WORLD

The various climatic regions of the world can widely be distributed as :
- Equatorial Region
- Tropical Grasslands or Savanna Region
- Tropical Desert Region
- Tropical Monsoon Region
- Mediterranean Region
- Cool Temperate Continental Region or Mid-latitude Grassland
- Taiga Region
- Tundra Region

Equatorial Region

Location

The Equatorial Region is located on both sides of the Equator between 10°N and 10°S latitudes.

Areas

The Equatorial Region areas are spread over the parts of three continents, Asia, Africa and South America *(Fig. 16.1)*.

- **South America :** The region includes the Amazon lowlands between Guiana and Brazilian highlands and coastal lowlands of North-eastern Brazil, coastal Colombia and parts of adjoining Ecuador.
- **Africa :** This region covers the entire Zaire (Congo) basin and the Guinea Coast in West Africa.

- **Asia :** This region includes Malaysia, Singapore, Indonesia, Papua Newguinea, parts of Philippines, peninsular Thailand, Nicobar Islands and some parts of Sri Lanka.

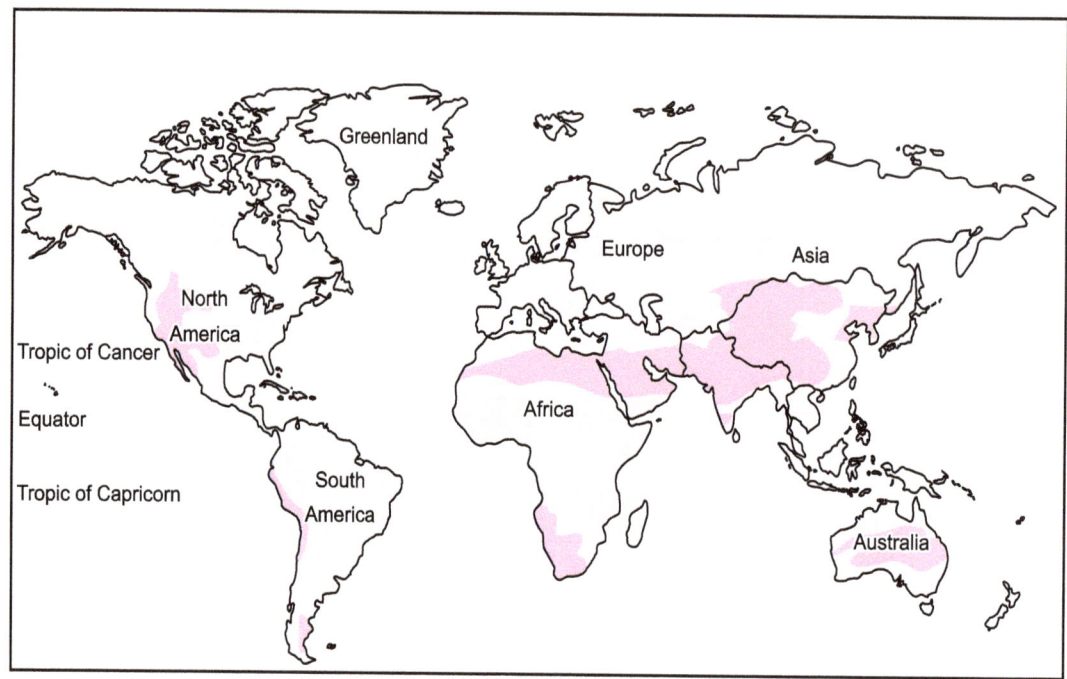

Fig. 16.1 : Equatorial Regions of the World

Climate

The Equatorial Region is a hot and wet region. The mornings are bright and sunny, with gradually increasing temperature. In the afternoon, the sky is overcast, followed by heavy downpours of convectional rain. The nights are cool with a clear sky. There is no winter season. Cloudiness and heavy rainfall help to moderate the daily temperature. Regular land and sea breezes help in maintaining an equable climate.

Temperature

As the Sun remains overhead throughout the year, the Equatorial region experiences a uniform high temperature round the year. The mean monthly temperature is around 25°C to 30°C with very little variation. The annual range of temperature (difference between the warmest and coldest months) is around 2°–3°C.

Rainfall

These regions are known for heavy rainfall, which is usually convectional. Rainfall averages between 150–350 cm and is well-distributed throughout the year. Manaus, lying in the interior of the Amazon lowlands, has an annual rainfall of 160 cm, while Belem, at the mouth of the Amazon has 220 cm and Singapore has 230 cm. The high temperature condition favours the convectional movement of the air, these convectional currents are at their maximum height by the afternoon. So, the rainfall occurs almost every day by 3 or 4 p.m. It occurs in torrential downpour with heavy showers and thunderstorms. On an average, there are 100 to 200 thunderstorms a year. There is no month without rain and there are two periods of maximum rainfall, July and September, which occur shortly after the equinoxes. Least rain falls in January and December solstices.

Natural Vegetation

- These are the largest evergreen forests in the world. These forests always look green, as there are no prescribed seasons for growing, flowering and shedding of leaves. These forests are also known as Equatorial or Evergreen rainforests.

- The high temperature and heavy rainfall produce luxuriant vegetation in these areas. There are dense equatorial forests known as the Selvas.

- The most remarkable feature of the Equatorial forests is the great variety of trees. Sometimes, several varieties of trees are found in a very small area.

- As the trees struggle for the sunlight, they grow to a tremendous height of about 40 to 50 meters. The trees usually form a thick canopy, and the sunlight is prevented from reaching the forest floor.

- The vegetation grows in four distinct layers, namely, emergent layer, canopy layer, understory layer, and forest floor *(Fig. 16.2)*.

Fig. 16.2 : Layers of Equatorial Rainforest

- There are various types of lianas (climbing plants) and parasitic plants, which also prevent the penetration of the sunrays to the lowest floor *(Fig. 16.3)*. Thus, the whole region appears to be dark, damp and gloomy. When light can penetrate to the forest floor, thickets of low trees, shrubs etc., grow.

Fig. 16.3 : Lianas

- Nearly, all the trees are of the broad-leafed evergreen type. Most of them are hardwood trees like Mahogany, Rosewood, Ebony, Ironwood, Greenheart, Cinchona, Rubber, etc.

- Palms and tree ferns are also found in most equatorial forests *(Fig. 16.4)*. In coastal areas and swamps, mangrove forests thrive.

Fig. 16.4 : Palms and tree ferns

Human Adaptations

- In the Equatorial regions, the natives remain cut off from the areas of great progress and eke out their living as primitive hunters, fish catchers or shifting cultivators and food gatherers.

- Resources are well developed in parts of Indonesia and Malaysia, but in most other parts, shifting agriculture is practiced and rivers are the only means of transport.

- In various areas, shifting agriculture is known by different names, like *Milpa* in South America, *Fang* in Africa and *Ladang* in Indonesia.

- The main crops are manioc (Cassava), yams, maize, bananas, groundnuts etc. Most of the farming is done by women, while men do hunting and fishing jobs.

- Many plantations have also been established widely in Indonesia, Malaysia, West Africa and Central America. The most notable plantation crop found in this region is rubber, mostly grown in Malaysia and Indonesia.

- The other products are Cocoa in Ghana and Nigeria, Coconuts in Philippine Islands and Indonesia, Palm oil in Indonesia and Malaysia, Manila hemp in Philippine Islands and Sugarcane in Indonesia.

Important Characteristics

- The Equatorial Region is located on both sides of the Equator between 10°N and 10°S latitudes.

- The Equatorial Region areas are spread over the parts of three continents, Asia, Africa and South America.

- The Equatorial Region is a hot and wet region. Cloudiness and heavy rainfall help to moderate

- the daily temperature. Regular land and sea breezes help in maintaining an equable climate.
- The mean monthly temperature is around 27°C with very little variation.
- These regions are known for heavy rainfall, which is usually convectional. Rainfall averages between 150–250 cm and is well-distributed throughout the year.
- These are the largest evergreen forests in the world. These forests always look green and therefore they are also known as Equatorial or Evergreen rainforests.
- Like vegetation, animal life in the equatorial regions is also found in abundance and varieties.

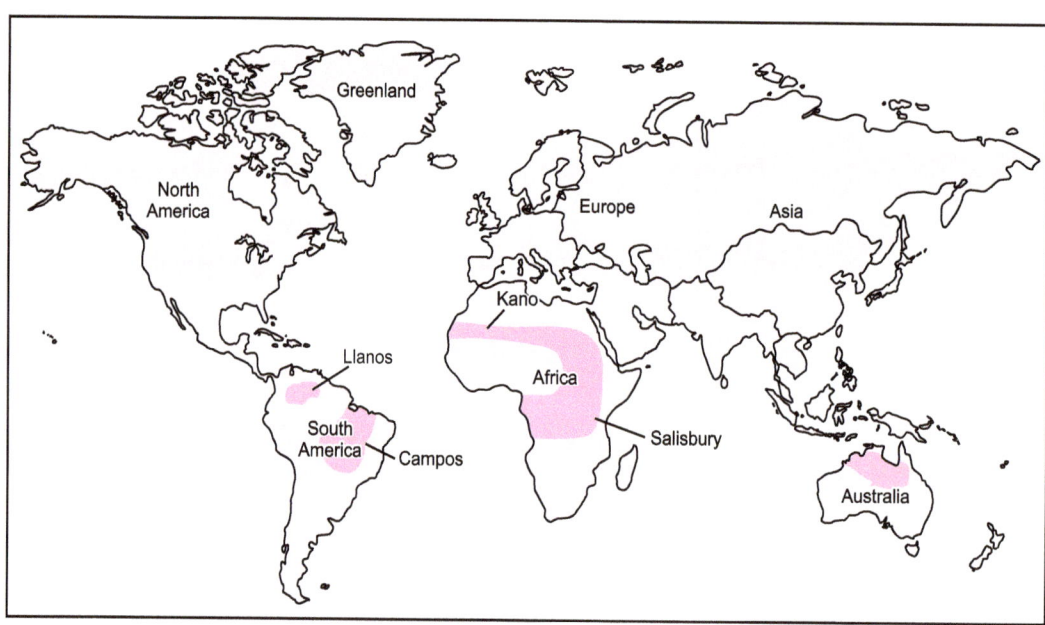

Fig. 16.5 : Tropical Grasslands of the World.

Tropical Grasslands or savanna Region

Location

Tropical Grasslands are also known as the Savannas. These grassland biomes are located between 10° to 20° north and south of the Equator. This belt borders the dry climate in the west and the monsoon climate in the East of an idealized continent. They lie in the transitional zone between the equatorial forest regions and the tropical deserts. As Sudan is a typical example of this region, it is also known as the Sudan type of climate.

Areas

The areas covered by the Tropical Grasslands are found across three continents, namely South America, Africa and Australia *(Fig. 16.5)*.

- **South America :** In this area there are two distinct regions of Savanna, North and South of the Equator, namely the Llanos of the Orinoco Basin and the Campos of the Brazilian Highlands, Guiana Highland, Venezuela, Columbia and highlands of Bolivia. In Central America, the main regions are Cuba, Jamaica and the Islands on the Pacific.
- **Africa :** In this area, it includes the southern part of Congo Basin, Central Nigeria, southern Kenya, Uganda, Central African Republic, Benin, Togo, Chad, Ghana, eastern Guinea, Tanzania, Mozambique, Zimbabwe, Zambia and Anglola.
- **Australia :** In this area, it includes the interior lands marginal to the desert in the northern parts of the continent including Northern Territory and Queensland.

Climate

The Tropical Grassland regions have two distinct seasons and do not get enough rain to support many trees.

Temperature

The mean temperature is high throughout the year ranging between 24°C to 32°C. The air is hot, dry and dusty. The annual range of temperature is greater than that of the Equatorial region. In this region three main seasons are found based on temperature and humidity.

- Cold dry season, having a high day temperature ranging between 26°C to 32°C, and low night temperature of about 20°C.
- Warm dry season, experiences vertical sunrays with high temperature ranging between 32°C to 38°C.
- Warm wet season, receiving about 80% of the total rainfall and has a relatively low temperature.

Rainfall

Rainfall in this region is convectional with very heavy downpours. It is concentrated to six or eight months of the year, followed by a long period of drought when fires can occur. It gets very hot and humid during this season. The average annual rainfall is about 30 cm on the desert border and about 120 cm on the forest's edge. The amount of mean annual rainfall decreases from east to west. There is heavier rainfall in the coastal areas and windward sides of the mountains. In the northern hemisphere, the rainy season begins in May and ends in September, while in the southern hemisphere, the rainy season occur from October to March.

The graph *(Fig. 16.6)* shows the average monthly temperatures and rainfall levels in the Savannah region of Mali (Africa). The temperature and rainfall patterns relate to each other. The hottest temperatures come just before heavy rainfall, and the coolest time of the year comes just after the rains. This pattern is typical of Savannah climates.

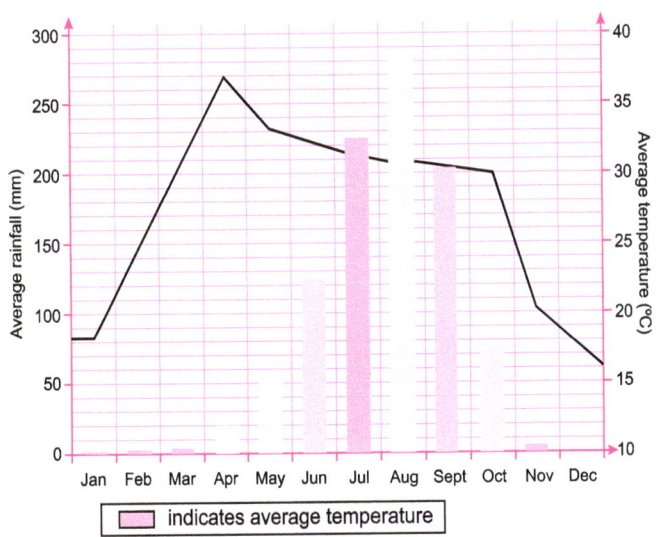

Fig. 16.6 : Average Monthly Temperatures and Rainfall Levels in Mali.

Natural Vegetation

There are several different types of Tropical grasslands around the world. They are called Campos in Brazil, Llanos in the Orinoco Basin and Savanna in Africa. The Serengeti Plains of Tanzania are some of the well-known, grasslands.

- Grasslands are regions of the world that are flat and dry, filled with grasses. They are located throughout the world and serve society mostly as farmland.
- Tall grasses and short trees characterize the tropical grasslands.
- The coarse tall grasses grow to a height of about 3 to 4 metres.
- The rainfall is neither sufficient nor well distributed to facilitate the growth of tall trees.
- Between the tall grasses, scattered short trees and low bushes grow.
- The trees are drought resistant and shed their leaves in the cool, dry season to prevent excessive loss of water.
- The main trees found in this region are Acacia, Baobabs, Eucalyptus, Tamarind, etc. *(Figs. 16.7 and 16.8)*.

Fig. 16.7 : Acacia Tree.

Human Adaptations

- Tropical grasslands are amongst the sparsely populated regions of the world. It is mostly inhabited by the tribal people who are engaged in cattle rearing and hunting. These people lead a nomadic life roaming about in search of pastures and water. The main tribal groups are Maasai of East Africa and Hausa of Nigeria *(Fig. 16.9)*.
- Though the region is mainly pastoral, cultivation of land has also increased.
- Some natives lead a settled life and work on plantations. The main crops produced in South

America are cotton, sugarcane and tobacco. In Africa, groundnut, millets and maize are grown.

Fig. 16.8 : Baobab Tree

- In West Africa, the main crops are groundnut, oil, palm, and cocoa. Other crops grown are peas, beans and sweet potatoes.
- Cattle rearing on a commercial scale have gained importance in South America. The Llanos form great cattle ranches in South America.

Fig. 16.9 : Maasai Tribe.

- In Australia, rearing of animal is an important occupation of people. They also grow maize and millets.

Important Characteristics

- These grassland biomes are located between 10° to 20° north and south of the Equator.
- Tropical Grasslands are found across three continents, namely South America, Africa and Australia
- The Tropical Grassland regions have two distinct seasons and do not get enough rain to support many trees.
- The mean temperature is high throughout the year ranging between 24°C to 32°C.
- The average annual rainfall is about 30 cm on the desert border and about 120 cm on the forest's edge.
- There are two very different seasons in a Savanna; a very long dry season (winter), and a very wet season (summer).
- Grassland regions of the world are flat and dry, filled with grasses. They are located throughout the world, serving the human society mostly as farmland for cultivation.
- The trees are drought-resistant and shed their leaves in the cool, dry season to prevent excessive loss of water.
- Tropical grasslands are amongst the sparsely populated regions of the world. It is mostly inhabited by the tribal people who are engaged in cattle rearing and hunting.

Tropical Desert Region

Location

The tropical deserts are located between 15° to 30° latitudes in both the hemispheres. Tropical Deserts are so called because this latitude zone mostly falls in the tropical zone. They occupy the western margins of the continents, the only exception being the Sahara Desert.

Areas

Tropical deserts are typically found under the subtropical ridge where there is largely unbroken sunshine for the whole year due to the stable descending air and high pressure. Their distribution is closely linked with the general atmospheric circulation and the arrangement of land and water bodies. It includes the following areas *(Fig. 16.10)* given below:

- **Africa :** Sahara Desert, Kalahari Desert and Namibian Desert.
- **Asia :** Thar Desert, Arabian Desert, large parts of Iran, southern and central Pakistan.
- **North America :** Mojave Desert, Colorado Desert and Mexican Desert.
- **South America :** Atacama Desert,
- **Australia :** The Great Australian Desert.

Climate

The tropical desert is an environment of extremes, thus it is the driest and hottest place on earth. This can be attributed to two reasons.

- There are no clouds in the atmosphere to scatter the insolation and no water vapour to absorb it.
- There is little moisture on the ground to be evaporated. Aridity also arises as distance from moisture sources increases.

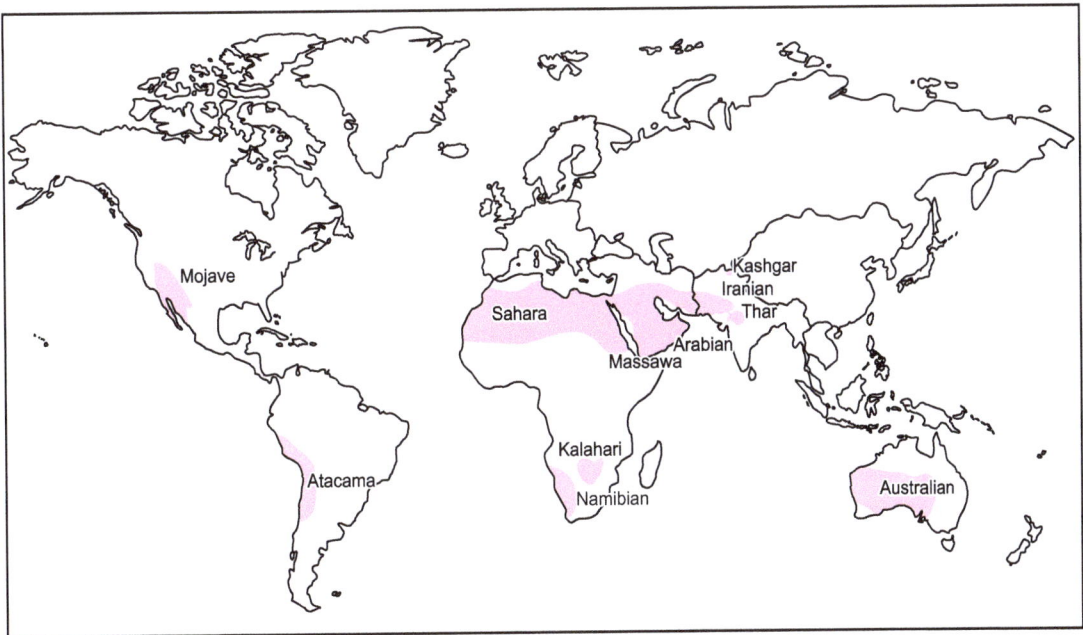

Fig. 16.10 : Tropical Deserts of the World.

Temperature

Tropical desert regions have the highest mean annual temperature than any climate on Earth. In summer, the average temperature ranges between 30° to 40°C and even goes up to 50°C in the noon. The temperature falls drastically at night. The sky in the tropical desert remains cloudfree due to the subsiding air of dominant high pressure resulting in large amounts of insolation. Without the absorptive blanket of clouds, radiation emitted from the Earth readily escapes into space, chilling the night time desert air. In winter, the day time temperature ranges between 15°C to 20°C, falling even further during the night. The diurnal range of temperature varies between 10°C to 29°C. The graph shows the average temperature of Tindouf, Algeria *(Fig. 16.11)*.

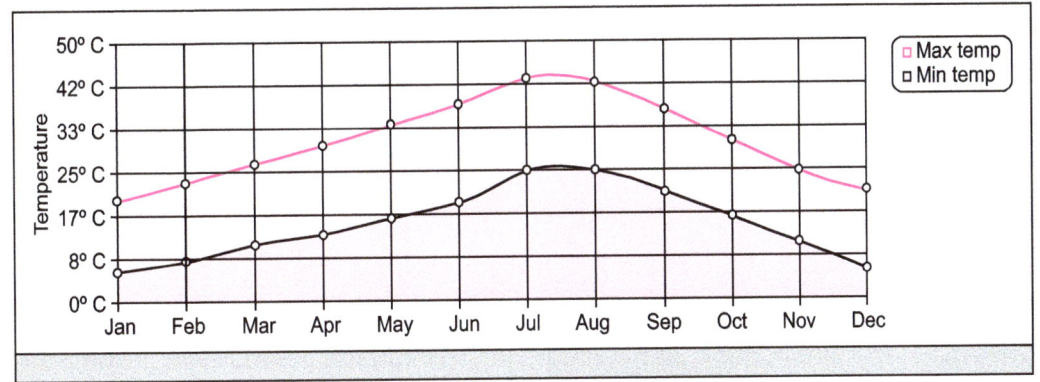

Fig. 16.11 : Temperature Graph of Tindouf, Algeria.

Rainfall

Rainfall in the tropical desert is very irregular and unreliable. Low latitude deserts receive an average rainfall of less than 25 cm (10 inch) a year. However, towards the humid margins, the annual average rainfall may vary from 50 to 75 cm. In these deserts, there may not be a drop of rain for several years in succession, but sometimes a single cloud-burst may yield so much rain that it may be more than the total amount of rain for a number of years. Air subsiding from the subtropical high is warmed, which reduces the relative humidity of the air. Relative humidity can drop to 10% or less. The extremely low relative humidity causes evaporation of whatever little surface water is present. The graph shows the average rainfall of Tindouf, Algeria *(Fig. 16.12)*.

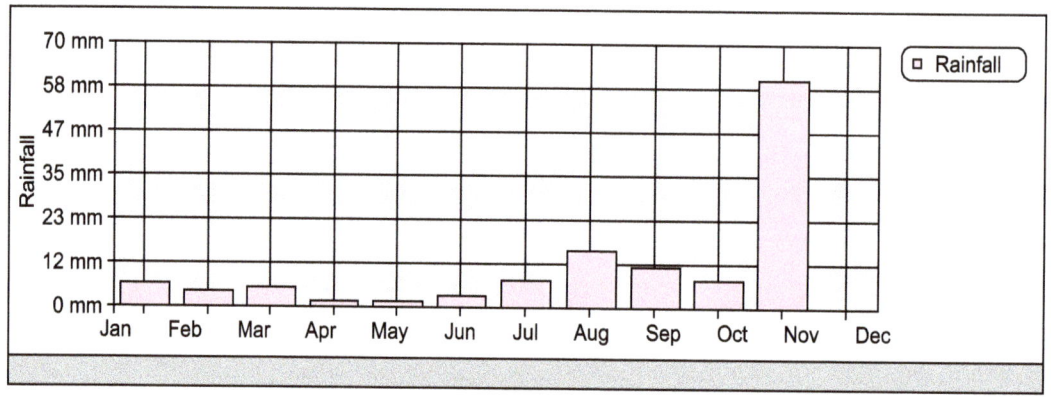

Fig. 16.12 : Rainfall Graph of Tindouf, Algeria

Since these deserts are located on the western margins of continents, Trade Winds that blow in the region shed their moisture on the eastern margins of continents. Therefore, they become dry by the time they reach the western side. Cold current, wash the coast on the Western side of the continent making the onshore winds stable as a result Kalahari, Atacama and Mexican desert regions receives very little amount of rainfall.

Natural Vegetation

- Since there is scarcity of water in the Tropical hot deserts, vegetation is sparse. Over large areas of these deserts, there may be little or no plant cover to be seen.
- The vegetation that grows in this region is of Xerophytic type. Plants that adapt to arid conditions are known as Xerophytic Plants. They have long roots, thick bark, waxy leaves, thorns, and small or no leaves *(Fig. 16.13)*.

- Typical desert plants, like cactus, adapt themselves to arid conditions by storing moisture in their stem or leaf cells.
- Some plants have leathery leaves, others have thorns and some have a repugnant smell as a means of protection against animal grazing.
- The main trees or bushes found in this region are Acacia, Cactus, Date palm, Kikar, etc. *(Fig. 16.14)*.

Fig. 16.14 : Palm Tree.

Human Adaptations

- The tropical deserts are agriculturally unproductive. Crops cannot be grown without irrigation in the deserts.
- Cultivation is mainly confined to regions where water is obtained from rivers, dams, oasis, or through a network of canals.
- In the extreme conditions, the native inhabitants have to struggle for means of livelihood.

Fig. 16.13 : **Desert Vegetation**

- Some of the primitive tribes are the Bushmen of the Kalahari, Aborigines of Australia and Bedouins of Sahara. They are nomadic hunters and food gatherers. They live in tents and migrate from place to place in search of water and pastures for their animals.
- The river Nile in Egypt allows the Egyptians to raise a number of crops. They cultivate cotton in summer, followed by wheat, barley, beans and other minor crops in winters. Millets, pulses, maize, beans, cotton, tobacco and fruits are the main crops.
- An oasis is a spot in the middle of a desert, where the elevation is low enough that the water table is right underneath the surface, resulting in the presence of springs *(Fig. 16.15)*.

Fig. 16.15 : Oasis.

- The most important plant in an oasis is the date palm. Farmers grow plants in different layers to make the best use of soil and water.
- The Sukkur dam of the Indus in Asia has led to farming of cotton, rice, wheat and oil seeds.

Important Characteristics

- The tropical deserts are located between 15° to 30° latitudes in both the hemispheres.
- Tropical deserts are typically found under the subtropical ridge where there is largely continuous sunshine for the whole year due to the stable descending air and high pressure.
- Tropical desert regions have the highest mean annual temperature than any climate on Earth.
- The ground temperature is so high that the raindrops get evaporated before they reach the ground.
- Both the annual and diurnal range of temperature remains high due to cloudless skies, sparse vegetation and very low humidity.
- Since there is scarcity of water in the tropical hot deserts, vegetation is sparse. Over large areas of these deserts, there may be little or no plant cover to be seen. Most of the vegetation that grows in this region is of Xerophytic type.

Tropical Monsoon Region

Location

The tropical monsoon region is located roughly between 10° to 30° North and South of the Equator. It is usually found in the eastern parts of the continents.

Areas

The areas covered by the tropical monsoon region include:

- **Asia :** This comprises the areas of India, Pakistan, Bangladesh, Myanmar, Thailand, Vietnam, Philippines, Sri Lanka and southern China.
- **North America :** It includes the areas of Mexico, Central America and West Indies.
- **South America :** It includes the areas of East Brazil.
- **Africa :** It covers the areas of East Africa and Malagasy.
- **Australia :** Northern Australia.

A major part of this region experiences a typical monsoon climate with seasonal reversal of winds, which occurs due to the differential heating of land and sea. This feature is much prominent in the Indian subcontinent *(Fig. 16.16)*.

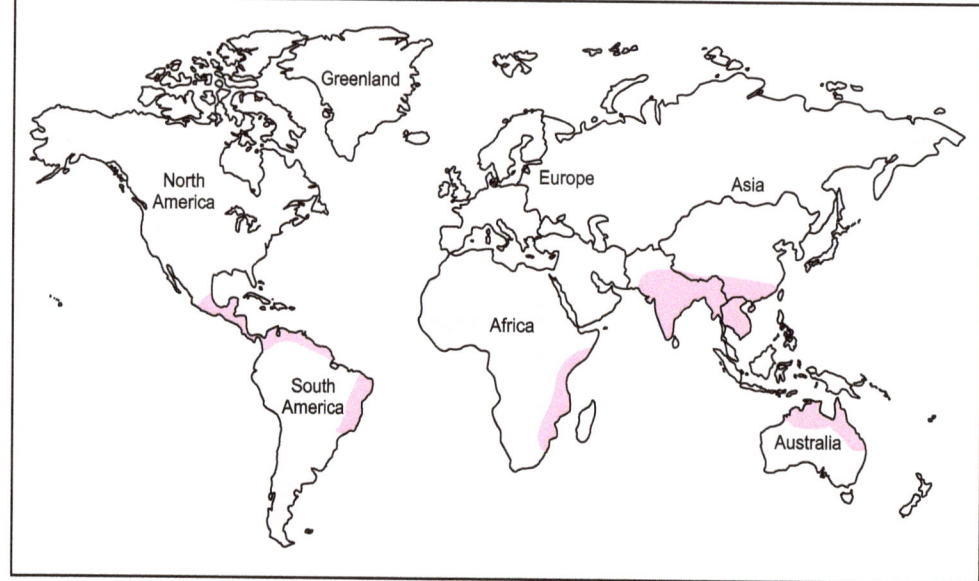

Fig. 16.16 : Tropical Monsoon Regions of the World.

Climate

The word 'monsoon' is derived from the Arabic word '*mausim*', which means 'season'. It is a seasonal wind that is associated with rain, hence it invariably means rainy season. Seasonal changes in the pressure system over Central Asia and Australia result in the seasonal reversal of winds between the two continents. This is the main feature of the Monsoonal Climate.

Temperature

Being located near the equator, the tropical monsoon climate experiences warm temperatures throughout the year. In this region, the average temperature varies from 27°C to 32°C. Annual range of temperature varies from 12°C to 17°C depending upon the location of the place.

Rainfall

This region comes under the influence of the Trade winds. It receives most of its rainfall from the southwest monsoon winds during the months of June-September. The average annual rainfall is 150 cm. In India, the annual amount of rainfall varies from 75 to 200 cm. The north-western parts of the Indian subcontinent receive rainfall during the winter season from the western disturbances coming from the Mediterranean Sea. Rainfall is heavy, but irregular in both time and place.

Seasons

Based on the temperature conditions and rainfall, the monsoon region enjoys three distinct seasons, especially in the Indian subcontinent.

- **Hot, Dry Summer Season (March to June)** : In summer, the average temperature ranges between 27°C to 32°C. In central India, it is around 35°C while in the interior states of Northern India, temperature soars to over 40°C. An intense low pressure is established over northern plains. The weather therefore remains hot and dry with local thunderstorms developing in coastal and mountain regions.

- **Rainy Season (July to October)** : During this period, the temperature ranges between 20°C to 38°C. By the first week of June, Kerala and Meghalaya receive the first monsoon showers. The southwest monsoon winds are drawn towards the low-pressure trough. These moisture-laden winds from the sea cause heavy relief rain to the western coastal plains and north-eastern states. On being obstructed by the mountains, these winds then blow along the plains of India. The amount of rainfall decreases as one move westward along the northern plains. Mumbai gets over 200 cm of rainfall as it lies on the windward side of the Western Ghats. Pune receives less than 100 cm as it lies in the rain shadow area.

- **Cool, Dry Winter Season (November to February)** : A feeble high pressure develops over northwest India by the end of October. Temperature begins to drop steadily with the average temperature ranging between 10°C to 20°C. Frost may occur at night in the higher altitudes. As such, cool dry offshore winds replace the warm moist winds. These are dry winds and bring little or no rain. These winds are called as the north-east monsoons or the Land Breeze. They pick up some amount of moisture from the Bay of Bengal and bring rainfall in Tamil Nadu. Chennai records heavy rainfall in the months of October-November. Similarly, Punjab and Haryana gets rain in winter, from western disturbances originating from the Mediterranean Sea.

Natural Vegetation

- This region is characterized by a wide variety of vegetation types. Many of the islands and coastal areas have forests.
- The trees found in these Monsoon forests are not as tall as the ones found in Equatorial or Tropical Rainforest, as there is lack of water during the dry season.
- Many tree species are present and may number between 30 to 40 species in a small tract. Common species of trees include Teak, Neem, Babul, Shisham, Sal, Sandalwood, Mahua and Bamboo.
- Areas where rainfall is not experienced throughout the year have a marked dry season and here, the Tropical Monsoon Deciduous Forests are found *(Fig. 16.17)*.
- The deciduous trees shed their leaves to prevent loss of water by transpiration.
- Commercially valuable timber is available, that can be exploited with ease.

Fig. 16.17. : Monsoon Forests

Human Adaptations

- The lowlands and river valleys are very fertile. These areas are intensively cultivated.
- Agriculture is the main occupation of the majority of people in the Tropical Monsoon region.

- Crops are grown on small farms in the plains and terraced hills.
- The major crops grown include rice, wheat, maize, millet, sorghum, gram and beans. A number of cash crops like sugarcane, cotton, tea, and coffee are also grown.

Important Characteristics

- The tropical monsoon region is located lies roughly between 10° to 30° North and South of the Equator in the Eastern margin of the Continents.
- This region experiences a typical monsoon climate with seasonal reversal of winds.
- Tropical monsoon climate experiences warm temperatures throughout the year.
- This region comes under the influence of the Trade winds. It receives most of its rainfall from the South-West monsoon winds during the months of June-September.
- Based on the temperature conditions and rainfall, the monsoon region enjoys three distinct seasons, especially in the Indian subcontinent.
- This region is characterized by a wide variety of vegetation types. Many of the islands and coastal areas have forests.
- Agriculture is the main occupation of the majority of people in the Tropical Monsoon region.

Mediterranean region

Location

The Mediterranean region generally refers to the lands around the Mediterranean Sea that have a Mediterranean climate. These are the countries bordering the Mediterranean Sea (plus Portugal) between about 27° to 47°N and 10°W to 37°E. The Mediterranean region basically covers portions of three continents, Europe, Asia and Africa. Mediterranean regions occur between approximately 30° to 45° north and south latitude on the west sides of these continents. Temperatures in these areas are from warm to hot in the high sun season with high evaporation rates and are mild in the low sun season with reduced evaporation rates. These regions have thus been called 'winter-rain and summer-dry' climates. Mediterranean types of lands occupy only about 1.7% of land area of the Earth. The region lies between Tropical desert on the Equatorward side and cool temperate west margin region on the poleward side.

Areas

The Mediterranean Sea is the largest of the semi-enclosed European seas. It is surrounded by 18 countries and has shores on three continents (Europe, Africa and Asia) *(Fig. 16.18)*.

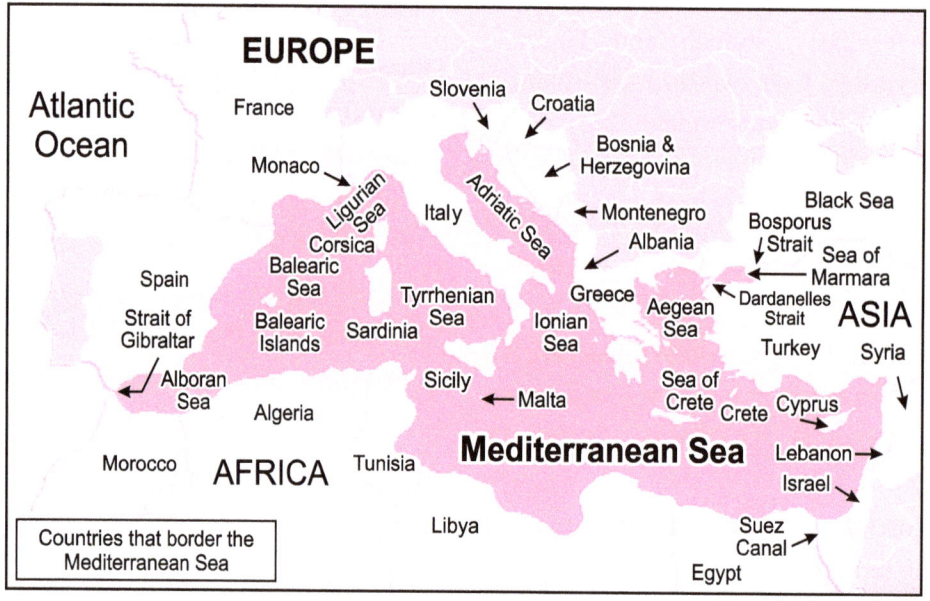

Fig. 16.18 : Countries Surrounding the Mediterranean Sea.

- **Europe :** Portugal, Spain, Italy, France and Greece. Albania, Bosnia-Hergovina, Croatia, Malta, Monaco, Serbia, Montenegro and Slovenia.
- **Asia :** Parts of coastal Turkey, Syria, Cyprus, Israel and Lebanon.
- **Africa :** Coastal regions of Algeria, Morocco, Tunisia and Libya.
- **North America :** Coastal California around San Francisco.
- **South America :** Central Chile.
- **South Africa :** Region around Cape Town.
- **Australia :** Southwest regions around Perth and Adelaide.

Climate

The climates in these areas are characterized by dry summers and wet winters from warm to hot in the high sun season with high evaporation rates and are mild to cool in the low sun season with reduced evaporation rates. These regions have thus been called 'winter-rain and summer-dry' climates. The dry summer climate of Mediterranean regions arises from the seasonal change in position of the semi-permanent subtropical high-pressure systems which are centered over the tropical deserts roughly over the Tropics of Capricorn and Cancer. The Westerlies that are produced provide a constant stream of dry and warm air to the Mediterranean regions, some like Santa Ana can be quite strong with real threats of fire. As the subtropical high retreats towards equator during the winter, maritime air masses and cyclonic storms developing along the polar front make their way into the Mediterranean region bringing coolness and moisture.

Temperature

Mean summer temperatures range between 20°C and 28°C. In the hottest month, the temperature may even reach to a maximum of 30°C. In winters, the mean temperature may be from 6° to 10°C. The temperature at night may fall below 0°C, owing to the destruction of forests in the region. Areas close to the oceans experience a lower temperature. Therefore, the mean annual range of temperature is 11°C to 17°C. In the Mediterranean climate mostly situated between the latitudes 30° and 40° North and South on the western margin of the continents, subtropical high-pressure systems cause the summer temperature to be higher. Many Mediterranean areas are influenced by their local winds. The berg prevails in South Africa, Mistral in Southern France, Sirocco blow across the Sahara desert over the Mediterranean Sea towards Europe.

The temperatures of the affected areas are modified by local winds.

Rainfall

Rainfall in the Mediterranean region is experienced mostly in winter. The annual average rainfall of this region varies between 35 cm to 75 cm. The rainfall in the Northern Hemisphere is received during winter between December to March while in Southern Hemisphere the rainy season lasts from May to August. Mediterranean climates experience both hot and cold local winds. Rainfall is more on the Poleward sides of the region.

Natural Vegetation

- The vegetation here is of deciduous type. It is adapted to withstand a long period of summer drought.
- Mediterranean summers are hot and dry and make the plant growth difficult. However, the plants in this region have adapted themselves to the summer drought, by storing water obtained from winter rains.
- Short stature, moisture retentive trees grow here especially citrus fruits. The grape plant is well suited for the Mediterranean climate. Many plants have small needle type of spiny leaves to cut down rate of transpiration. Other plants have taproots, which can reach down to the moist rock layer below the surface.
- In the drier forests, the vegetation is scrub-like and consists of sweet smelling herbs and shrubs such as Oleander, Rosemary, Thyme and Lavender.
- In the wetter parts, e.g., Coniferous trees are found on mountain slopes. The dominant trees in the Mediterranean region of Europe include Oak, Laurel, Cork, Oleander, Beech and Ash. All these are evergreen trees. Olive is the most common tree. Eucalyptus, introduced from Australia is also now commonly found.
- In Europe, most of the natural vegetation has been replaced by cultivated plants like orange, lemon and laurel. The North American Mediterranean region is still rich in flora.
- The Mediterranean biome is divided into five floristic biome subtypes, according to the various floristic realms into which each fall :

- **Mediterranean Flora :** These comprise two main types: Maquis – dense shrub formations, and Garrique – more open, healthy and aromatic shrubs (Lavender, Thyme). Trees and shrubs include: Holm's oak, Cork oak, Pines, Holly, Atlas cedar, Boxwood, Arbutus, Olives, etc.
- **Californian Flora :** 'Chaparral' – shrub/tree vegetation. Trees and shrubs include: *Quercus dumosa* (and other oaks), Rhamnaceae, Manzanita, Chamis, etc. Annuals or geophytes inlude: Clarkia, Calochortus, Brodiaea and California poppy.
- **Chilean Flora :** 'Matorral' – shrub/tree vegetation. Woody vegetation includes: *Lithraea caustica* (Anacardiaceae), *Quillaja saponaria* (Rosaceae), *Jubaea chilensis* (Chilean wine palm). Other vegetations includes: *Colletia armata* (Rhamnaceae), *Ephedra andina*, *Mesembryan themum* (Aizoaceae), etc.
- **Capensic (South Africa) Flora :** 'Fynbos' – healthy vegetation, very few trees, 'Veld' – more shrubby vegetation. Protea (proteas, Proteaceae), Erica (600 species, Ericaceae), Restionaceae, Pelargonium (florist geranium), Iridaceae, Amaryllidaceae, etc.
- **Australian Flora :** 'Mallee' – healthy vegetation on poor soil. It includes Banksia (and other Proteaceae), *Eucalyptus diversicolor* (karri) and *Eu. marginata* (jarrah), Desert oak, grass trees, Epacridaceae, Orchidaceae and other herbaceous families.
- Mediterranean region is famous for fruit cultivation. Citrus fruits like Orange, Lime and Lemon are grown. Other fruits grown are Figs, Peaches, Pears, Apricots, Cherries, etc.
- Several nut trees are also grown in this region. Walnut, Chestnut, Hazelnut, Almonds, etc., are important nut crops. Olives are grown in plenty and are used as fresh fruit as well as used for oil.
- Grapes are grown abundantly in Mediterranean region. They are used in several forms, fresh as well as dried. The Mediterranean lands are famous for their varieties of wine, which are known by the names of their producing areas. Suerry, Chianti, Champagne and Burgundy, are some famous brands.

Human Adaptation

- The Mediterranean, which literally means 'sea between lands', offers favourable environmental conditions, such as climate, biological diversity, and natural resources.
- The effect of moderate rainfall in this region is marked by the pleasant climate and bright sunny weather, especially in winter, which is most favoured by tourists who flock in great numbers to the region.
- Due to warm bright summers and cool moist winters, wide varieties of crops are cultivated in the Mediterranean region.
- This region is particularly famous for orchard farming and fruit cultivation where a wide variety of citrus fruits like oranges, limes, lemons and grapefruit are grown. In fact, the Mediterranean regions accounts for 70% of the world's export of citrus fruits. Besides citrus fruits, the other important fruits cultivated in the Mediterranean region are olives, grapes, walnuts, hazelnuts and almonds.
- The crops grown in the Mediterranean regions include wheat, barley, rice, cotton and tobacco. These factors make human adaptation in this area much comfortable.

Important Characteristics

- The Mediterranean region is defined as countries bordering the Mediterranean Sea.
- Mediterranean climate is famous for its warm dry summers and mild rainy winters.
- Offshore trade winds blow in the summer, whereas Onshore Westerly winds blow in the winter bringing cyclonic rain.
- Because of its unique climate, these lands are known for growing citrus fruits.
- The Mediterranean region supports a deciduous type of vegetation.
- Mediterranean regions accounts for 70% of the world's export of citrus fruits.
- Grapes are an important vine crop in this area, grown for fruit and to make wine.

Cool Temperate Continental Region or Mid-latitude Grassland

Location

The cool temperate continental regions lie Poleward of the warm East Margin region. These areas are found in the interior parts of the continents in the temperate zone of 40° to 55° North and South of the Equator. They lie in the transition zone of desert and humid climates. The characteristic of this type of climate is that they experience the continental or extreme type of climate.

Areas

The cool temperate continental region is found on the periphery of mid-latitude deserts and the leeward side of mountain systems in inner Asia, South America, and the Western United States. North-eastern United States and adjoining parts of Canada, North China, Manchuria are the main areas included in this region. A vast expanse of this climatic region occurs in the following: *(Fig. 16.19).*

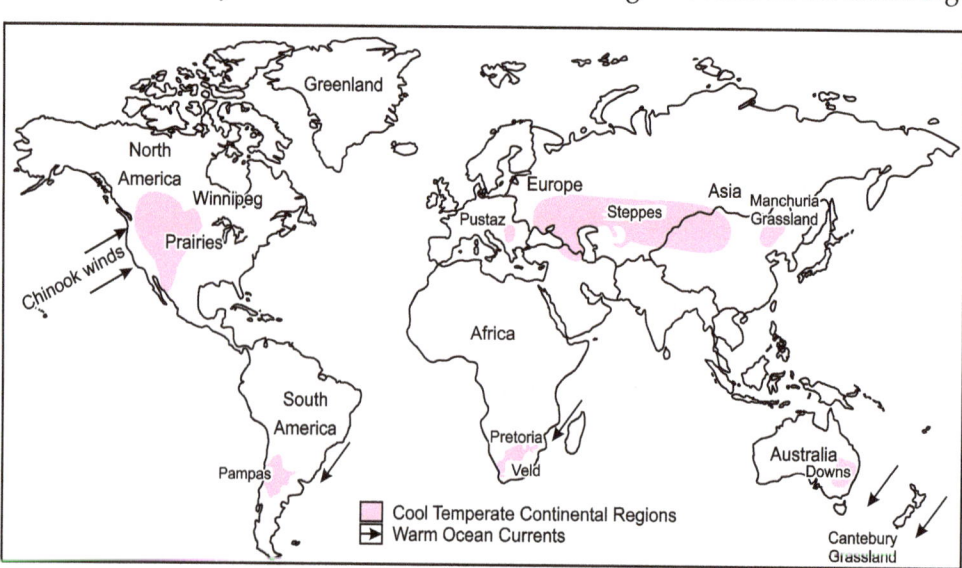

Fig. 16.19 : Cool Temperate Continental Regions (Steppes and Prairies).

- **North America :** An area around the great lakes of USA and Canada upto the Rockies in the West, covering the great plain of N. America. It is known as Prairies.
- **South America :** The parts of Argentina and Uruguay are as Pampas.
- **Australia :** In the Murray–Darling river basin is known as Downs.
- **South Africa :** On the leeward side of the Drakensburg mountain, is known as Veld.
- **Asia :** Western Siberia , North West China and Manchurian plains are known as Steppes.
- **Europe :** North of Black Sea and Caspian sea and a small area in the Hungarian plains are known as Steppes.

Climate

As regards to climate, all humid continental climates have cold winters. The region usually has warm wet summers and long cold dry winters. Short summer humid climates have long winters and they are severe too, but the summers are short.

Temperature

Winter temperature in January is 5°C. Though summers are short, yet during this short period, they bring enough warmth and during the day time, the maximum temperature reaches 30°C. Summer temperatures are high and July temperatures are as high as 24°C.

Summers here are somewhat wet and winters are cold, with January temperature averaging about 4°C. The areas located poleward or in the interior have colder winters than the areas located on the coasts or on the margins, which are equatorward. The extremes of temperatures are greater in the Northern hemisphere than in the Southern hemisphere. The annual range of temperature is 20 to 25 °C.

Rainfall

Rainfall in short summer humid climate is maximum varying from 25 to 60 cm annually, but northward regions have less than 20 inches precipitation. Winter rainfall in these regions is in the form of snowfall, which continues for 60 to 80 days and the region remains covered with snow sometimes for more than four months. Strong winds, during the winter, cause snow particles to whirl high into air and the result are in the form of invisibility. Visibility is reduced to zero. The rainfall is of convectional origin and mostly of light showers in the summer season.

Natural Region

- Due to scanty rainfall, long periods of drought and cold winters, it is a treeless area.
- Various species of grasses are found, as they are able to withstand low rainfall and seasonal variations.
- Short trees like willows, alders and poplars may be seen along the water course.
- In dry areas, scrubs and thorny plants are found.

Human Adaptation

- This region experiences extreme weather conditions and scanty rainfall, mainly suited for extensive mechanized farming and grazing.
- These areas at one time were covered by grass, because of many changes brought by man and animals, little of the original grass remains.
- Currently, these lands have emerged as the world's greatest food producing areas. Agriculture on these grasslands is highly mechanized.
- Extensive farms for producing wheat have been started under the system of collective farms. Most of the wheat produced in USA and Canada comes from the Prairies region. They are called the 'granaries of the world'.
- Other crops that farmers grow are maize, cotton, oats, corn, rye , sugarbeet , barley and potatoes.

Important Characteristics

- These climates are affected by their interior continental or leeward orographic position.
- The controlling factors over the geographical distribution and climatic characteristics of the cool temperate continental region are similar to that of the mid-latitude deserts.
- The region has warm wet summers and cold dry winters.
- The vegetation mostly consists of tall grasses.

Taiga Region or Coniferous Forest Region

Location

The Coniferous Forest region is located in the Northern Hemisphere, situated between 55°N to 70°N latitudes, while in the Southern Hemisphere these latitudes are covered by sea. These forests stretch in a continuous belt across the Northern Europe, Canada and Russia. Therefore, this cold temperate region of coniferous forests is also known as Siberian or Taiga Region.

Areas

The Coniferous forest belt has the greatest extent in the northern part of Eurasia covering Siberia. The areas covered by the Coniferous forest are widespread *(Fig. 16.20)*.

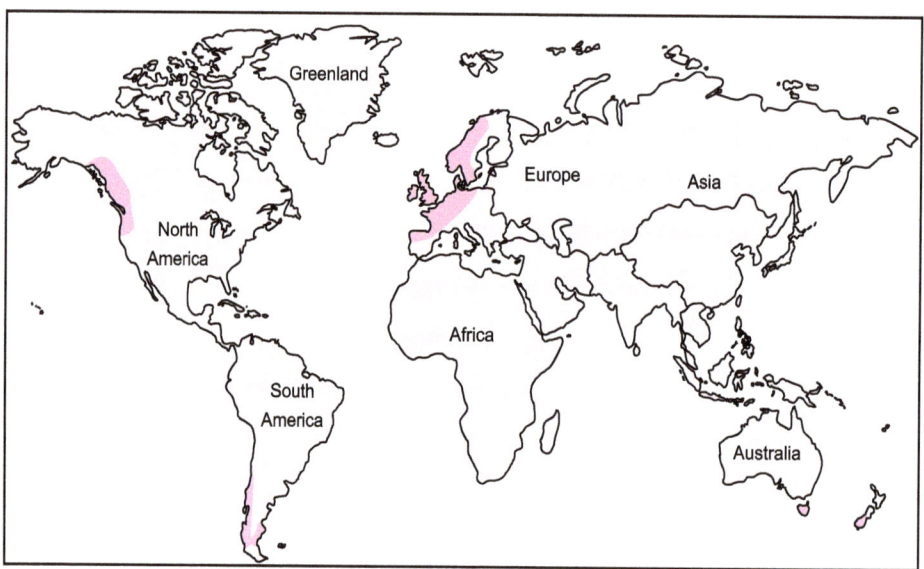

Fig. 16.20 : Coniferous Forest Regions of the World.

- **Asia :** Coniferous forest belt is found along North Siberia, covering the Sakhalin Island and the Kamchatka Peninsula.
- **Europe :** Coniferous forest belt stretches over northern part of European Russia, Poland, Finland and Sweden.
- **North America :** Coniferous forest region extends from South Alaska along South Canada to Labrador.

Climate

Only in the Northern Hemisphere experiences the Siberian type of climate because of the narrowness of the southern continents in the high latitudes *(Fig. 16.21)*.

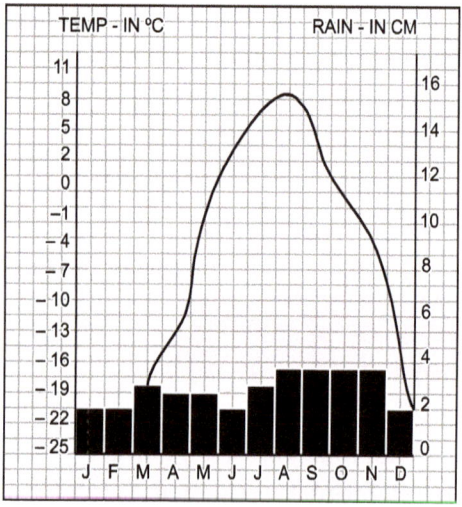

Fig. 16.21 : Taiga Region Climate.

Temperature

The Siberian type of climate is marked by very long winters and short summers. It experiences severe winters of long duration lasting from October to April, temperature falling to $-30°C$ or less. It is further lowered by northerly Polar Winds like the Blizzards of Canada and Burans of Eurasia. The summers are brief and cool, lasting only 3 to 4 months, the average temperature of the warmest month seldom rising above 15°C. Heavy snowfall occurs during the winter, frost occurs as early as August, and by September lakes and ponds get frozen. The daily snowfall causes thick cover of ice on land, blocking the flow of water, hence hindering the transport system. Verkhoyansk is a Siberian station where the minimum temperature is recorded to be $-50°C$. On account of such a low record of temperature that is even lower than that of the Polar Region, Verkhoyansk is known as the Cold Pole of the Earth. The winter season nights are very long but the days are very short. On the other hand, the summer season nights are very short and the sun shines for as long as eighteen hours. The days are seldom warm due to the slanting rays of the sun.

Rainfall

The Coniferous Forest region is situated in the belt of westerly winds. In this region, the relative humidity is generally high and the rate of evaporation is very slow because temperatures are generally low. Most of the rain comes from cyclonic weather. The rainfall is greater near the coast, decreasing towards the interior parts. The average annual rainfall ranges between 25 cm to 75 cm. Most of the precipitation is received during summer months from June to September, whereas during the winters precipitation is received too, but in the form of snowfall as the winter temperatures are generally below the freezing point.

Natural Vegetation

Taiga region receives precipitation throughout the year, but in small amount. Even this small amount of precipitation is more than sufficient for tree growth. During summers, the middle course of the Siberian River melts and the water released from melting of snow spreads far and wide, creating marshes. This moisture is utilized by vegetation. Therefore, this region is capable of supporting evergreen trees. These trees are called Coniferous trees *(Fig. 16.22)*.

Fig. 16.22 : Coniferous Trees

- The Coniferous Forests have several distinctive features that makes it easy to exploit. Hence, this region has become commercially very important.
- The trees are usually evenly spaced, attaining a usual size and stature and are seldom higher than 35 meters.
- There is no undergrowth as the soils of this region are practically devoid of humus and are very poor because the ground is frozen to a depth of about a meter and a half where shallow rooted plants cannot survive. Thus, undergrowth has hardly any scope of development.
- The evergreen trees of the Coniferous Forests do not have a specific season or duration for shedding leaves. So, it is called Evergreen coniferous forest.
- Leaves of Coniferous Trees are needle shaped known as conifers and hence the trees bearing such leaves are called coniferous. They are tough and hard, and do not wither even in the face of gusty polar winds that are full of snowflakes.
- The coniferous trees acquire a cone like shape by the typical development of branches stretching downwards. Due to the conical shape of trees, the snow slides downwards and does not remain suspended on tree-tops or on the branches. The trees, therefore, remain safe and secure from the impact of snowfall.

Fig. 16.23 : Pine Cone (closed)

- The trees contain a high percentage of pitch resulting in the break out of forest fires during summers.
- The coniferous forests of Eurasia and North America are the richest sources of softwood, which is used in furniture making, building construction purposes, paper and pulp, rayon, etc.

Fig. 16.24 : Pine Cone (open).

- The major trees of the coniferous forests are limited to Pine, Fir, Spruce and Larch. Pine trees are of several varieties, namely White pine, Red pine, Jack pine, Scots pine, Lodge pine, etc. Similarly, Fir trees are also of several varieties, namely Balsam fir and Douglas fir *(Fig. 16.23 and 16.24).*

Human Adaptation

- The coniferous forest region does not support a favourable climatic environment for population concentration. Most of the area is covered by forests and marshes, which put obstacle in the way of development of means of transport, etc.
- Farming is not considered as an important economic activity due to the intense cold prevailing in most part of the year, short growing season of about 90 days and low fertility of the soil covered with snow.
- However, the soil is favourable, in some parts of Canada, where the soil is covered with sand, clay, gravel, deposited by the melting glaciers of past ages or in the sheltered valley and lowlands bordering the Steppes.
- In these areas where the soil is favourable for agriculture, some crops like barley, oats, rye, potatoes, etc., are grown.
- These Coniferous Forest regions are potential areas for the supply of several economic products, especially wood. Lumbering is, therefore, the predominant occupation of this region.
- The valuable variety of soft woods found in this region is of great commercial value. Today there are a number of non-conventional purposes for which wood is used. Even the seeds of some pines furnish food for man. Thus, in this way wood is conserved and put to useful purposes.

Important Characteristics

- The Coniferous Forest region is located in the Northern Hemisphere, situated between 55°N to 70°N latitudes, while in the Southern Hemisphere these latitudes are covered by sea.
- These forests stretch in a continuous belt across the Northern Europe, Canada and Russia.
- The Siberian type of climate has very long winters and short summers. The winters are bitterly cold and even summers are cool (far from being warm). Temperatures are generally below freezing point during the long winter.
- The Coniferous Forest region is situated in the belt of westerly winds, thus the rain is received throughout the year but in the small quantity.
- Taiga region receives precipitation throughout the year, but in small amount. Therefore, this region is capable of supporting evergreen trees known as Coniferous trees.
- The major trees of the coniferous forests are limited to pine, fir, spruce and larch.
- The coniferous forest region does not support a favourable climatic environment for population concentration.
- Farming and agriculture is not considered as an important economic activity due to the intense cold prevailing in most part of the year.
- Coniferous Forest regions are potential areas for the supply of soft wood.

Tundra region

Location

The word 'Tundra' is derived from a Russian term, which means a flat treeless plain which is boggy. The Tundra region is located roughly beyond the Arctic Circle (66° 30′ N) in the Northern Hemisphere, while there is no Tundra region in the Southern Hemisphere.

Areas

The Tundra region areas are stretched over the coastal lands of the Arctic Ocean in Eurasia and North America and the Southern coastal fringe of Greenland and several groups of islands, situated in the Arctic Ocean near the northern coasts of the northern continents *(Fig. 16.25).*

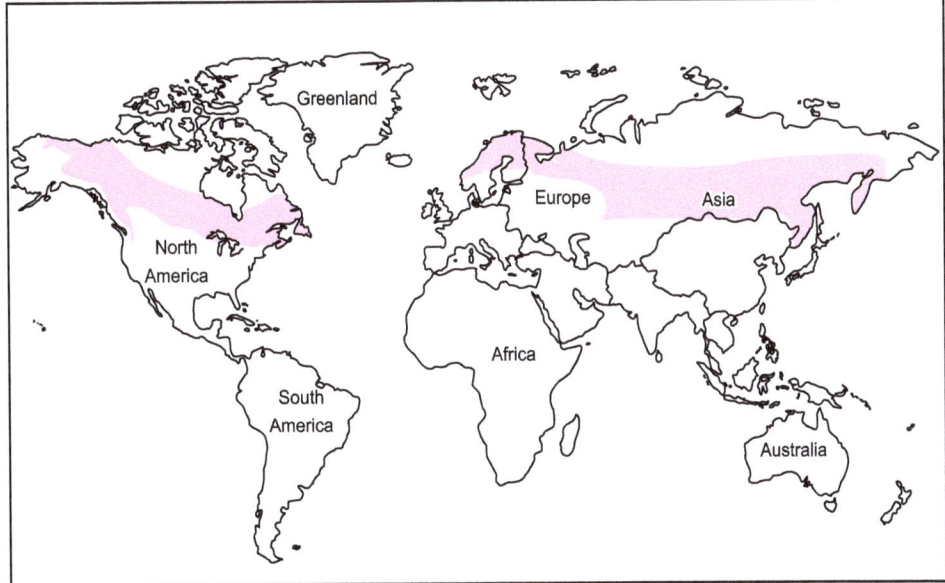

Fig. 16.25 : World map showing the Tundra Region areas of the World.

- **North America :** Northern coastal region of Alaska and Canada and also the group of Islands, located nearby and the coastal fringe of Greenland.
- **Europe :** Northern Scandinavia, Iceland, Spitsbergen Islands, northern coastal region of European Russia.
- **Asia :** Northern coastal region of Siberia.

Climate

The Tundra climate is also known as the Arctic or Polar type of climate. It is found mainly north of the Arctic Circle in the Northern hemisphere. The climate is characterized by long, severe winters; cool, brief summers and scarce rainfall. Due to the rise of harmful activities like, excessive use of CFCs, fossil fuels, deforestation, global temperatures, etc., there has been noticed great changes in the climate and rainfall patterns *(Fig. 16.26)*.

Fig. 16.26 : Tundra Region.

Temperature

The chief characteristic of Tundra climate is very low mean annual temperature. Here winters are severe and long, while summers are cool and short, lasting hardly for two to three months when the sun does not set at all. The warm months have a temperature ranging between 2°C to 10°C. Although during summer the area receives continuous sunlight, the sun hardly comes up the horizon due to the slanting rays of the sun. During winters, the surface usually remains covered with snow for nine to ten months as temperatures are as low as –40°C. At the North Pole, there are about six months without light in winter. This is because temperatures remain as low as the Sun is low in the sky and much of the warmth of its faint rays is either reflected by the ground snow. It is twilight which is furnished by the reflection of heavenly bodies on the white sheets of snow and ice, and also by brilliant and colourful illuminating curtains of the *Aurora Borealis*, which is a phenomenon of higher latitudes. It occurs when the charged particles from the sun interact with gases in the earth's atmosphere. *Aurora Borealis* are seen only in latitudes beyond 65° in both North and South hemispheres.

Rainfall

As the polar region is a high pressure region, it does not favour precipitation. Precipitation is very low, about 9.1 inches only, falling mainly in the second half of the year both as rain and snow. Rainfall is scarce, usually below 25 cm annually. Most of the rain is cyclonic in origin and brought by the Westerlies that are strongest in winter. Rain generally falls in the form of drizzle and is received mainly in summer, whereas in coastal areas, where the cyclones are strongly felt, most of the rain falls in winter exceeding the normal limit of 12 inches. In winter, rainfall takes the form of snow that does not melt due to severe cold. Snowfall varies with locality; it may fall either as ice crystals or large, combined snowflakes. Evaporation is also very little due to the low temperature. Due to low rate of evaporation and lack of moisture in the air, no convectional rainfall occurs. Figure shows the rhythm of temperature and precipitation of a Tundra region taken at Upernavik, Greenland (72°N, 56°W) *(Fig. 16.27)*.

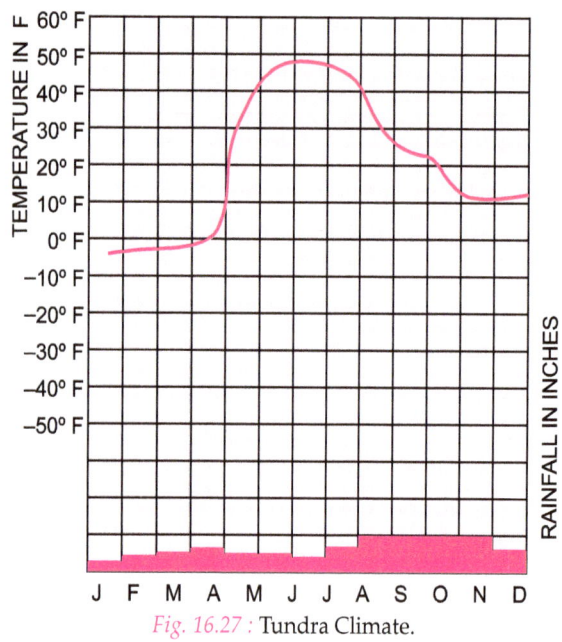

Fig. 16.27 : Tundra Climate.

Fig. 16.28 : Moss and Lichen on Rocks.

Natural Vegetation

- In Tundra region weather conditions are not favourable for vegetative growth. The growing season available during summers is too short and the temperatures are too low for the germination of seeds.

- The area is often marshy with permanently frozen sub-soil. These marshy areas are known as muskegs. The vegetation here is rare as the ground remains frozen throughout the year. Even then some sort of vegetation is visible that has remarkably adapted itself to the environment.

- In Tundra region most of the vegetation found is xerophytic as water is not available on account of frozen environment. Only few plants survive including Mosses, Lichens and Sedges. Some hardy grasses grow in the more favourable coastal lowlands *(Fig. 16.28)*.

- With the onset of winter, the grass cover disappears and the animals and birds migrate towards south to the warmer regions in search of food.

  In Tundra region, three types of vegetation are found.

- **Bush Tundra :** This type of vegetation includes dwarf trees that look like scrubby bushes, namely Alders, Birches, Willows and Junipers. Sometimes they take a creeping form and cover the ground by a network of their branches.

- **Grass Tundra** *:* This type of vegetation includes a special type of grass, namely, Moss, Lichen and Sedges. This is such a hardy vegetation that it thrives with minimum possible moisture and can survive under any amount of cold, so much that it remains alive even beneath the snow cover.

- **Flowering Plants :** During summers some berry bushes and limited flowering plants are able to grow and display their colourful sight before they die down. They are extremely short-lived plants, e.g., Poppies, Lilies, Buttercups and Violets.

Human Adaptation

- Tundra regions are unsuitable for man due to various reasons like, extremely cold climate, virtually absent vegetation, and hardly manageable food resources with formidable hazards.

- Population in this region remains very sparsely populated. Although this is a very extensive region, yet its total population is limited to hardly one lakh.

- The Tundra region is inhabited by primitive people who lead a semi-nomadic life. In Alaska, Greenland and northern Canada, these semi-nomadic people are called the Eskimos. They live as hunters, fish gatherers, deriving their food from fish, seals, walruses and polar bears. They even hunt reindeer and other animals, which provide them with milk, meat, fat, skins and bones. They also rear fur-bearing animals on a commercial scale.

- The Lapps of the Scandinavian Tundra are slightly more cultured and they are mainly the reindeer-herders and fishermen. The Siberian Tundra-dwellers are the Samoyeds, the Yakuts and the Chuckchis. All of them are hunters and fishermen.

Important Characteristics

- The Tundra region is located roughly beyond the Arctic Circle (66° 30′ N) in the Northern Hemisphere, while there is no Tundra region in the Southern Hemisphere.
- The Tundra region areas are stretched over the coastal lands of the Arctic Ocean in Eurasia and North America and the Southern coastal fringe of Greenland and several groups of islands, situated in the Arctic ocean near the Northern coasts of the Northern continents.
- The climate is characterized by long, severe winters; cool, brief summers; and scarce rainfall.
- The chief characteristic of Tundra climate is very low mean annual temperature. Here winters are severe and long, while summers are cool and short, lasting hardly for two to three months when the sun does not set at all.
- Precipitation is very low, about 9.1 inches only, falling mainly in the second half of the year both as rain and snow.
- In Tundra region weather conditions are not favourable for vegetative growth. The growing season available during summers is too short and the temperatures are too low for the germination of seeds.
- Population in this region remains very sparsely populated. Although this is a very extensive region, yet its total population is limited to hardly one lakh.
- The Tundra Region is inhabited by primitive semi-nomadic people like the Eskimos, the Lapps, the Samoyeds, the Yakuts and the Chuckchis.

EXERCISES

PART - (A)

A. Answer the following questions

1. State the location of the Equatorial climate region.
2. Give the other names by which these regions are also popular.
3. Which parts of Asia are included in this region?
4. Give a brief account of the Rainforests together with their location and types of trees.
5. Why has the Equatorial Region the hottest climate?
6. What type of rainfall occurs in Equatorial Regions and why?
7. State in brief, the characteristics features of the Equatorial type of climate.
8. Name a few important trees found in this region.

B. Define the following terms

1. Evergreen forest
2. Selvas
3. Milpa

C. Give reasons for the following

1. There is a uniform high temperature in the Equatorial region.
2. The diurnal range of temperature in the Equatorial region is low.

D. Mapwork

1. On an outline map of the world, shade the portions of Equatorial climate.

PART (B)

A. Answer the following questions

1. What is the latitudinal extent of Tropical Grasslands?
2. Mention the areas covered under Tropical Grasslands.
3. Describe the rainfall pattern of the Savanna region.
4. Mention the different types of vegetation found in the Savanna region.
5. Describe about the inhabitants of the region and their occupation.

B. Define the following terms

1. Savanna
2. Llanos
3. Campos

C. Give reasons for the following

1. The tropical grasslands are also called as Sudan type of climate.
2. Tall trees are not found in the savanna region.

D. Map work

1. On an outline map of the world, shade the areas covered under tropical grasslands.

PART (C)

A. Answer the following questions

1. What is the extent of the tropical desert region?
2. Name the areas that are covered under it.
3. Describe the characteristics of the vegetation of hot deserts.
4. What are xerophytic plants?
5. Name the important crops grown in the tropical deserts.
6 What is an oasis?
7. Name the tribes that are native to the tropical deserts.

B. Define the following terms

1. Xerophytic plants
2. Oasis

C. Give reasons for the following

1. Hot deserts are regions of scanty rainfall.
2. Hot deserts are generally found along the western margins of the continents.
3. In the tropical desert climate region, Trade winds are dry.

D. Map work

1. On an outline map of the world, shade and name the tropical deserts.

PART (D)

A. Answer the following questions

1. Give the extent of the tropical monsoon lands.
2. Name the areas that are covered under it.
3. What is the temperature pattern for this region?
4. Discuss the seasons experienced in monsoon climate.
5. Describe the characteristics of the vegetation of this region.
6. Name some of the crops grown in this region.

B. **Give reasons for the following**
   1. Northeast Monsoon winds are practically dry.
   2. Mumbai receives more rainfall than Pune.

C. **Map work**
   1. On an outline map of the world, shade the areas experiencing monsoon climate.

PART (E)

A. **Answer the following questions**
   1. What is the main feature of the Mediterranean climate?
   2. List out the main types of Mediterranean vegetation.
   3. Discuss the rainfall pattern in the Mediterranean region.

B. **Give reasons for the following**
   1. Mediterranean regions are called as 'winter-rain and summer-dry' climates.
   2. Human adaptation is much comfortable in the Mediterranean region.

C. **Map work**
   1. On an outline map of the world, shade and name the countries bordering the Mediterranean Sea.

PART (F)

A. **Answer the following questions**
   1. List out the areas covered by the cool temperate continental region.
   2. Discuss vegetation patterns in the cool temperate continental region.
   3. Discuss the climatic features of the cool temperate continental region.

B. **Give reasons for the following**
   1. Prairies are called as granaries of the world.

C. **Map work**
   1. On an outline map of the world, shade and name the Prairies and Steppes.

PART (G)

A. **Answer the following questions**
   1. Describe the location of the Coniferous Forest region.
   2. Name the chief Coniferous Forest areas of the world.
   3. What are the summer conditions in the Coniferous Forest region?
   4. What are the winter conditions in the Coniferous Forest region?
   5. Mention the distribution of rainfall in the Coniferous Forest region.
   6. How are the trees of the Coniferous Forests adapted to the climatic conditions?
   7. Name some common Coniferous Forest trees.
   8. What are the main human responses to the Coniferous Forest environment?

B. **Define the following terms**
   1. Taiga
   2. Cold Pole

C. **Give reasons**
   1. The Taiga region is sparsely populated.
   2. Coniferous Forest regions are not favourable for agriculture.
   3. Coniferous Forest regions have long, cold winter season.
   4. Coniferous Forests are of great commercial value.

D. Map Work

1. On an outline map of the world, mark the distribution of the Coniferous Forests of the world.

PART (H)

A. Answer the following questions

1. Describe the location of the Tundra region.
2. Which parts of the world are included in the Tundra region?
3. What are the summer conditions in the Tundra region?
4. What are the winter conditions in the Tundra region?
5. Describe the natural vegetation of Tundra region.
6. What is meant by Aurora Borealis? Where do they occur?

B. Define the following terms

1. Bush Tundra
2. Eskimos
3. Muskegs
4. Cold Desert

C. Give reasons

1. There are no trees in the Tundra region.
2. In the Tundra region there is continuous twilight for many weeks.
3. Polar Tundra region is known as the Cold Desert.

D. Map Work

1. On an outline map of the world, mark the Tundra regions of the world.

E. Board Questions

1. To which natural regions of the world are the following associated ?
   (i) Conical-shaped soft wood trees.
   (ii) 4 O'clock rains.
2. (a) (i) Name the type of rainfall that occurs in the Amazon basin.
       (ii) Mention one important characteristic feature of the climate of the Amazon basin.
   (b) (i) What is Campos ?
       (ii) Name the most important economic activity practised in this region.
   (c) (i) Mention two characteristic features of the natural vegetation found in the Kalahari Desert.
       (ii) Name the primitive people of the Kalahari Desert.
   (d) (i) Which Natural region is called 'The Granary of the world' ?
           Why is it called so ?
   (ii) Why agriculture is not a main occupation in the Tundra region ?
3. In which of the natural regions of the world would the following be found :
   (i) Pine trees
   (ii) Tall grass
   (iii) Olive trees
4. Give a reason for the following :
   (i) Tropical deserts are found on the western margins of the continents.

www.ingramcontent.com/pod-product-compliance
Ingram Content Group UK Ltd.
Pitfield, Milton Keynes, MK11 3LW, UK
UKHW050418240426
12048UKWH00014B/702